"Schneider has written the first thorough study of *On Love and Self-Control* (with English translation), carefully comparing it to related Pachomian texts and also to similar material in the *Apocalypse of Samuel of Qalamun*. The detailed review of the monastic manuscripts in which these texts are preserved also raises many interesting questions. Her work will certainly encourage further work on fourth- and fifth-century ascetic contexts in Egypt."

—Dr. Janet A. Timbie
The Catholic University of America

"In this excellent book of meticulous scholarship, Carolyn Schneider restores a neglected Coptic text to its original context in early Egyptian monasticism. Schneider persuasively argues that *On Love and Self-Control* originated within the Pachomian monastic community, probably during the turmoil that followed Pachomius's death in 346, and that the leader Horsiesios could have been its author. She then traces the history of the text and its reception, from late antiquity, to a medieval scriptorium in the White Monastery, to its rediscovery by modern scholars. A clear and accurate English translation makes this rich discourse available to a wide range of readers interested in the history and spirituality of early Christian monasticism."

—David Brakke
Joe R. Engle Chair in the History of Christianity and Professor of History
The Ohio State University

CISTERCIAN STUDIES SERIES: NUMBER TWO HUNDRED SEVENTY-TWO

The Text of a Coptic Monastic Discourse, *On Love and Self-Control*

Its Story from the Fourth Century to the Twenty-First

Carolyn M. Schneider

Cistercian Publications
www.cistercianpublications.org

LITURGICAL PRESS
Collegeville, Minnesota
www.litpress.org

A Cistercian Publications title published by Liturgical Press

Cistercian Publications
Editorial Offices
161 Grosvenor Street
Athens, Ohio 54701
www.cistercianpublications.org

Scripture texts, prefaces, introductions, footnotes, and cross-references used in this work are translated by the author.

1 2 3 4 5 6 7 8 9

Library of Congress Cataloging-in-Publication Data

Names: Schneider, Carolyn M., 1963– author. | Athanasius, Saint, Patriarch of Alexandria, –373 dubious author.
Title: The text of a Coptic monastic discourse, On Love and self-control : its story from the fourth century to the twenty-first / Carolyn Schneider.
Other titles: On love and self-control. English.
Description: Collegeville, Minnesota : Cistercian Publications, Liturgical Press ; 21 cm. | Series: Cistercian studies series ; number two hundred seventy-two | In English; with some material translated from Coptic. | Includes bibliographical references.
Identifiers: LCCN 2016051049 (print) | LCCN 2016053669 (ebook) | ISBN 9780879070724 | ISBN 9780879075262 (ebook)
Subjects: LCSH: On love and self-control—Criticism, Textual. | Love—Religious aspects—Christianity. | Self-control—Religious aspects—Christianity. | Coptic monasticism and religious orders. | Athanasius, Saint, Patriarch of Alexandria, –373.
Classification: LCC BX137.2 .S346 2017 (print) | LCC BX137.2 (ebook) | DDC 248.4/8172—dc23
LC record available at https://lccn.loc.gov/2016051049

This book is dedicated to the Christians of the Middle East,
who have much to teach about love and self-control.

Contents

Preface

This book is an introduction to a beautiful fourth-century Coptic discourse on love and self-control. Although the Coptic text has been known to scholars for almost a hundred years, it appears here in an English translation for the first time, with the hope of making it better known to more people. I share this as one newcomer to Coptic studies to others who might be exploring Egyptian Christianity, although I hope that even seasoned Coptic scholars can find something new in the pages of this book.

It was the discourse's insistence that estrangement from one's neighbor is estrangement from God that captured me and plunged me into the study of the Coptic language and history. That study resulted in this book, which seeks to build on the hard, careful work of many others over a long period of time. A chronological review of the scholarly work that has already been done on the text of *On Love and Self-Control* will both acknowledge the value of that work and clarify the contribution of this present study.

The scholarly study of *On Love and Self-Control* began with Arnold van Lantschoot, who first published the Coptic text, along with a French translation, in 1927. Lantschoot dated the manuscript paleographically to the eleventh or twelfth century. He noted that it was part of a dismembered codex and listed other works that had been identified as part of the same codex. Although Lantschoot mentioned that the heading attributes the text to Athanasius, Bishop of Alexandria from 328 to 373, he deliberately set aside questions of genuine authorship and other literary issues.[1] These were taken up later by Louis-Théophile Lefort.

In 1933, Lefort published an article exploring the relationship between *On Love and Self-Control* and another text, *Instruction concerning a Spiteful Monk*.[2] He did so because he had noticed that the two works share a large portion of text, sometimes exactly word for word. But the heading of the *Instruction concerning a Spiteful Monk* attributes that work to Pachomius (289–346 CE), the founding father of a monastic network in Upper Egypt. Lefort pursued the question of which work came first, *On Love and Self-Control* or *Instruction concerning a Spiteful Monk*. After comparing the two texts, he concluded that *On Love and Self-Control* came first and that Pachomius was quoting extensively from it when he delivered his *Instruction concerning a Spiteful Monk*. Lefort based this conclusion on two main observations. First, imprecisions in *On Love and Self-Control* are clarified in *Instruction concerning a Spiteful Monk*. Second and more important, *Instruction concerning a Spiteful Monk* is addressed to a single male monk, so the pronouns in that work are second-person singular except in the section shared with *On Love and Self-Control*, where they are second-person plural, reflecting the fact that this work is addressed to a community of monks. Lefort thus argued that a segment of *On Love and Self-Control* had been extracted, paraphrased, and inserted into *Instruction concerning a Spiteful Monk*.

Lefort dated *Instruction concerning a Spiteful Monk* to the early 330s on the basis of information about its context provided by its heading:

[1] Arnold van Lantschoot, "Lettre de saint Athanase au sujet de l'amour et de la tempérance," *Le Muséon* 40 (1927): 265–92.

[2] Louis-Théophile Lefort, "S. Athanase écrivain copte," *Le Muséon* 46 (1933): 1–33.

> Instruction pronounced by our most excellent holy father, Apa Pachomius the holy archimandrite, for a brother monk bearing a grudge to another. This happened in the time of Apa Ebonh, by whom he was brought to Tabennesi. [Our father] addressed these words to him in the presence, and to the great joy, of other elder fathers. In the peace of God! May his holy blessing and that of all the saints come over us! May we all be saved! Amen.[3]

Tabennesi was the first Pachomian monastery and the original headquarters of the federation until it became too crowded. Construction of a new headquarter at Pbow began around 330, and Pachomius moved there a few years later. It was also shortly after 330 that the monastery of Sheneset joined the Pachomian *koinonia*. So the fact that *Apa* Ebonh, who was the superior of the monastery of Sheneset, brought his troublesome monk to Pachomius while Pachomius still resided at Tabennesi suggested to Lefort a date in the early 330s for the *Instruction concerning a Spiteful Monk*. That would place *On Love and Self-Control* some time earlier than 330.

Lefort found in this dating what he considered an excellent reason to consider *On Love and Self-Control* genuinely Athanasian. The *Life of Pachomius* records that Athanasius visited the newly established Pachomian community around 329 as a new

[3] Translation by Armand Veilleux, *Instructions, Letters, and Other Writings of Saint Pachomius and His Disciples*, in *Pachomian Koinonia: The Lives, Rules, and Other Writings of Saint Pachomius and his Disciples*, CS 47 (Kalamazoo, MI: Cistercian Publications, 1982), 3:13. The text was first published by E. A. Wallis Budge, "The Instructions of Apa Pachomius the Archimandrite," in *Coptic Apocrypha in the Dialect of Upper Egypt* (Oxford: Oxford University Press, 1913), 145–77, with an English translation on pages 352–82. The heading is on pages 145 (Coptic) and 352 (English). In 1956, Louis-Théophile Lefort published a revised edition of the Coptic with a French translation in *Oeuvres de s. Pachôme et de ses disciples*, CSCO 159, pp. 1–24 (Coptic), and CSCO 160, pp. 1–26 (French) (Louvain: L. Durbecq, 1956). The heading is in CSCO 159, p. 1 (Coptic), and CSCO 160, p. 1 (French).

bishop seeking to consolidate support in Upper Egypt.[4] Lefort saw this visit as the occasion for the letter *On Love and Self-Control* and asserted that its attribution to Athanasius was accurate.

Turning to linguistic matters, Lefort demonstrated that in spite of its many loanwords from Greek, *On Love and Self-Control* was composed in the Sahidic dialect of Coptic, spoken in the south of Egypt in the fourth century. He found support for a Sahidic original mainly in the fact that several of the scriptural quotations in the discourse can have come from only the Sahidic translation of the Scriptures, not from the Greek. These passages use expressions that do not occur in the Greek Scriptures but only in the Sahidic version.

Lefort acknowledged, however, that the fact that the text was composed in the Sahidic language might call into question its Athanasian authorship, since there is no evidence that Athanasius knew Coptic. Lefort called for a reassessment of the literature attributed to Athanasius and of the assumption that ascetic discourses in Coptic attributed to Athanasius were either translations from Greek or were not authentic. He argued that only a bishop who could speak Coptic could have gained the trust and deep loyalty of the Egyptian monks that Athanasius gained, since most of the monks communicated only in Coptic.

In 1955 Lefort republished the Coptic text of *On Love and Self-Control*, again with a French translation.[5] He smoothed out

[4] Armand Veilleux, *The Life of Saint Pachomius and His Disciples*, in *Pachomian Koinonia: The Lives, Rules, and Other Writings of Saint Pachomius and His Disciples*, CS 45 (Kalamazoo, MI: Cistercian Publications, 1980), 1:51–52 (SBo 28) and 317 (G[1] 30); Louis-Théophile Lefort, *S. Pachomii vita bohairice scripta*, CSCO 89 (Louvain: L. Durbecq, 1952–1953), 28–29; and Francis Halkin, *Sancti Pachomii vitae graecae*, Subsidia hagiographica 19 (Brussels: Société des Bollandistes, 1932), 19–20.

[5] Louis-Théophile Lefort, "Sur la charité et la tempérance," in *S. Athanase: Lettres festales et pastorales en copte*, CSCO 150 (Louvain: L. Durbecq, 1955), 110–20, and CSCO 151 (Louvain: L. Durbecq, 1955), 88–98.

the irregularities of the text, which Lantschoot had chosen to reproduce, and he added diacritical marks. In the footnotes he identified the scriptural quotations and references in the text. He updated the list of other works included in the codex with *On Love and Self-Control* and affirmed Lantschoot's dating of the manuscript, preferring the twelfth to the eleventh century because irregularities in the text suggested that the scribe who copied it was more at home in the northern dialect of Bohairic, which became dominant in the south only in the twelfth century. In reintroducing the text, Lefort summarized his findings regarding the connection between *On Love and Self-Control* and *Instruction concerning a Spiteful Monk* and reiterated his assertion that Athanasius wrote to Egyptian monks in Coptic.

Subsequent scholarly discussions about *On Love and Self-Control* addressed the question of whether or not Athanasius was the real author of the text by focusing on whether or not Athanasius knew Coptic. Lefort's view that Athanasius spoke and wrote in Coptic when communicating with the monks of Upper Egypt has become a minority view among scholars of Egyptian Christianity in late antiquity.[6] Intensive study of this historical era since Lefort's time can be summarized by the argument of Annick Martin that the traditional distinction between a literate, Greek-speaking Alexandrian clergy and an illiterate, Coptic-speaking monastic leadership along the Nile valley is inaccurate. Rather, the leaders of fourth-century Egyptian monasticism were literate and often bilingual. Even those *apas* who did not know Greek, such as Pachomius, had translators among their followers. Thus Martin concludes that

[6] Other scholars who entertain the idea that Athanasius spoke and wrote in Coptic are W. H. C. Frend, "Athanasius as an Egyptian Christian Leader in the Fourth Century," in *Religion, Popular and Unpopular in the Early Christian Centuries* (London: Variorum Reprints, 1976), XVI:28, 33–34; and Johannes Quasten, *Patrology*, 4 vols. (Westminster, MD: Christian Classics, Inc., 1986), 3:47–48.

Athanasius would not have used Coptic in Alexandria and would not have needed to learn it in order to carry on his contacts with the monks of Upper Egypt. She points out that all the universally acknowledged Athanasian literature is in Greek, including his letters to monks and his Easter letters to the Egyptian church at large.[7]

However, as Lefort had already noted, there was not yet consensus about the authenticity of several ascetic works attributed to Athanasius, some preserved in Coptic. These included *On Love and Self-Control*. David Brakke set out to evaluate these ascetic writings in an important article from 1994.[8] For most of the works he found evidence of a Greek original, but not for the original Coptic *On Love and Self-Control*. Leaving open the question of whether Athanasius could have written in Coptic, Brakke found that there were reasons to accept *On Love and Self-Control* as Athanasian. Internal evidence for an early-to mid-fourth-century date and content compatible with genuine Athanasian works spoke in favor of Athanasian authorship. First, a passage in the text speaks of three kinds of monks, virgins [ϩⲉⲛⲡⲁⲣⲑⲉⲛⲟⲥ], renunciants [ϩⲉⲛⲁⲡⲟⲧⲁⲕⲧⲓⲕⲟⲥ], and anchorites [ⲁⲛⲁⲭⲱⲣⲏⲧⲏⲥ]; this monastic terminology was typical of the early to mid-fourth century, a time frame consistent with Athanasian authorship. Second, Brakke found three themes in the text that were discussed in a manner coherent with Athanasius's handling of the

[7] Annick Martin, *Athanase d'Alexandrie et l'église d'Égypte au IVe siècle (328–373)* (Palais Farnèse: École française de Rome, 1996), 667–69. Other scholars who think that Athanasius probably did not know Coptic are Tito Orlandi, *Elementi di lingua e letteratura copta* (Milan: La Goliardica, 1970), 76; Martin Tetz, *Theologischer Realenzyklopädie* (1979), s.v. "Athanasius von Alexandrien"; and Timothy Barnes, *Athanasius and Constantius: Theology and Politics in the Constantinian Empire* (Cambridge, MA, and London: Harvard University Press, 1993), 13–14.

[8] David Brakke, "The Authenticity of the Ascetic Athanasiana," *Orientalia,* n.s., 63, no. 2 (1994): 17–56.

themes in his genuine works: the use of navigational imagery for the Christian life, the parable of the five wise and five foolish virgins from Matthew 25:1-12, and the exhortation to drink wine only in small amounts. Finding nothing in the text that contradicted Athanasius's views expressed elsewhere, Brakke accepted the authenticity of *On Love and Self-Control* as a work of Athanasius, but he did so "with hesitation."[9]

After this, in a series of articles published between 2007 and 2009, Christoph Joest indirectly advanced the study of *On Love and Self-Control* by directly advancing the study of its near relative, *Instruction concerning a Spiteful Monk*. Joest demonstrated clearly that *Instruction concerning a Spiteful Monk* was not a single composition by Pachomius containing a long quotation from *On Love and Self-Control*, as Lefort had assumed. Rather, it was a compilation of three parts woven together and revised by an editor, only the first part of which was the original instruction by Pachomius. Joest carefully compared the discursive styles of the text's three sections with the styles of Pachomius and two of his successors as *Apa* of the *koinonia*, Theodore and Horsiesios. Joest showed that the last part of *Instruction concerning a Spiteful Monk* in particular was most consistent with the style of Horsiesios. He suggested that Horsiesios was not only the author of the last section but also the editor who made the compilation, reworking the material from *On Love and Self-Control* and inserting it into the middle. Joest did not question Athanasius's responsibility for the original version of *On Love and Self-Control*.[10] One effect that Joest's work had on the study of *On Love and Self-Control* was to unmoor the text

[9] Brakke, "Authenticity," 36.

[10] Christoph Joest, "Horsiese als Redaktor von Pachoms Katechese 1 'An einen gröllenden Mönch': Eine stilkritische Untersuchung," *Journal of Coptic Studies* 9 (2007): 61–94; "Pachoms Katechese 'an einen gröllenden Mönch,'" *Le Muséon* 120 (2007): 91–129, and "Die sog. 'Règlements' als Werk des Pachomianers Horsiese († nach 386)," *Vigiliae christianae* 63 (2009): 480–92.

from the date of Pachomius's original instruction to a spiteful monk in the early 330s. Since the final redacted form of *Instruction concerning a Spiteful Monk* containing the selection from *On Love and Self-Control* came from a later time, *On Love and Self-Control* itself might have come from a later time. Thus the occasion for its composition might not have been Athanasius's trip to Upper Egypt at the beginning of his episcopate.

In a tantalizingly brief article from 2010, Malcolm Choat suggested that the context of *On Love and Self-Control* was thoroughly Pachomian from the start. Taking note of the threefold monastic terminology highlighted by Brakke (virgins [ϩⲉⲛⲡⲁⲣⲑⲉⲛⲟⲥ], renunciants [ϩⲉⲛⲁⲡⲟⲧⲁⲕⲧⲓⲕⲟⲥ], and anchorites [ⲁⲛⲁⲭⲱⲣⲏⲧⲏⲥ]), Choat observed that, although these terms were indeed characteristic of the mid-fourth century and were used in the Pachomian community, Athanasius himself completely avoided the term ἀποτακτικος. Choat argued that *On Love and Self-Control* could have been written by Athanasius in Greek, translated into Sahidic, and revised by a Pachomian. But he found it more likely that *On Love and Self-Control* was not a letter from Athanasius to the Pachomians at all but a discourse originally delivered by a Pachomian to the Pachomians.[11]

My research has supported Choat's proposal, and this book seeks to put flesh on the bones of that proposal by contextualizing *On Love and Self-Control* in as many ways as possible. In introducing the discourse, I first review the history of the Pachomian community in the fourth century, paying special attention to its conflicts and finding a possible occasion for *On Love and Self-Control* in an ideological struggle that engulfed the community following Pachomius's death in 346. A central

[11] Malcolm Choat, "Athanasius, Pachomius, and the 'Letter on Charity and Temperance,'" in *Egyptian Culture and Society: Studies in Honor of Naguib Kanawati*, vol. 1, ed. Alexandra Woods, Ann McFarlane, and Susanne Binder, Supplément aux Annales du service des antiquités de l'Egypte, cahier no. 38 (Cairo: Conseil suprême des antiquités de l'Egypte, 2010), 97–103.

figure in the crisis was Horsiesios, the designated leader of the community at that time.

Next, I seek to show that Horsiesios was a more likely original orator of the discourse than Athanasius, beginning with a study of the heading of *On Love and Self-Control*, which attributes the text to the "Archbishop" Athanasius. Since this title was applied to the bishop of Alexandria only from the turn of the fourth to the fifth century onward, its use reveals that the heading was probably not an original part of the mid-fourth-century text but was added later. Furthermore, comparison of the heading of *On Love and Self-Control* with the extant headings of the other works in the codex with which *On Love and Self-Control* was bound reveals that they were almost certainly written by the same scribe and thus were probably added at the time the codex was made. The nature of this anthology and the list of authors whose works it contains point to the turn of the sixth to seventh centuries as a possible date of compilation. The place of compilation is most likely to have been the Monastery of Saint Shenoute of Atripe, which is the source of the sole extant eleventh- to twelfth-century copy of the codex containing *On Love and Self-Control*.

In arguing that the attribution to Athanasius may not be accurate, I do not mean to suggest that it was an unreasonable attribution or that the scribe was deliberately trying to deceive. As many scholars have shown, there are good reasons to see an Athanasian hand in *On Love and Self-Control*. I review these but go on to demonstrate that there are even better reasons to see in it the hand of Horsiesios, whose mother tongue was Sahidic. All three of the themes that Brakke found in common between *On Love and Self-Control* and the writings of Athanasius can be found likewise in the writings of the Pachomians. Of these three themes, the parable of the five wise and five foolish virgins from Matthew 25:1-12 is especially noteworthy. It and several other scriptural passages cited in *On Love and Self-Control* are used only by Horsiesios in the Pachomian literature. Furthermore, there are features in the discourse that are incompatible with Athanasian usage: not only does the discourse use the monastic term ⲁⲡⲟⲧⲁⲕⲧⲓⲕⲟⲥ, which is lacking in the genuine Athanasiana, but it also uses the term "image of God" (ⲑⲓⲕⲱⲛ ⲙ̄ⲡⲛⲟⲩⲧⲉ) as a synonym for "human being." In his genuine works, Athanasius limits that title to the second person of the Trinity, incarnate in the Savior; he can say of humanity that it was made *according to* God's image before sin, and that after sin it can be called God's image by spiritual participation in *the* image of God, but for Athanasius, a sinful human being per se is no longer the image of God. In *On Love and Self-Control,* in contrast, a human being, even a sinful human being, is the image of God without qualification. This is Pachomian usage.

In order to complete the introduction to *On Love and Self-Control,* I examine the moments in which the text appears in the historical record past the seventh century all the way to the present scholarly effort to reconstruct the codex after its dismemberment in the nineteenth century. The processes of copying, codifying, and borrowing from *On Love and Self-Control* are treated as hermeneutically important moments and, using clues from historical context, I make attempts to discern what *On Love and Self-Control* might have meant to scribes and readers at those times. Of particular interest is the discovery that the portion of the discourse that deals with wine and is common to *On Love and Self-Control* and *Instruction concerning a Spiteful Monk* was included in the *Apocalypse of Samuel of Qalamun,* an eleventh-century Coptic text, now extant only in an Arabic translation. Appendix A allows the reader to see the different ways in which the passage about wine is recorded in each of the three texts in English translation. Appendix B provides summaries of the contents of the codex to which *On Love and Self-Control* belongs, insofar as it has been reconstructed, adding the identification of a previously unidentified text as well as summaries of works that have not yet been edited or translated from Coptic.

Today, access to *On Love and Self-Control* is difficult for those who are not trained in Coptic studies. It is the goal of this study to make the text more easily accessible. But this study is surely imperfect. So, like many a Coptic scribe, I attach a colophon here, pleading for the mercy of the readers. The words are borrowed from Abū al-Barakāt, the fourteenth-century synthesizer of Egyptian ecclesiastical practice, in his book *The Lamp of Darkness.* He concluded his introduction by addressing those who knew his subject well: "I ask whoever examines this book to fill its gaps, to repair its defects, and to correct what could be found false in it because of error or of negligence, placed too early or too late."[12]

[12] Louis Villecourt, *Livre de la lampe des ténèbres et de l'exposition (lumineuse) du service (de l'église) par Abû'l-Barakât connu sous le nom d'Ibn Kabar*, PO 20, fasc. 4 (Paris: Firmin-Didot, 1929), 628.

Acknowledgments

I first encountered *On Love and Self-Control* in French as I was working on my PhD dissertation on the intimate connection between Christ and Christians in Athanasius and Luther. I completed the dissertation in 1999 and always intended to go back to that lovely discourse on love and self-control, which at that time I assumed was Athanasian. But the journey back was long and took place in baby steps. Many people helped me to steady myself as I inched forward, and I would like to thank them.

First of all, the Hugo and Georgia Gibson committees of 2001–2003 at Texas Lutheran University gave me funding and encouragement to begin exploring the original context of *On Love and Self-Control* by examining the relationship of Athanasius to the Pachomian community. I am grateful to the committee members of those years, those still living (Charles Eckert, Dorothy Baubach, Lori Gallegos, Phil Ruge-Jones, and John Thorson) and those who have since died (Milton Mayer, James Witschorke, and Robert Haugen). I sent the resulting draft for review to Janet Timbie, now adjunct associate professor in the Department of Semitic and Egyptian Languages and Literatures at The Catholic University of America. She responded by telling me that I could not do what I was trying to do without learning Sahidic and translating the discourse directly from the Coptic. She was right, of course. That was only the first piece of wise counsel that Janet Timbie has given me; for all of her advice I thank her immensely.

So the process of learning Coptic began and eventually led me to the Collegeville Institute for Ecumenical and Cultural

Research in the fall of 2011. There I was able to complete the translation of *On Love and Self-Control* and begin what was intended to be a brief accompanying article until I realized that contextualizing the discourse would be far more complex than I had anticipated and would defy brevity; it was going to be a book instead. I thank David Brakke for his help in checking the draft of my translation at this time, and I thank Janet Timbie for her extensive comments and suggestions regarding the translation. I am also grateful for the support of the staff of the Collegeville Institute, particularly the executive director, Don Ottenhoff, and the program manager and communications associate, Carla Durand. I thank also my colleagues there for their lively conversation and input: John Keenan, Lauren and David Matz, Michael McGregor, Glen Miller, James Powers, and Kathleen Norris. Up the hill from the Institute, Adam McCollum (at that time lead cataloger, Eastern Christian Manuscripts) and Matt Heintzelman (curator of Austria/Germany Study Center and cataloger of rare books) graciously welcomed me to the Hill Museum and Manuscript Library and helped me gain access, both personal and electronic, to ancient texts and nearly ancient secondary sources.

My debt to librarians is enormous. I would like to thank especially Janine Lortz, interlibrary loan associate at Alcuin Library of Saint John's University; Monica Blanchard, curator at the Semitics/ICOR Library of The Catholic University of America; and Nadine Cherpion, responsable des Archives scientifiques at the Institut français d'archéologie orientale. With the help of Nadine Cherpion, Anne Boud'hors (directeur de recherche at the Institut de recherche et d'histoire des textes), and Catherine Louis, I was able to look at the fragments of MONB.CP held in the archives of the Institut français d'archéologie orientale (IFAO) in Cairo. I could not have completed Appendix B of this book without the generosity of Catherine Louis in sharing with me the meticulous work she has done in cataloguing the manuscripts held at IFAO.

My debt to other scholars is also enormous. I must wait for the day of resurrection to thank properly the late William Harmless of Creighton University. He graciously agreed to read an early draft of this book and with great patience and wisdom taught me how to make it better. The revised version was sent to Rebecca Krawiec, chair of the Religious Studies and Theology Department of Canisius College, and Caroline Schroeder, associate professor of religious and classical studies at the University of the Pacific. I am grateful to both for their insightful comments and questions that helped me to hone my argument so that it is sharper and more clear.

This process of improvement continued with the careful editing of Marsha Dutton, executive editor at Cistercian Publications. I am glad for the privilege of having worked with Marsha as the editor of this book. She made me think again not only about what I was saying but also about how I was saying it. Thanks to her prodding, the book you are reading is significantly clearer than the book I gave to her initially.

While the work on editing was ongoing, Gabriel Moss, the director of the Ancient World Mapping Center at the University of North Carolina, was expertly and cheerfully creating the map that appears in this book to help readers locate the places associated with *On Love and Self-Control*. I obtained the coordinates for the map in several different sites, as follows:

The Monastery of St. Samuel of Qalamun and the Monastery of St. Shenoute at the Coptic Research Site, www.ambilacuk.com/coptic/gpslist.html, thanks to Howard Middleton-Jones, 2007, The Multi-Media Coptic Database Project.

I found the other monastic coordinates through individual searches at the Pleiades website: pleiades.stoa.org/, with thanks to:

M. Drew Bear, DARMC, R. Talbert, Sean Gillies, Johan Åhlfeldt, Jeffrey Becker, and Tom Elliott, "Panopolis/Schmin: a Pleiades place resource," *Pleiades: A Gazetteer of Past Places*, 2015, pleiades.stoa.org/places/756613 (accessed Oct. 6, 2016);

M. Drew Bear, R. Talbert, T. Elliott, and S. Gillies, "Bau/Pboou: a Pleiades place resource," *Pleiades: A Gazetteer of Past Places*, 2012, https://pleiades.stoa.org/places/756540 (accessed Oct. 6, 2016);

M. Drew Bear, R. Talbert, T. Elliott, and S. Gillies, "Chenoboskion: a Pleiades place resource," *Pleiades: A Gazetteer of Past Places*, 2012, pleiades.stoa.org/places/756545 (accessed Oct. 6, 2016);

M. Drew Bear, R. Talbert, T. Elliott, and S. Gillies, "Mouchonsis/Tmushons: a Pleiades place resource," *Pleiades: A Gazetteer of Past Places*, 2012, pleiades.stoa.org/places/756604 (accessed Oct. 6, 2016);

M. Drew Bear, R. Talbert, T. Elliott, and S. Gillies, "Nagos: a Pleiades place resource," *Pleiades: A Gazetteer of Past Places*, 2012, pleiades.stoa.org/places/756607 (accessed Oct. 6, 2016);

J. Keenan, S. E. Sidebotham, T. Wilfong, R. Talbert, T. Elliott, and S. Gillies, "Phnoum: a Pleiades place resource," *Pleiades: A Gazetteer of Past Places*, 2012, pleiades.stoa.org/places/786090 (accessed Oct. 6 2016);

J. Keenan, S. E. Sidebotham, T. Wilfong, R. Talbert, T. Elliott, and S. Gillies, "Tabennisis: a Pleiades place resource," *Pleiades: A Gazetteer of Past Places*, 2012, pleiades.stoa.org/places/786125 (accessed Oct. 6, 2016).

As I was writing I was privileged to teach for two semesters at the Evangelical Theological Seminary in Cairo. President Atef Gendy was a most thoughtful and gracious host, along with Dean Magdi Gendy, my supervisor Mark Nygard, at that time director of the Graduate Studies Program, and my colleague Willem De Wit, assistant professor of biblical studies and systematic theology. I am full of gratitude for them and for my students for enabling me to enter into the life of the Egyptian Christian community. I treasure that experience.

Finally, I thank my family for giving me time and space as I finished the book. My sister, Sue Schneider, was especially generous in opening her house to me, while my father, David Schneider, diligently hunted down rare journal articles on my behalf.

Abbreviations

An Boll	*Analecta Bollandiana*
BL	British Library
BL Or.	British Library, Oriental collection
BSAC	*Bulletin de la Société d'archéologie copte*
CCSL	Corpus christianorum, series latina
Cl. Pr.	Clarendon Press
CS	Cistercian Studies series
CSCO	Corpus scriptorum christianorum orientalium
IFAO	Institut français d'archéologie orientale
JCS	*Journal of Coptic Studies*
Mémoires	Mémoires publiés par les membres de la mission archéologique française au Caire
MONB.CP	Monastero Bianco, Codex CP
NPNF	A Select Library of Nicene and Post-Nicene Fathers
OCP	*Orientalia christiana periodica*
PG	Patrologia cursus completus, series graeca, edited by J.-P. Migne
PO	Patrologia orientalis
ROC	*Revue de l'Orient chrétienne*
SAC	Studies in Antiquity & Christianity
SBo	Sahidic-Bohairic

2

Or. 8802, f.2 (© The British Library Board, Or. 8802, f.2)

Introduction

> Is there not only one God over all of us? Why has each of us left his brother behind to defile the covenant of life and peace that is with us? . . . "Come and be reconciled with one another," says the Lord.* So, understand that the one who is reconciled to his brother is reconciled to God, and the one who is separated from his brother is separated from God: "For the one who does not love his brother, whom he sees, cannot love God either, whom he does not see."* . . . If the Lord has commanded us to love our enemy and to bless those who curse us and to do good to those who hate us, then what sort of danger are we in if we hate our brothers, our holy members and our coheirs, children of God, chosen shoots of the true grapevine, lost and scattered sheep, to whom the only-begotten son of God came forth. Having rescued them from the enemy, he offered himself up as a sacrifice for them. This very form, namely, the human being, the image of God, this one for whom the living Word bore these troubles, you hate because of jealousy and empty glory or greatness, in which the enemy has bound you so that he might make you a stranger to the living God.

*Isa 1:18

*1 John 4:20

So an *Apa* [father] spoke in the mid-fourth century to a monastic community in conflict, the monks of the famous federation of monasteries organized by Pachomius (292–346 CE) in Upper

Egypt. The *Apa*'s discourse on love and self-control was written down in Sahidic (the Coptic dialect of Upper Egypt in late antiquity) and kept for reflection. Decades later, part of it emerged, closely paraphrased, in the *Instruction concerning a Spiteful Monk*, a compilation made from an instruction of Pachomius's against spite, the section from *On Love and Self-Control*, and another discourse on forgiveness. Then *On Love and Self-Control* seems to have gone underground, like a lost river, for around seven hundred years before coming up again in the hand of a copyist in another famous Upper Egyptian monastery, the Monastery of Saint Shenoute of Atripe. By that time it had been attributed to Athanasius, bishop of Alexandria (298–373 CE), and copied, perhaps several times, although only a single known copy survives. This copy was placed in a book or codex that was an anthology of ascetic writings by authority figures of the fourth to seventh centuries. All the writings in the anthology were in Sahidic, although some were translations of pieces originally written in Greek. The discourse *On Love and Self-Control* next appeared in the nineteenth century in the British Museum, separated from most of the other pieces of its codex. Since then, two scholarly editions of the text have been published, each with a French translation, and the manuscript has been moved to the British Library, where it is catalogued as Or 8802 (fols. 1^r–4^v, line 24).[1]

[1] The editions are by Arnold van Lantschoot, "Lettre de saint Athanase au sujet de l'amour et de la tempérance," *Le Muséon* 40 (1927): 265–92; and Louis-Théophile Lefort, "Sur la charité et la tempérance," in *S. Athanase: Lettres festales et pastorales en*

On Love and Self-Control was not written for scholarly examination but for spiritual use in reconciling members of a monastic community in conflict. No community escapes conflict, and so the *Apa*'s concern has lasting relevance. Conflict is perennial even in monastic communities. In exploring modern Egyptian monasticism one author notes that still "one of the hardest things for monks to get accustomed to is not sexual abstinence but keeping their tempers in check."[2] The monastic community that first heard the discourse *On Love and Self-Control* was fraying because of anger and resentment and needed to be healed and brought back together. With this discourse, their *Apa* took the role of a pharmacist, dispensing the medicine prescribed and provided by God for the cure of hatred.

Taking a look into a theological medicine chest of the Egyptian monks of old days may uncover some remedies that have not yet reached their expiration date. But opening this chest and deciphering its contents is not easy. We no longer live in the community that first heard the discourse *On Love and Self-Control*. So now we do need scholarly work

---

copte, CSCO 150, 110–20. Lefort provides a French translation in *S. Athanase: Lettres festales et pastorales en copte*, CSCO 151, 88–98. The catalogue entry for the manuscript is in Bentley Layton, *Catalogue of Coptic Literary Manuscripts in the British Library Acquired since the Year 1906* (London: The British Library, 1987), #175, pp. 216–18. Plate 23 in this catalogue contains an image of the manuscript from fol. 4^r.

[2] Sana S. Hasan, *Christians versus Muslims in Modern Egypt: The Century-Long Struggle for Coptic Equality* (Oxford and New York: Oxford University Press, 2003), 65.

to make such a text more accessible. Coptic studies is a notoriously complex field with many subfields that must be integrated in presenting the translation of a text like *On Love and Self-Control*: translation of the Coptic text, examination of issues of authorship and dating of the text, contextualization of the text in the history of Egyptian Christianity, particularly in its monastic form, reflection on the theology expressed in the text, and attention to codicological efforts to reconstruct the text's dismembered codex. This introduction to the translation examines the text at these various layers so that those who want to discover this discourse *On Love and Self-Control* and the ancient Egyptian monastic communities that were inspired by it may understand its contents more easily.

Summary of the Text

The discourse opens with thanks that God does not hate humanity but has mercifully reconciled with humans through the Son and continues to guide them lovingly through the Holy Spirit. It continues by noting how often in the Scriptures God has urged people to love each other in the same way. This scriptural urgency is expressed in two ways, the *Apa* says: through threats and encouragements. He gives examples of the evil that happens to and through hateful people, such as the rich man who despised Lazarus in his poverty.* Here the *Apa*, following the Sahidic translation of the Bible, names the rich man Nineve.

*Luke 16:19-31

Next come examples of the goodness that happens to and through gentle people, like Joseph and Moses, who returned good for evil toward those who hated them. By means of texts like Matthew 25:41-43, in which Jesus identifies with the hungry, the thirsty, the foreign, the naked, the sick, and the imprisoned, the *Apa* reminds the community that to love the least is to love God. Then why, he cries, turning to his present situation, is there a rift in the community that claims to love God? Because of Christ, one's neighbor is God's divine Son, he tells them, so to be separated from one's neighbor is to be separated from God. God wills forgiveness instead. Fasting without forgiving is unacceptable to God. The real fast is repentance, which looses the chains of violence toward the neighbor in which the devil has bound up the heart. God wants hearts to walk in free simplicity and love toward the brothers whom the only-begotten Son of God has rescued. The *Apa* calls these brothers "the image of God." Healing will happen when every form of violence is replaced by the "living cures" of kindness, he says, citing letters of Paul, and 1 Peter 1:25–2:2 in its Sahidic version.

These words of encouragement are followed by words of threat depicting the final Judgment, at which those who have condemned others find themselves condemned. In a string of questions, the *Apa* asks his monks to consider the sins against God's image for which they might be held accountable in front of the whole world and all the angels on that day. He admonishes them to fear God, remembering that God is the real judge, not they themselves. The *Apa* goes on to warn that mere monastic status, whether as virgins (ϩⲉⲛⲡⲁⲣⲑⲉⲛⲟⲥ), renunciants (ϩⲉⲛⲁⲡⲟⲧⲁⲕⲧⲓⲕⲟⲥ), or anchorites (ⲁⲛⲁⲭⲱⲣⲏⲧⲏⲥ), will not excuse the monks, because an ascetic life stripped of the "human-loving

Christ" is not the real virginity that they promised to God. Disciples of Christ are given a deposit from God: each other. This they dare not despise and destroy.

Through a series of rhetorical questions placed in God's mouth, the *Apa* reminds the community that God has given them the "virtues of the virgin Spirit of Christ" with which to care for one another and fight off the devil. These will "pilot" them "in the middle of the bitter waves." He lists these virtues: faith and knowledge, intelligence and wisdom, fasting and self-control, purity and caution, love and peace, patience and gentleness, joy, and generosity and kindness, prayer and steadfastness, modesty and simplicity, silence and the withholding of judgment, difficulty and injustice.

Although he is not yet finished with the list, the *Apa* pauses after the surprising inclusion of "difficulty and injustice" in an otherwise positive recital of the gifts of the Spirit. He recalls the suffering of "our fathers," who denied themselves even the relief of wine because of its potential to unleash the tongue and cause harm to the community. He acknowledges that the "great self-controlled one, Timothy," drank a little wine because of illness, but this fact does not mean that a healthy person should let himself be drowned because his love of wine makes him hate the piloting virtue of self-control.

Returning to the list of virtues, the *Apa* concludes with humility, depicting it as a rough haircloth cord used to guide the splendid curtain of the tabernacle. Here the *Apa*'s predilection for the term *guide* or *pilot* (ⲣ̄ϩⲙ̄ⲙⲉ) comes to the fore, because the description of the tabernacle in Exodus 26 does not mention any such guiding cord but speaks instead of a haircloth covering for the tabernacle. But the thread of ⲣ̄ϩⲙ̄ⲙⲉ, whether used as a noun or a verb, leads through this whole discourse *On Love and Self-Control*, from its first lines, where God "guides us lovingly," to this place, where humility is the guiding rope of the curtain in the tent where God's Spirit dwells.

The discourse concludes with a warning not to become careless but to keep on struggling in repentance and humility toward the image of God until the crown of righteousness is given. The final scriptural example is of the wise virgins, who kept oil in their lamps to meet the bridegroom at last and to be received into the bridal chamber in the "city of our Lord Jesus Christ."

The Language and Fourth-Century Date of the Text

Although it contains a large number of loan words from Greek, *On Love and Self-Control* is in Sahidic Coptic. In addition to the fact that it is stylistically Coptic, it also contains some scriptural quotations that are distinctively from the Sahidic Bible, not the Greek. One example is the reference to Nineve, the name that the Coptic tradition gives to the rich man whom the Greek Scriptures leave unnamed in Jesus' parable about a rich man and his poor neighbor, Lazarus.[3]* *On Love and Self-Control*

*Luke 16:19-31

[3] The important third-century Greek manuscript of the gospel according to Luke, *Papyrus Bodmer XIV* (P^{75}), is an exception to the rule because in it the rich man is named *Neue*, which is probably a corruption of the name *Nineve*. See the variants

also uses the Coptic versions of Isaiah 1:18, "Come and be reconciled with one another" ("Come and let us converse" in the Greek Septuagint), and 1 Peter 2:2, "love the holy, spiritual milk in which there is no deceit" ("love the holy, spiritual milk" in the Greek Septuagint).[4] The discourse is so saturated with biblical quotations and allusions, whether uniquely Coptic or not, that one could say that the Scriptures themselves are the language of the text.

The terminology used in the discourse to identify various types of monks as virgins (ϩⲉⲛⲡⲁⲣⲑⲉⲛⲟⲥ), renunciants (ϩⲉⲛⲁⲡⲟⲧⲁⲕⲧⲓⲕⲟⲥ), and anchorites (ⲁⲛⲁⲭⲱⲣⲏⲧⲏⲥ) provides the strongest clue to the dating of the text, since, as David Brakke points out, this "three-fold distinction is characteristic of the early and middle fourth century."[5] The term ⲁⲡⲟⲧⲁⲕⲧⲓⲕⲟⲥ (renouncer or renunciant), which refers

---

of Luke 16:19 in Eberhard Nestle, Erwin Nestle, Kurt Aland, Matthew Black, Carlo M. Martini, Bruce M. Metzger, and Allen Wikgren, eds., *Novum Testamentum Graece*, 26th ed. (Stuttgart: Deutsche Bibelgesellschaft, 1979).

[4] Louis-Théophile Lefort first drew attention to the peculiarities of the Sahidic version of the passages from Luke and Isaiah. See his *S. Athanase*, CSCO 151, 88n7 and 91n32. To compare the Coptic and Greek scriptures, see George Horner, *The Gospel of S. Luke*, in *The Coptic Version of the New Testament in the Southern Dialect*, 7 vols. (Oxford: Clarendon, 1911), 2:314–20; Émile Amélineau, "Fragments de la version thébaine de L'Écriture (Ancien Testament)," *Recueil de travaux relatifs à la philologie et à l'archéologie égyptiennes et assyriennes* 9 (1887): 116; Horner, *The Catholic Epistles and the Apocalypse, The Coptic Version of the New Testament* (Oxford: Clarendon, 1924), 7:16; and the corresponding passages in *Septuaginta*, ed. Alfred Rahlfs (Stuttgart: Deutsche Bibelgesellschaft, 1979).

[5] David Brakke, "The Authenticity of the Ascetic Athanasiana," *Orientalia*, n.s., 63, no. 2 (1994): 35.

to a communal ascetic who has renounced some aspects of societal involvement but not necessarily all aspects, fell out of use by the fifth century.[6] The discourse's internal witness to its fourth-century origin is precious because *On Love and Self-Control* has survived only in a single manuscript, copied in the eleventh or twelfth century. Fortunately, there is one ancient, external witness that likewise points to the existence of *On Love and Self-Control* in the fourth century. A Sahidic *Instruction concerning a Spiteful Monk* (London, British Library, Or. 7024), probably compiled at the turn of the fourth to fifth century, made use of the pre-existing *On Love and Self-Control* by including a long paraphrase of the last two-thirds of *On Love and Self-Control*.[7] The

[6] Ewa Wipszycka, "Moines et communautés monastiques en Égypte (IVe–VIIIe siècles)," *The Journal of Juristic Papyrology*, Supplement XI (Warsaw: Warsaw University, Faculty of Law and Administration, Chair of Roman and Antique Law, Institute of Archaeology, Department of Papyrology, and the Raphael Taubenschlag Foundation, 2009), 313. On the ἀποτακτικοί see also James Goehring, *Ascetics, Society, and the Desert: Studies in Early Egyptian Monasticism*, Studies in Antiquity & Christianity (Harrisburg, PA: Trinity, 1999), 20–26, 53–72.

[7] *Instruction concerning a Spiteful Monk* is published in E. A. Wallis Budge, "The Instructions of Apa Pachomius the Archimandrite," in *Coptic Apocrypha in the Dialect of Upper Egypt*, 145–77, with an English translation on pages 352–82; and Louis-Théophile Lefort, *Oeuvres de s. Pachôme et de ses disciples*, CSCO 159, 1–24 (Coptic), and CSCO 160, 1–26 (French). A modern English translation is in Armand Veilleux, *Instructions, Letters, and Other Writings of Saint Pachomius*, in *Pachomian Koinonia: The Lives, Rules, and Other Writings of Saint Pachomius and his Disciples*, CS 47 (Kalamazoo, MI: Cistercian Publications, 1982), 3:2–3, 13–46. In "S. Athanase écrivain copte," *Le Muséon* 46 (1933): 1–33, Lefort

confluence of the internal and external witnesses make it very likely that *On Love and Self-Control* came from the middle of the fourth century.

The Pachomian *Koinonia*: The Community to which *On Love and Self-Control* Was First Addressed

The *Instruction concerning a Spiteful Monk* also unintentionally reveals the community for which *On Love and Self-Control* was probably intended. *Instruction concerning a Spiteful Monk* is attributed to Pachomius, the founder and first *Apa* of a large federation of monasteries near the Nile in Upper Egypt. In its present form, Pachomius's original instruction has been extended by two additional parts: the paraphrase from *On Love and Self-Control* and a further discourse on forgiveness, probably by Horsiesios, the third *Apa* of the Pachomian community.[8] An editor glued these together probably at the turn of the fourth to fifth centuries, when controversy raged in Egypt over whether sinful

---

put the corresponding passages from *On Love and Self-Control* and *Instruction concerning a Spiteful Monk* in parallel columns for easy comparison.

[8] Christoph Joest has clearly laid out the tripartite structure of the *Instruction concerning a Spiteful Monk* and has made a strong argument on stylistic grounds for Horsiesios's hand in the last section. See Joest, "Horsiese als Redaktor von Pachoms Katechese 1 'An einen gröllenden Mönch': Eine stilkritische Untersuchung," *Journal of Coptic Studies* 9 (2007): 61–94; and Joest, "Pachoms Katechese 'an einen gröllenden Mönch,'" *Le Muséon* 120 (2007): 91–129. But I disagree with Joest's conclusion that Horsiesios was the final editor of *Instruction concerning a Spiteful Monk* and with his assumption that Athanasius was the author of *On Love and Self-Control*, as will become clear.

humans retain the image of God. All three sections speak of humans as the image of God, implying that the answer is *yes*.[9] Since the monks of the Pachomian community clearly had a copy of *On Love and Self-Control* and were using it, and since it is not cited by any other ancient source, it seems that *On Love and Self-Control* was intended for the Pachomians.

The thriving Pachomian monasteries established in Upper Egypt in Pachomius's lifetime were (in Coptic) Tabennesi, Pbow, Sheneset, Thmoushons, Tse, Shmin, Tsmine, Thbew, and Phnoum.[10] These

[9] Carolyn Schneider, "The Image of God in *On Love and Self-Control* and *Instruction concerning a Spiteful Monk*," in *Coptic Society, Literature and Religion from Late Antiquity to Modern Times: Proceedings of the Tenth International Congress of Coptic Studies, Rome, September 17–22, 2012, and Plenary Reports of the Ninth International Congress of Coptic Studies, Cairo, September 15–19, 2008*, vol. 2, ed. Paula Buzi, Alberto Camplani, and Federico Contardi, Orientalia Lovaniensia Analecta 247 (Leuven: Peeters, 2016), 929–36.

[10] Armand Veilleux, *The Life of Saint Pachomius and his Disciples*, in *Pachomian Koinonia: The Lives, Rules, and Other Writings of Saint Pachomius and his Disciples*, CS 45 (Kalamazoo, MI: Cistercian Publications, 1980), 1:71–78 (SBo 49–58) and 334–35, 352–54 (G[1] 54 and 80–83); Louis-Théophile Lefort, *S. Pachomii vita bohairice scripta*, CSCO 89, 51–57; and Francis Halkin, *Sancti Pachomii vitae graecae*, 36–37, 54–57. See also Annick Martin, *Athanase d'Alexandrie et l'église d'Égypte au IVe siècle (328–373)*, 124–27; Derwas J. Chitty, "A Note on the Chronology of the Pachomian Foundations," in *Papers Presented to the Second International Conference on Patristic Studies Held at Christ Church, Oxford, 1955*, part 2, ed. Kurt Aland and F. L. Cross, Studia Patristica 2, Texte und Untersuchungen zur Geschichte der altchristlichen Literatur 64 (Berlin: Akademie-Verlag, 1957), 379–85; Susanna Elm, "*Virgins*

were the names of the villages in or near which the monasteries were built.[11]

Tabennesi was the site of the first Pachomian monastery, which was built around 323 as a male monastery, to which a female monastery was soon added under the leadership of Pachomius's sister, Mary. Because of this origin, in late antique Egypt Pachomians were often called Tabennesiotes, even if they were from one of the other Pachomian monasteries. When Tabennesi got too crowded, Pachomius began to construct a new male monastery at Pbow around 329. Meanwhile, around 330, two independent monasteries requested and gained admission to the Pachomian community: Sheneset and Thmoushons. A monk named Ebonh had been and continued to be the father of the monastery at Sheneset, while Pachomius functioned as the father over the entire growing community. It was for one of Ebonh's monks that Pachomius delivered his original *Instruction concerning a Spiteful Monk* at Tabennesi in the early 330s, after Sheneset

---

of God": The Making of Asceticism in Late Antiquity, Oxford Classical Monographs (Oxford: Clarendon, 1994), 289–92; and James E. Goehring, "The Ship of the Pachomian Federation: Metaphor and Meaning in a Late Account of Pachomian Monasticism," in *Christianity in Egypt: Literary Production and Intellectual Trends: Studies in Honor of Tito Orlandi*, ed. Paola Buzi and Alberto Camplani, Studia ephemeridis augustinianum 125 (Rome: Institutum patristicum augustinianum, 2011), 295–98.

[11] For maps, see Philip Rousseau, *Pachomius: The Making of a Community in Fourth-Century Egypt*, The Transformation of the Classical Heritage, ed. Peter Brown (Berkeley: University of California Press, 1985), 56, map 2; and William Harmless, *Desert Christians: An Introduction to the Literature of Early Monasticism* (New York: Oxford University Press, 2004), 123, Figure 5.1.

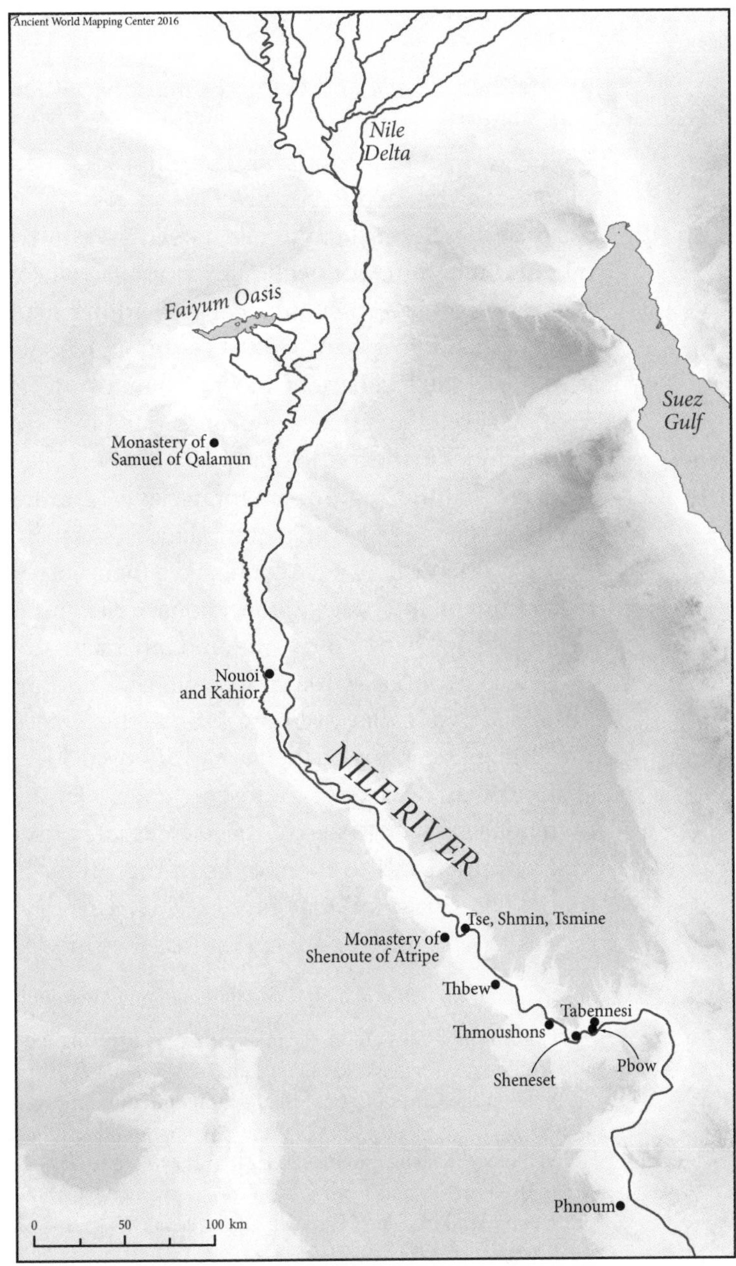

Monasteries associated with *On Love and Self-Control:* the early Pachomian network, the Monastery of Shenoute of Atripe, and the Monastery of Samuel of Qalamun (map credit: Ancient World Mapping Center, WNC-Chapel Hill)

joined the *koinonia* and before Pachomius settled into Pbow.[12]

Later, Pachomius appointed a monk named Horsiesios, destined to be one of his successors, as *apa* of Sheneset.[13] Pachomius had moved to Pbow by 336, and it became the headquarters for the whole community. He appointed a capable young man named Theodore, also destined to be one of his successors, as the local *apa* of Tabennesi in his place. Writing about the number of people living in these communities in the fourth century, Philip Rousseau declares that the "figures are impressive," and indeed they are: "The two early foundations of Tabennesi and Phbow may have contained a thousand or more [inhabitants] each. Other monasteries numbered perhaps two or three hundred inhabitants."[14]

These groups shared an ascetic rule and an authoritative leader at Pbow. Under the *Apa* of the *koinonia* each monastery had its own local *apa* and was divided into houses, each with its own housemaster.[15] Weekly, the individual housemasters preached to the monks in their houses on Wednesday and Friday nights. The *apa* of each monastery preached once on Saturday and twice

[12] Helpful timelines are in Harmless, *Desert Christians*, 119; and Veilleux, *Pachomian Koinonia*, 1:466–73. See also Chitty, "A Note on the Chronology of the Pachomian Foundations," 379–85.

[13] Veilleux, *Pachomian Koinonia*, 1:248 (SBo 199) and 381–82 (G^1 119); Lefort, *S. Pachomii vita bohairice scripta*, CSCO 89, p. 196; and Halkin, *Sancti Pachomii vitae graecae*, 77.

[14] Rousseau, *Pachomius*, 74–75.

[15] In this book, when *Apa* is capitalized, it refers to the superior of a monastic federation; when it is not capitalized, it refers to the superior of a particular monastery.

on Sunday, when the community gathered to celebrate the Eucharist. The *Apa* of the whole network delivered catecheses when he made the rounds of the monasteries.[16]

On what occasion might a Pachomian *apa* have perceived a need for a discourse on love and self-control and fulfilled that need so compellingly that his discourse was written down and preserved by the community? What follows is an attempt to answer this question, first by describing an annual opportunity for confession, forgiveness, and reconciliation among the Pachomians as part of an event known as the Remission, then by tracing a period of particularly intense rancor in Pachomian life. It occurred around the year 350, in the changes of leadership following the death of Pachomius. A similar moment of crisis, although more muted, took place in 368, following the death of Theodore, one of Pachomius's successors as *Apa* of the community. The conditions of the division in the community in 350 seem to reflect the concerns addressed in *On Love and Self-Control* and may have elicited the discourse's plea for reconciliation. The conflict of 368 cannot be ruled out, however, as an alternative possibility. Perhaps the discourse was delivered during the Remission at one of these times of conflict.

The Pachomian Remission: An Annual Opportunity for a Discourse On Love and Self-Control

When Pbow became the headquarters, the community gathered there twice a year. They fasted

[16] Harmless, *Desert Christians*, 129.

together there during Holy Week, and they met again for what was known as the Remission in the Coptic month of Mesore (now called Misra), which corresponds roughly to August. The Remission was an annual accounting undertaken in Egypt by the secular authorities just before the start of the new fiscal year. The practice as adopted by Pachomius for his own community involved stock taking of the monasteries' material possessions and mutual accounting of their stewardship. But soon the resolution of conflict and the forgiving of sin became an integral part of the Pachomian Remission.[17] The seventh of Pachomius's extant letters calls the monks to the Remission with these words:

> The time is coming near for us to assemble together, according to the custom of the remission, following the early prescriptions to convene together in order to carry out the remission and pardon. Let then everyone pardon his brother according to the commandment of God and in conformity with the laws which were written for us by God. Let everyone *totally open his heart* to his brother.* Let the brothers share their judgments with one another. Let their souls be cleansed in sanctification and the fear of God. . . . So will they be prepared to receive the heritage of the saints who held the present life in contempt in order to receive the life of the age to come. . . . It is written,

*Rom 14:5

[17] Bernadette McNary-Zak, *Letters and Asceticism in Fourth-Century Egypt* (Lanham, MD: University Press of America, 2000), 53–59; and McNary-Zak, "Pachomian Remission," *Coptic Church Review* 23, no. 4 (2002): 107–10.

> *If you forgive men their sins, your heavenly Father will forgive you yours.** Again, *Let each one forgive his brothers from his heart.**[18]

*Matt 6:14

*Matt 18:35

Perhaps the discourse *On Love and Self-Control*, with its emphasis upon accountability for what has been entrusted to the monks and upon forgiveness of the sins of others, was delivered at an August Remission during a time of heightened conflict in the community.

A Potential Context for On Love and Self-Control *in the Pachomian Conflicts following Pachomius's Death*

The Pachomian network was thriving in the mid-fourth century. But it also experienced periods of serious conflict that could have spurred a discourse on love and self-control. Particularly fractious moments were the leadership crises following the deaths of the *Apas*, beginning with Pachomius's death from a plague that killed hundreds of the monks and their leaders in 346. Before he died, Pachomius named his successor as general *Apa*. Many of the monks had expected and hoped that he would choose Theodore, the *apa* of Tabennesi.

[18] Veilleux, *Pachomian Koinonia*, 3:69–71 (in Veilleux's *Pachomian Koinonia*, biblical quotations are in italics). See also Hans Quecke, *Die Briefe Pachoms: Griechischer Text der Handschrift W. 145 der Chester Beatty Library*, Textus Patristici et Liturgici 11 (Regensburg: Friedrich Pustet, 1975), 107–8; and Amand Boon, *Pachomiana latina: Règle et épitres de s. Pachome, Épitre de s. Theodore et "Liber" de s. Orsiesius, Texte latin de s. Jérôme*, Bibliothèque de la Revue d'histoire ecclésiastique 7 (Louvain: Bureaux de la Revue, 1932), 95–96.

But Pachomius was disciplining Theodore in humility at the time because Theodore had prematurely accepted the office of general *Apa* in a prior conversation with the leaders of the community. So Pachomius named Petronius, *apa* of Tsmine, as his successor. Petronius, however, lived only three months longer, and named Horsiesios, the *apa* of Sheneset, as his successor. But Horsiesios did not feel capable of handling this responsibility, and many of the monks agreed with him. In fact, there had been grumbling that he was only a "neophyte" and not one of the "ancients" (the founders) when Pachomius appointed him earlier as *apa* at Sheneset. Pachomius is said to have responded to the murmuring with these words, "Do not think that the kingdom of heavens belongs only to the ancients. An ancient who murmurs against his brother is not an ancient; he has not even made a beginning at being a monk. For *God wants* nothing from men but *fear and love* [Deut 10:12]; and *love does not do harm to the neighbor* [Rom 13:10]."[19]

The Greek version of the *Life of Pachomius* reports that Horsiesios did his best and was known especially as a master of the scriptures.[20] But he had trouble holding the community together. The monastery at Thmoushons was particularly difficult for him to handle. Briefly, the conflict centered

[19] Veilleux, *Pachomian Koinonia*, 1:381–82 (G^1 119); Halkin, *Sancti Pachomii vitae graecae*, 77. See also Veilleux, *Pachomian Koinonia*, 1:248 (SBo 199); Lefort, *S. Pachomii vita bohairice scripta*, CSCO 89, pp. 195–96.

[20] Veilleux, *Pachomian Koinonia*, 1:406 (G^1 149); and Halkin, *Sancti Pachomii vitae graecae*, 94–95. See also Joest, "Pachoms Katechese 'an einen gröllenden Mönch,'" 94.

on the problem of disobedience to the rules of the community among some of the monastic leaders.

Underlying this conflict was the expansion of the Pachomian community both in terms of numbers of monks and in terms of the land on which they lived and worked. As long as Pachomius was alive his federation acquired no agricultural land. He had instated monastic poverty in order to equalize the monks and monasteries, thus aiming to prevent pride, the greatest enemy of community.[21] The monks worked on the land of others for pay.[22] After Pachomius's death Thmoushons began acquiring agricultural land and was becoming prosperous.

In the conflict, the rules requiring accountability to the chief Steward at Pbow seem to have been violated.[23] Thmoushons in particular wanted to

[21] Bernward Büchler, *Die Armut der Armen: Über den ursprünglichen Sinn der Mönchischen Armut* (Munich: Kösel, 1980), 26, 40–41, 59, 62–82.

[22] Ewa Wipszycka, "Les Terres de la congrégation pachômienne dans une liste de payments pour les apora," in *Le Monde grec: Hommages à Claire Préoux*, ed. Jean Bingen, Guy Cambrier, and Georges Nachtergael (Brussels: Éditions de l'Université de Bruxelles, 1975), 635.

[23] Precept 27 of the Pachomian rules required the superior of each monastery to keep account of the work done or neglected in his monastery and to bring it to the annual Remission, "when an account shall be given and sins forgiven everyone." See Armand Veilleux, *Pachomian Chronicles and Rules*, in *Pachomian Koinonia: The Lives, Rules, and Other Writings of Saint Pachomius and his Disciples*, CS 46 (Kalamazoo, MI: Cistercian Publications, 1981), 2:149–50; Boon, *Pachomiana Latina*, 19–20. Regulations 28 and 29 of *The Regulations of Horsiesios* say in part, "It behooves [you] also not to sell or to buy or to do anything, large or small, without [the permission of] the superior of the community and the . . . [*lacuna*]. Let everything, small or large, be registered at the steward's office, clearly and

stock its own supplies over and above those allotted to each monastery by the chief steward, and it wanted to keep its own accounts of these supplies. When Horsiesios refused to let Thmoushons operate independently it threatened to break away from the community.

In *The First Greek Life of Pachomius* the story begins just after Petronius has died. It records that after Horsiesios became the *Apa* of the *koinonia*, he urged the monks

> to keep the rules of the Community which Abba Pachomius had established for its constitution while he was still alive, as well as the decisions of the fathers, the housemasters, and the seconds of the monasteries. And these he appointed at the two moments of the year: at the Passover and at the time of the great remission of the accounts of their bodily needs and of their work and their expenditure, [which they do] so that the steward of the Great Monastery might know how to carry out his administration.[24]

After noting that the chief Steward, Paphnouti, had died, and that Horsiesios had appointed Psahref in his place, the story continues:

> And it happened after this, as the brothers had greatly increased in numbers, that they

---

legibly, so that God's name may be glorified in everything we undertake." See Veilleux, *Pachomian Koinonia*, 2:207; Lefort, *Oeuvres de s. Pachôme et de ses disciples*, CSCO 159, p. 90.

[24] Veilleux, *Pachomian Koinonia*, 1:384–85 (G^1 122); Lefort, *S. Pachomii vitae sahidice scriptae*, CSCO 99–100 (Louvain: L. Durbecq, 1952), 303–4.

> began to expand in fields and many material things in order to feed the multitude. And each monastery began to be a little negligent as other preoccupations increased. A certain Apollonius, father of the monastery of Thmoušons, wanted to buy himself superfluous commodities. Questioned about this by Horsiesios and reprimanded by him, he was vexed. By the enemy's temptation, he wanted to separate his monastery from the Community and he persuaded many elders of the monastery to do so. Many other monasteries were harmed by him because he had seceded, saying, "We no longer belong to the *Koinonia* of the brothers." And because he would not listen to Abba Horsiesios trying to persuade him, the temptation grew stronger.[25]

The Coptic *Life of Pachomius* picks up the story at this point, while Horsiesios is grieving at the loss of "certain monasteries" that had separated from the community and at their disobedience to his guidance. It says that he "was very worried that he himself might be the cause of the dissolution of the *koinonia*" because Apollonius, leader of Thmoushons and his followers, were saying, "We will have nothing to do with Horsiesios nor will we have anything to do with the rules which he lays down."[26]

Overwhelmed by his inability to rein in Thmoushons, Horsiesios despaired and sequestered himself at Sheneset, indicating that Theodore

[25] Veilleux, *Pachomian Koinonia*, 1:387–88 (G[1] 127); Halkin, *Sancti Pachomii vitae graecae*, 80–81.

[26] Veilleux, *Pachomian Koinonia*, 1:195 (SBo 139); and Lefort, *S. Pachomii vitae sahidice scriptae*, 99–100, p. 268.

had the necessary charisma to lead the community and that Theodore was the true successor to Pachomius. Theodore took up the responsibilities of leadership but was always careful to continue acknowledging the ongoing validity of Horsiesios's authority. Among Theodore's first words as *Apa* was a call to repentance: "Now then, brothers, if we have sinned, let us repent. You see, I am going to make a covenant with you today before the Lord concerning the granting of forgiveness for the contempt into which some of you have fallen. For you have raised your hands to tear apart the holy place which the Lord bestowed on our holy father Pachomius because of the prayers and tears which he had offered Him on our behalf."[27]

In time, Theodore was able to reconcile the monks at Thmoushons to the community. One of the practices he established in order to prevent further rebellion was the rotation of the *apas* of the monasteries at the Easter and August gatherings.

In 363 Horsiesios sent Theodore with a delegation of Pachomians to greet Bishop Athanasius of Alexandria as he made a celebratory tour of the Thebaid during Easter after the death of the emperor Julian. The monks welcomed him into their newly founded monasteries of Nouoi and Kahior near Shmoun. After touring and admiring the monasteries, Athanasius sent Theodore back to Horsiesios with a letter in which Athanasius greeted Horsiesios and expressed his joy at meet-

[27] Veilleux, *Pachomian Koinonia*, 1:200 (SBo 142); and Lefort, *S. Pachomii vitae sahidice scriptae*, CSCO 99–100, pp. 188–89. For the Greek version, see Veilleux, *Pachomian Koinonia*, 1:390–91 (G[1] 131); Halkin, *Sancti Pachomii vitae graecae*, 82–83.

ing Horsiesios's "coworker" Theodore, along with the other monks.[28] In this way, Athanasius showed respect for Horsiesios's nominal position as *Apa* and contributed toward Horsiesios's subsequent reintegration into the community.[29]

Horsiesios came back to Pbow in 363, and five years later, in 368, Theodore became ill and died. Horsiesios's anxiety at that time surfaces in two of his four surviving letters. In his third letter, written when Theodore was sick, Horsiesios pleads that there be no disorder but that all be reconciled to God and to each other. To love one another is to be prepared for the return of the bridegroom, he says, like the five wise virgins who were ready with oil in their lamps in Jesus' parable in Matthew 25:1-12.[30] Horsiesios was afraid that Theodore's death, like the deaths of Pachomius and Petronius, would once again cause the community to be fractured. Horsiesios's fourth letter is fragmentary, but he clearly wrote it after the death of Theodore, when Horsiesios became the sole leader again. Horsiesios called on the monks to remember their fathers Pachomius (whom he compares to Moses the lawgiver), Petronius, and Theodore, all of whom taught them to care for each other.[31] There

[28] Veilleux, *Pachomian Koinonia*, 1:253–54 and 402 (SBo 204 and G[1] 144); Lefort, *S. Pachomii vita bohairice scripta*, CSCO 89, p. 202; Halkin, *Sancti Pachomii vitae graecae*, 91.

[29] David Brakke, *Athanasius and Asceticism* (Baltimore and London: Johns Hopkins University Press, 1995), 126; Rousseau, *Pachomius*, 189; Harmless, *Desert Christians*, 139.

[30] Veilleux, *Pachomian Koinonia*, 3:157–58 (Horsiesios, Letter 3.1).

[31] Veilleux, *Pachomian Koinonia*, 3:163–64 (Horsiesios, Letter 4.5).

are some hints in this letter that the unpopular practice of the rotation of *apas* was being challenged after Theodore's death. Horsiesios wrote, "Let no one say, . . . 'I want to remain in this place' or else say, 'I want to go into that community'; but let us all remain in what is established and commanded."[32]

Yet in spite of possible dissatisfaction among the local *apas*, Horsiesios remained undisputedly the general *Apa* of the community. Horsiesios's leadership was affirmed by a letter from Bishop Athanasius of Alexandria, consoling the Pachomian community at the death of Theodore. Athanasius entrusted the care of the community to Horsiesios, since during Theodore's lifetime, he said, the two had been "as one."[33] In both the Bohairic and Greek *Lives* of Pachomius, Athanasius's letter has the last word, and his subtle intervention smoothes the transition of leadership.[34] Horsiesios died during the years that Theophilus was Bishop of Alexandria (385–412 CE).[35]

[32] Veilleux, *Pachomian Koinonia*, 3:164 (Horsiesios, Letter 4.7). See also Heinrich Bacht, *Das Vermächtnis des Ursprungs*, Studien zum frühen Mönchtum 1 (Würzburg: Echter, 1972), 24; Goehring, *Ascetics*, 230, 232.

[33] Veilleux, *Pachomian Koinonia*, 1:264–66 and 406–7 (SBo 210 and G^1 150); Lefort, *S. Pachomii vita bohairice scripta*, CSCO 89, p. 215; and Halkin, *Sancti Pachomii vitae graecae*, 95–96.

[34] Brakke, *Athanasius and Asceticism*, 127–29.

[35] Sometime between 395 and 399 CE Theophilus received a letter about the Pachomians from a bishop named Ammon. It fails to mention Horsiesios at all, perhaps a clue that he had already died by then. For the text of the *Letter of Ammon*, see Veilleux, *Pachomian Koinonia*, 2:2–3, 71–109; and Halkin, *Sancti Pachomii vitae graecae*, 97–121. I follow Jon Dechow in his dating of the *Letter of Ammon* in *Dogma and Mysticism in*

The deaths of the *Apas* triggered dangerous moments of crisis for the Pachomians, threatening the dissolution of their community. A discourse like *On Love and Self-Control* would have been an appropriately urgent call to reconciliation at an August Remission during one of these crises. It may have been delivered after the deaths of Pachomius and Petronius or after the death of Theodore, but it is not possible to say beyond a doubt which of these two transitions of leadership the discourse fits better. Both times of bereavement caused immense anguish, especially for Horsiesos, the common successor of Petronius and of Theodore.[36]

Pachomian Use of On Love and Self-Control *in the Editing of* Instruction concerning a Spiteful Monk

Some time after the discourse *On Love and Self-Control* was delivered and recorded, a large portion of it was slightly altered and sandwiched in between Pachomius's *Instruction concerning a Spiteful Monk* and another sermon calling a monk to vigilance with himself and peace with others. The changes made to *On Love and Self-Control* as it went through this process and was refitted to a

---

Early Christianity: Epiphanius of Cyprus and the Legacy of Origen, Patristic Monograph Series 13 (Macon, GA: Mercer University Press, 1988), 186–87.

[36] *On Love and Self-Control* contains a subtle anti-Arian note, but it does not help to determine whether it should be dated around 350 or 368, since at both times there were Arian emperors on the throne in the eastern half of the Roman empire (Constantius II in 350 and Valens I in 368), making Arianism a continuing issue in Egypt.

new purpose in the Pachomian community hint that as part of the literary compilation *Instruction concerning a Spiteful Monk, On Love and Self-Control* may have been used to address a new situation of conflict, namely, a controversy over the phrase *the image of God,* which enveloped Egyptian monasticism in 399–400 and soon merged into a larger controversy over the theology of Origen of Alexandria (185–254 CE). Initially the question was whether sin has obliterated the image of God in human beings. The section below shows how the Pachomian editor's use of *On Love and Self-Control* in the compilation of *Instruction concerning a Spiteful Monk* highlights references to human beings, even sinners, as the image of God, and thus points indirectly to the editor's stance in the controversy.

There was no single tradition among the Pachomians regarding the concept of the *image of God,* but a dual tradition. The authors of the various *Lives* of Pachomius attribute the term *image of God* almost exclusively to Pachomius himself,[37] who, as Jon Dechow points out, sometimes speaks of the image of God in a non-Origenist way (to refer to a human being per se) and sometimes in an Origenist way (to refer to Christ as the human being par excellence).[38] Since references to human beings

[37] The only exception is Theodore's third instruction, where Theodore quotes Romans 8:29 to speak of people divinely chosen to conform to the image of God's son. See Veilleux, *Pachomian Koinonia,* 3:112 (§31); Lefort, *Oeuvres de s. Pachôme,* CSCO 159, p. 55.

[38] Jon Dechow, *Dogma and Mysticism,* 198–99.

The source of the phrase *image of God* for Pachomius is Genesis. But it would be fascinating to explore the source of Pachomius's interpretation of this phrase. Cassian accused

per se as the image of God emerge in Pachomian literature on occasions of conflict (such as rejections of applicants for admission to the community, expulsions of monks, exorcisms, and reflections upon human sinfulness), it is clear that these human images of God are post-lapsarian, as illustrated in several incidents and teachings from the *Lives* of Pachomius and the *Paralipomena* (a selection of Pachomian anecdotes).

In the first Sahidic *Life*, Pachomius prays for his unruly early community in Tabennesi, remembering that God made even soil into God's image.[39]

Egyptian anti-Origenists of retaining influences from traditional Egyptian religion in their understanding of *the image of God* (Elizabeth Clark, *The Origenist Controversy: The Cultural Construction of an Early Christian Debate* [Princeton, NJ: Princeton University Press, 1992], 56). Could he have been at least partly correct? Might Pachomius have been influenced by the traditional Egyptian religion in which he was raised? Erik Hornung and Boyo Ockinga have studied the concept of the image of God in Pharaonic times (and its potential influence on the Old Testament), noting that the concept applied normally to the ruler, but sometimes also to any human being, who could house a god in his or her heart. Hornung points out that although the image was usually linked to actions reflective of the god Re, such as listening and exercising wisdom, in rare instances human beings were called the image of God regardless of their qualities. See Erik Hornung, *Conceptions of God in Ancient Egypt: The One and the Many*, trans. John Baines (Ithaca, NY: Cornell University Press, 1982), 138–39 and 229–30; Boyo Ockinga, *Die Gottebenbildlichkeit im alten Ägypten und im alten Testament*, Ägypten und altes Testament: Studien zu Geschichte, Kultur und Religion Ägyptens und des altes Testaments 7 (Wiesbaden: Otto Harrassowitz, 1984), 1–2, 142–45, 147–48, and 153.

[39] Veilleux, *Pachomian Koinonia*, 1:434; Lefort, *S. Pachomii vitae sahidice scriptae*, CSCO 99–100, p. 114.

The Bohairic *Life* contains a series of episodes concerning darnel in the community, a metaphor taken from Jesus' parable about the wheat and the weeds growing together in Matthew 13:24-30. First, Pachomius has a vision that inspires him to expel from the community the darnel "who defile the image of God."[40] Then he reluctantly accepts into the community an Alexandrian whom he knows through special insight to be darnel, even though God created him in God's image. One of the other monks questions Pachomius about his refusal to accept some people as monks. Pachomius assures him that it is not because he disregards "God's image" but for the sake of the community.[41] Later, Pachomius is presented with a demon-possessed man. The man is healed when Pachomius prays that God have mercy on him, "because he is your image and likeness."[42] In the *Paralipomena*, Pachomius says that God has sent warnings and witnesses to humanity throughout history because God has always loved humanity, God's image.[43]

But the Sahidic *Lives* of Pachomius in particular also express the contrasting idea that Christ is the sole untarnished image of God. S[3c] C, a set of anonymous homiletic fragments of a Sahidic *Life of Pachomius* not translated by Veilleux, teaches that although humanity was created in the image

[40] Veilleux, *Pachomian Koinonia*, 1:150 (§106); Lefort, *S. Pachomii vita bohairice scripta*, CSCO 89, p. 139.

[41] Veilleux, *Pachomian Koinonia*, 1:153–54 (§107); Lefort, *S. Pachomii vita bohairice scripta*, CSCO 89, pp. 142–44.

[42] Veilleux, *Pachomian Koinonia*, 1:162 (§109); Lefort, *S. Pachomii vita bohairice scripta*, CSCO 89, p. 152.

[43] Veilleux, *Pachomian Koinonia*, 2:63 (§39); Halkin, *Sancti Pachomii vitae graecae*, 162–63.

of God, sinful human beings are now in the image of God only when they are in Christ by faith. Quoting 2 Corinthians 4:4, the first fragment asserts that Christ is the image of God and the tree of life from which Adam and Eve are able to eat only when they take "the pattern [ⲧⲩⲡⲟⲥ] of humans who walk in faith." Fragments two and three both say that Adam was made in the image of God but nevertheless disobeyed God. Until their disobedience, humans had known only good. Since then, they have continued to turn to corrupt use everything God made good. Thus, in commenting on Genesis 3:22, where God observes that the human beings have "become like one of us, knowing good from evil," the text observes that "the Lord did not want Adam to become like him in this way, knowing good and evil." For as fragment one says, the "tree of the knowledge of good and evil is the pattern [ⲧⲩⲡⲟⲥ] of erring humans and heretics."[44]

Further Sahidic references to Christ alone as the image of God in the *Life of Pachomius* appear in a prayer and a vision. In one of his prayers, Pachomius addresses God as the Lord, who "sent us in the world your holy Word, Truth and Life, the true Light, the Invisible who is conformed to your image in everything, our Lord, your beloved Son Jesus Christ who died for us and is risen in order to raise us."[45] In a vision about the future of his

[44] Louis-Théophile Lefort, *Les Vies coptes de saint Pachôme et de ses premiers successeurs*, Bibliothèque du Muséon 16 (1943; reprint, Louvain: Université de Louvain, Institut orientaliste, 1966), 360–70.

[45] Veilleux, *Pachomian Koinonia*, 1:436 (§16); Lefort, *S. Pachomii vitae sahidice scriptae*, CSCO 99–100, p. 115; Lefort, *Les Vies coptes de saint Pachôme et de ses premiers successeurs*, Bibliothèque du

community, Pachomius sees the brothers walking in a dark place with only a small light to guide them. The Lord tells him that the light is "the Gospel of
2 Cor 4:4 the glory of Christ who is the image of God."[46]

On Love and Self-Control nowhere applies *image of God* to the Son or Word of God or to Christ. Rather, it consistently uses this term to refer to human beings, and sinners at that, lost sheep whom the "living Word" has rescued. *Instruction concerning a Spiteful Monk* takes over this usage and intensifies it in a way that suggests that its editor made his composition during the monastic controversy in Egypt over the proper understanding of *image of God*.

This controversy about whether human beings retain the image of God erupted in Egypt in 399. *The Life of Aphou* records that in his festal letter for that year Theophilus, bishop of Alexandria, wrote that human beings, because of their weakness in contrast to God's glory, are not in the image of God.[47] The theological anthropology expressed by Theophilus was part of an inheritance from Origen, the church's influential Alexandrian scholar and teacher in

Muséon 16 (1943; repr. Louvain: Université de Louvain, Institut orientaliste, 1966), 67; Dechow, *Dogma and Mysticism in Early Christianity*, 198–99.

[46] Veilleux, *Pachomian Koinonia*, 1:144 (§103); Lefort, *S. Pachomii vitae sahidice scriptae*, CSCO 99–100, p. 259; Lefort, *Les Vies coptes*, 174. (The reflection on 2 Cor 4:4 was omitted from the Bohairic *Life*.)

[47] Tim Vivian, *Four Desert Fathers, Pambo, Evagrius, Macarius of Egypt, and Macarius of Alexandria: Coptic Texts Relating to the* Lausiac History *of Palladius*, Popular Patristics Series (Crestwood, NY: St. Vladimir's Seminary Press, 2004), 183.

the third century. But not all Egyptians shared this theological anthropology, as John Cassian wrote in his fifth-century work on Egytian monastic spirituality, saying that the festal letter was received with "great bitterness by nearly all the various sorts of monks who were living throughout the province of Egypt."[48] Cassian accuses the non-Origenist monks of anthropomorphism, but as Georges Florovsky has pointed out, the monks were not insisting that God somehow has a body; rather, they were insisting that human beings are still somehow in the image of God.[49] This issue soon became enmeshed with a number of other issues stemming from Origen of Alexandria, and the controversy lurched on and spread.[50] Theophilus

[48] Boniface Ramsey, *John Cassian: The Conferences*, Ancient Christian Writers 57 (New York, and Mahwah, NJ: Paulist Press, 1997), 371. As an Origenist himself, Cassian was exaggerating the amount of opposition to the festal letter. In fact, many Egyptian monks at the time were Origenist (see Samuel Rubenson, *The Letters of St. Antony: Monasticism and the Making of a Saint,* Studies in Antiquity and Christianity [Minneapolis: Fortress, 1995], 37, 190).

[49] Georges Florovsky, *Aspects of Church History*, vol. 4 of *The Collected Works of Georges Florovsky* (Belmont, MA: Nordland, 1975), 119.

[50] In commenting on Genesis 1:26 in his Homilies on Genesis, Origen asserts that the image of God is strictly speaking only the eternal Word and Son of God. The intellectual form of humanity was created according to this image before the formation of the human body, which is not part of the image of God. But in humanity, he said, the image of God was "laid aside" because of evil. So the Savior became incarnate, taking the image of humanity in order to enable humanity to regain the likeness of the image of God through participation in the Savior's "spiritual image." See Origen, *Origen: Homilies on Genesis and Exodus*, trans. Ronald E. Heine, The Fathers of the

conceded to monastic pressure on the issue of the image of God and subsequently launched an anti-Origenist campaign that had a profound impact on Egyptian monasticism.

On Love and Self-Control exemplifies the monastic stance equating "human being" with "image of God" when it bases its call for mutual love on the assumption that each person is the image of God. Three times it speaks of human beings as the image of God:

1. This very form, namely, the human being, the image of God, this one for whom the living Word bore these troubles, you hate because of jealousy and empty glory or greatness, in which the enemy has bound you so that he might make you a stranger to the living God.[51]
2. For how many wrongdoings will you be able to give account, O human? For the . . . adulteries of the heart toward the image of God?[52]
3. Paul said, "I fought the good struggle, I completed the course, I guarded the faith, so now the crown of righteousness is placed before me."* And not for him alone, but for us also, if we endure in grief and humility: grief because of the passions that are at work in the body, and humility because of our neighbor, the image of God.[53]

*2 Tim 4:7-8

Church (Washington, DC: The Catholic University of American Press, 1981), 61–67.

[51] Lantschoot, "Lettre de saint Athanase," 271; Lefort, "Sur la charité et la tempérance," CSCO 150, p. 114.

[52] Lantschoot, "Lettre de saint Athanase," 272–73; Lefort, "Sur la charité et la tempérance," CSCO 150, p. 115.

[53] Lantschoot, "Lettre de saint Athanase," 278; Lefort, "Sur la charité et la tempérance," CSCO 150, p. 120.

These references to human beings as the image of God all occur in the section of *On Love and Self-Control* that was added to *Instruction concerning a Spiteful Monk*. When the compiler attached his paraphrased version of *On Love and Self-Control* to *Instruction concerning a Spiteful Monk,* he cut off the first third of the discourse *On Love and Self-Control,* beginning his selection precisely where the text begins to use the phrase *the image of God*. Then, in his adaptation of *On Love and Self-Control,* the editor added to it a fourth reference to human beings as the image of God. Since the original *Instruction concerning a Spiteful Monk* at the beginning of the compilation already contained two references to humans as the image of God, and the piece of a discourse at the end of the compilation contained one more reference to humans as the image of God, all sections of the compilation *Instruction concerning a Spiteful Monk* contain a consistent reference to people as the image of God in spite of their sinfulness.

The editor seems to have been working during the controversy over the image of God. Furthermore, he seems to have been working at a stage of this controversy when the original issue of the image of God had become part of a larger conflict over Origenism. The evidence for this inference is the fact that he deleted a passage from *On Love and Self-Control* that stresses the ineffability of God in a manner very reminiscent of Origen's comments on prayer. The passage excised from *On Love and Self-Control* says, "We have been given prayer and steadfastness, which fill the eyes of the soul with light up to the place where God sits, so that we might gaze at the glory of the unseen one himself and fear before his unnameable fatherhood."[54] In the adaptation of the text for his compilation, the monk cut this passage short to "We have been given holy prayer and steadfastness, which fill the soul with light,"[55] deleting the reference to the eyes of the soul gazing at the "glory of the unseen one."

It seems that when *On Love and Self-Control* was first delivered, there was space in the Pachomian community for Origenist ideas and non-Origenist ideas to dwell together; the discourse used the term *image of God* in a non-Origenist way to refer to sinful humanity while simultaneously alluding to Origen on prayer. But in the heat of the controversy at the turn of the century, the Pachomian editor who added part of *On Love and Self-Control*

[54] Lantschoot, "Lettre de saint Athanase," 275; Lefort, "Sur la charité et la tempérance," CSCO 150, pp. 117–18. In the ninth chapter of his treatise *On Prayer*, Origen wrote, "'To you have I lifted up my eyes, you who dwell in heaven' (Ps. 123:1) and 'To you, O God, have I lifted up my soul' (Ps. 25:1). For the eyes of the mind are . . . so exalted that they peer beyond the created order and arrive at the sheer contemplation of God . . . . How would things so great fail to profit those eyes that gaze at the glory of the Lord with unveiled face and that are being changed into his likeness [εἰκόνα] from glory to glory (cf. 2 Cor. 3:18)? For then they partake of some divine and intelligible radiance. This is demonstrated by the verse 'The light of your countenance, O Lord, has been signed upon us' (Ps. 4:6)." See Rowan Greer, *Origen: An Exhortation to Martyrdom, Prayer, First Principles: Book IV, Prologue to the Commentary on the Song of Songs, Homily XXVII on Numbers*, Classics of Western Spirituality (New York, Ramsey, and Toronto: Paulist Press, 1979), 99; Paul Koetschau, *Origenes Werke*, vol. 2, Die griechischen christlichen Schriftsteller der ersten drei Jahrhunderte (Leipzig: J. C. Hinrichs'sche Buchhandlung, 1899), 318–19.

[55] Veilleux, *Pachomian Koinonia*, 3:34; Budge, *Coptic Apocrypha*, 167; Lefort, *Oeuvres de s. Pachôme*, CSCO 159, p. 18.

to *Instruction concerning a Spiteful Monk* chose to focus on the non-Origenist element of *On Love and Self-Control* and to delete the Origenist element in his paraphrasing of the text, suggesting that for him the two elements could no longer coinhabit the mind.

The way that the Pachomian editor altered the text of *On Love and Self-Control* in adding it to his compilation with *Instruction concerning a Spiteful Monk* also reflects a shift in the engagement of the Pachomian community with ideological issues and questions of heresy. In drawing attention to this shift, James Goehring observed that theological diversity was accepted in the early days of the Pachomian community because Pachomius's original emphasis "was on an orthodox practice and not on an orthodox theology."[56] But after Pachomius's death, the community had to institutionalize the charismatic leadership of its founder. It did so under the leadership of Theodore through increased stress on the rules of the *koinonia* and through increasingly close ties with the wider ecclesiastical leadership, especially with the bishop of Alexandria, who at that time was Athanasius. Doctrinal uniformity according to episcopal standards of theological orthodoxy grew to be important among the Pachomians, and their literature reflects it, sometimes even anachronistically. For example, the Greek *Life of Pachomius* portrays Pachomius himself as an opponent of Origenism, suggesting that the text was written during the Origenist controvery and its authors wanted to

[56] Goehring, *Ascetics*, 160.

depict themselves as a community that was anti-Origenist from the start.[57]

The same dynamic seems to have been at work in the editing of *On Love and Self-Control*: an earlier text that included both Origenist and non-Origenist ideas was purged of its Origenism and fortified in its non-Origenism, indicating that the historical setting for the editing of material to create the compilation *Instruction concerning a Spiteful Monk* as it exists today was the Egyptian controversy over the image of God and its intersection with the wider Origenist controversy at the turn of the fourth to fifth century. The original *On Love and Self-Control* contains an injunction not to "participate in conversation with any heresy in argument, lest the inexpressible glory of divinity be blasphemed." This warning against involvement in theological controversy, too, was deleted by the later editor, who appears to have been involved in theological controversy.

The Dissolution of the Pachomian Community

Conflict wracked the Pachomian community from time to time. Ultimately ideological conflict destroyed it. I here describe its dissolution as a result of controversy over the Council of Chalcedon in order to show that the manuscript of *On Love and Self-Control* has not come down directly from the Pachomians but rather indirectly through a non-Pachomian monastery as part of an anti-Chalcedonian codex.

The Council of Chalcedon (451 CE) had made two decisions that were offensive to most Egyptian

[57] Goehring, *Ascetics*, 208–18.

Christians: it had deposed Dioscorus, archbishop of Alexandria (444–454 CE), and it had adopted a formula describing Christ in two natures (divine and human) rather than in one indissoluble nature out of the two. Nevertheless, Egyptian supporters of the council could also be found, including among the Pachomians, whose community seems to have tolerated various views of Chalcedon for a time. But in the sixth century something went wrong. The call of *On Love and Self-Control* for the monks to love one another and to be reconciled seems to have gone unheeded.

The story of Elias of Samhud in an Upper Egyptian *synaxarion* reveals tension within the Pachomian community at that time. As a young man, Elias entered the monastery of the Pachomians at Pbow and lived an ascetic life, but he left when he found that "the holy memory had been changed and that dissension and discord existed in the monastery."[58] An account of the sixth-century Pachomian *Apas* says that after an *Apa* named Pshentbahse died, "the schism happened in the community," after which Abraham was appointed

[58] A *synaxarion* is a calendar of saints' days and other commemorations in the Coptic church, including stories about the saints. Elias of Samhud was commemorated on the 13th of Kiyahk (December 9). See René Basset, *Le Synaxaire arabe jacobite (rédaction copte) II: Les Mois de Hatour et de Kihak*, PO 13, tome III, fasc. 3 (Paris: Firmin-Didot, 1909), 436–41, especially 440; *The Coptic Encyclopedia*, vol. 3, s.v. "Elias of Samhud, Saint," by René-Georges Coquin; Iacobus Forget, *Synaxarium alexandrinum* I.3, CSCO 49, Scriptores arabici 5 (Louvain: L. Durbecq, 1954), ٣٣٢-٣٢٩, especially ٣٣١; and Iacobus Forget, *Synaxarium alexandrinum* I, CSCO 78, Scriptores arabici 12 (Louvain: L. Durbecq, 1953), 222–25, especially 224–25.

as *Apa*.[59] Once again the transition of leadership was a time of crisis for the Pachomians, this time leading to a schism that appears to have been a breach between Chalcedonian and non-Chalcedonian Pachomians.

After Emperor Justinian acceded to the throne (527–565 CE), he attempted to reunify his cracked and fragile empire under Chalcedonian Christianity, providing occasion for previously latent theological conflict in the Pachomian community to break out into the open. A fragmentary *Panegyric on Manasseh* records that when Abraham, a non-Chalcedonian, was *Apa*, some Pachomian monks brought a complaint against him to Emperor Justinian. What happened next is lost. But apparently, Justinian sent representatives to investigate Pbow, because when the textual fragments pick up the story again, one of the complainants is reporting to the emperor that when the representatives left, Abraham ordered the monks to wash the "meeting place" with water "as though it were polluted by you our lord, the emperor, and all who are under the authority of the Roman Empire."[60]

[59] ⲙⲛ̄ⲛ̄[ⲥⲁⲛⲁ]ⲓ̈ ⲁⲡⲥⲭⲓⲥⲙⲁ [ϣⲱ]ⲡⲉ ϩⲛ̄ⲧⲕⲟⲓ[ⲛⲱ]ⲛⲓⲁ. Lefort, *S. Pachomii vitae sahidice scriptae*, CSCO 99–100, p. 361; Lefort, *Les Vies coptes de saint Pachôme*, 406; and Émile Amélineau, *Monuments pour servir à l'histoire de l'Égypte chrétienne aux IVe, Ve, VIe, et VIIe siècles*, Mémoires publiés par les membres de la mission archéologique française au Caire, tome 4, fasc. 2 (Paris: Ernest Leroux, 1895), 743–44.

[60] James E. Goehring, "Keeping the Monastery Clean: A Cleansing Episode from an Excerpt on Abraham of Farshut and Shenoute's Discourse on Purity," in *The World of Early Egyptian Christianity: Language, Literature, and Social Context, Essays in Honor of David W. Johnson*, ed. James E. Goehring and

The reporter suggests that since he and his fellow complainants shared the emperor's theological convictions, the emperor ought to remove Abraham and give his office to them.[61]

The emperor grasped the opportunity of this "internal ideological dispute within the Pachomian federation," Goehring says, to offer "the pro-Chalcedonian Pachomians the occasion to gain the upper hand and extend their control of the federation in Upper Egypt by seizing power in the central Monastery of Pbow."[62] Justinian summoned Abraham to Constantinople and gave him an ultimatum: he could commune with the emperor and return home with his rank, or he could refuse and never return to his monastery. Abraham wrote a letter to his monastic community, telling them that he was no longer their *Apa*. Justinian then sent Bankares, one of the monks who had originally complained about Abraham, to Pbow as the new *Apa*. When he arrived with soldiers who had orders to drive out any who would not recognize the faith of the emperor, many of the monks fled. The non-Chalcedonian Empress Theodora somehow managed to get Abraham back to Egypt, where he went to the Monastery of Saint Shenoute of Atripe to copy the monastic rules in

---

Janet Timbie, CUA Studies in Early Christianity (Washington, DC: The Catholic University of America Press, 2007), 159.

[61] Goehring, "Keeping the Monastery Clean," 160.

[62] James E. Goehring, "Remembering Abraham of Farshut: History, Hagiography, and the Fate of the Pachomian Tradition," 2005 NAPS Presidential Address, *The Journal of Early Christian Studies* 14, no. 1 (2006): 17.

the *scriptorium* in order to found a new monastery at a place called Farshut.[63]

Although reduced in numbers, the Pachomian community continued in Chalcedonian form for a while but eventually dissolved. By the eleventh century even its former headquarters of Pbow was a deserted ruin.[64] No books have been found there.[65] The ruins of the other Pachomian monasteries have yet to be located and excavated.

[63] René Basset, *Le synaxaire arabe-jacobite (redaction copte) III: Les Mois de Toubeh et d'Amchir*, PO 56, tome XI, fasc. 5 (Paris: Didot, 1915), 684; and Forget, *Synaxarium alexandrinum* I.3, CSCO 49, Scriptores arabici 5, ٤١٢-٤١١; Forget, *Synaxarium alexandrinum* I, CSCO 78, Scriptores arabici 12, pp. 402–3; Émile Amélineau, *Vie d'Abraham*, in *Monuments pour servir*, 746; Goehring, *Ascetics*, 247–48.

[64] Basil T. A. Evetts and Alfred J. Butler, *The Churches and Monasteries of Egypt and Some Neighboring Countries, Attributed to Abû Sâlih, the Armenian* (Oxford: Clarendon, 1895; repr. London: Butler & Tanner, 1969), 281–82; Kurt J. Werthmuller, *Coptic Identity and Ayyubid Politics in Egypt, 1218–1250* (Cairo and New York: The American University in Cairo Press, 2010), 23–25; Goehring, *Ascetics*, 86; and *The Coptic Enclclopedia*, s.v. "Pbow: Archaeology," by Peter Grossmann.

[65] James M. Robinson has suggested that in the remains of the library of Pbow are a stash of documents known as the Dishna Papers and that these were buried after Justinian imposed Chalcedonianism on the community; they include several of the letters of Pachomius, Theodore, and Horsiesios. See James M. Robinson, "The First Christian Monastic Library," in *Coptic Studies: Acts of the Third International Congress of Coptic Studies, Warsaw, 20–25 August, 1984*, ed. Wlodzimierz Godlewski (Warsaw: Pánstwowe Wydawnictwo Naukowe, 1990), 371–78; and Robinson, *The Story of the Bodmer Papyri: From the First Monastery's Library in Upper Egypt to Geneva and Dublin* (Eugene, OR: Cascade, 2011), esp. 130–84. The Dishna Papers were discovered accidentally by locals around 1952 in a village near the ruins of Pbow and gradually sold piecemeal to antiquities

The ruined church of the monastery of Pbow in the surrounding village known in Arabic as Faw. (Photograph by Carolyn M. Schneider, 2012.)

---

dealers. The uncontrolled nature of the discovery and distribution of this find, however, has led to debate about which manuscripts are actually part of the collection. Rudolph Kasser summarizes the doubts in *The Coptic Encyclopedia*, vol. 8: Appendix, s.v. "Bodmer Papyri," 48–53. In any case, the manuscripts do not include *On Love and Self-Control*.

Debate also continues over whether the collection of texts discovered at Nag Hammadi, also near Pbow, once belonged to the Pachomians. Because of the Origenist nature of many of the texts, it has been suggested that Origenist Pachomians hid them when the Alexandrian bishops imposed anti-Origenism on monastic communities in the fifth century. See Hugo Lundhaug and Lance Jenott, *The Monastic Origins of the Nag Hammadi Codices*, Studien und Texte zu Antike und Christentum 97 (Tübingen: Mohr Siebeck, 2015). Like the Dishna papers, the Nag Hammadi documents do not include *On Love and Self-Control*.

On Love and Self-Control ***and Its Codex (MONB.CP)***

The Provenance of the Manuscript of On Love and Self-Control

The manuscript of *On Love and Self-Control* comes from the Monastery of Saint Shenoute of Atripe, located north of the ruins of Pbow, further down the Nile, near the modern city of Sohag. (See the map, p. 13 above.) This still-active monastery is often called the White Monastery because of the light-colored stone used to build its enormous church.[66] It is named after its most renowned leader, *Apa* Shenoute (ca. 348–ca. 464 CE). It was in this monastery that the sole remaining manuscript of *On Love and Self-Control* was copied, probably in the late eleventh or early twelfth century, when Sahidic was still in use in the monastery. During the twelfth century Sahidic was gradually replaced in Upper Egypt by Bohairic, the Coptic dialect of Lower Egypt, and by Arabic.[67]

[66] The first extant literary occurrence of the name *White Monastery* is from the work of the Muslim historical geographer Yaqut (1179–1229), but he was using a term already known. See Stefan Timm, *Das christlich-koptische Ägypten in arabischer Zeit*, part 2, Beihefte zum Tübinger Atlas des vorderen Orients, Series B, no. 41/2 (Wiesbaden: Dr. Ludwig Reichert, 1984), 622.

[67] Emmanuel Lanne, *Le grand euchologe du Monastère Blanc*, PO 135, tome XXVIII, fasc. 2 (Paris: Firmin-Didot, 1958), 273; Ugo Zanetti, "Bohairic Liturgical Manuscripts," 61, no. 1 (1995): 67; and Heinzgerd Brakmann, "Fragmenta graeco-copto-thebaicq: Zu Jutta Henners Veröffentlichung alter und neuer Dokumente südägyptischer Liturgie," *Oriens christianus* 88 (2004): 136n70; Samuel Rubenson, "Translating the Tradition: Some Remarks on the Arabization of the Patristic Heritage in Egypt," *Medieval*

The monastic network that Shenoute led was younger than the Pachomian network. It was founded sometime in the mid-fourth century by a man named Pcol, who adapted the evolving rule of Pachomius to establish a stricter rule in his own community.[68] Ebonh (not the Pachomian) succeeded Pcol, and Shenoute then became the third archimandrite of the community around the year 385, further adapting the rule of *Apa* Pcol. Shenoute's federation consisted of the Monastery of Shenoute (the White Monastery), the Monastery of *Apa* Pshoi, known in Arabic as *Anba* Bishay (the nearby Red Monastery), a women's monastery slightly south of the White Monastery, and "a cluster of male and female hermits."[69] The Monastery of Shenoute had a *scriptorium* that was very active, and a large library from which about ten thousand leaves survive.[70] Archeological excavations are on-

---

Encounters 2, no. 1 (1996): 7; and Arietta Papaconstantinou, "'They Shall Speak the Arabic Language and Take Pride in It': Reconsidering the Fate of Coptic after the Arab Conquest," *Le Muséon* 120, nos. 3–4 (2007): 282–84.

[68] Bentley Layton, "Some Observations on Shenoute's Sources: Who Are Our Fathers?" *Journal of Coptic Studies* 11 (2009): 50.

[69] Bentley Layton, "The Ancient Rules of Shenoute's Monastic Federation," in *Akhmim and Sohag*, ed. Gawdat Gabra and Hany Takla, vol. 1 of *Christianity and Monasticism in Upper Egypt* (Cairo: The American University in Cairo Press, 2008), 75.

[70] Tito Orlandi, "The Library of the Monastery of Saint Shenoute at Atripe," in *Perspectives on Panopolis: An Egyptian Town from Alexander the Great to the Arab Conquest, Acts from an International Symposium Held in Leiden on 16, 17 and 18 December 1998*, ed. A Egberts, B. P. Muhs, and J. van der Vliet, Papyrologica Lugduno-Batava 31 (Leiden: Brill, 2002), 229.

going at the Monastery of Saint Shenoute of Atripe, but the room that served as the *scriptorium* has not yet been identified.

In 1883, four thousand parchment folio fragments were found in a small room above the monastery's church.[71] This room was too small to have been the full library, but it may have been used to hold books that were used in worship. Inscriptions found on the walls at the time but no longer visible listed the room's contents. Among other entries on the east wall were the "discourses of the archbishops." The west wall listed twenty copies of the *Life of Apa Pachomius*; further down the list was another copy of the *Life of Apa Pachomius* along with those of *Apas* Horsiesios and Theodore.[72] It is clear that the community of Shenoute treasured the Pachomian heritage and preserved its literature.

The Creation of the Codex in the Late Sixth or Early Seventh Century

When it was copied, the manuscript of *On Love and Self-Control* was part of a book, but in the nineteenth century the codex was dismembered and its pieces disseminated among several institutions. The work of identifying the texts that once belonged together in the codex is ongoing.

[71] Orlandi, "The Library of the Monastery of Saint Shenoute at Atripe," 212.

[72] Orlandi, "The Library of the Monastery of Saint Shenoute at Atripe," 213–15, 225; Walter Ewing Crum, "Inscriptions from Shenoute's Monastery," *The Journal of Theological Studies* 5 (1904): 564–66. See also Sofia Schaten and Jacques van der Vliet, "Monks and Scholars in the Panopolite Nome: The Epigraphic Evidence," in *Christianity and Monasticism in Upper Egypt*, 1:138.

Sunday school children visit the remains of the ancient church at the Monastery of Saint Shenoute of Atripe. From this view toward the east, one enters the small door to participate in the liturgy. Just above the worship space in the north corner is the room where *On Love and Self-Control* was found, among many other fragments. (Photograph by Carolyn M. Schneider, 2012.)

Scholars refer to this partially reconstructed codex as MONB.CP, where MONB indicates its provenance in the White Monastery (*Monastero Bianco* in Italian), and CP is simply the two-letter designation that identifies this particular codex.[73]

MONB.CP is an anthology of letters and "words" (discourses or homilies) by highly respected church leaders of the fourth century to the turn of the sixth-seventh centuries around the

[73] See Tito Orlandi, "MONB.CP:00FF," Corpus dei manoscritti copti letterari, http://rmcisadu.let.uniroma1.it/cgi-bin/cmcl/chiamata.cgi (accessed Jan. 2, 2012). See also Orlandi, "The Library of the Monastery of Saint Shenoute at Atripe," 230–31.

broad theme of living an ascetic life and developing the spiritual virtues. The contents of MONB.CP that have been identified so far are attributed to Athanasius of Alexandria (298–373 CE), Liberius of Rome (?–366 CE), Gregory of Nyssa (ca. 335–ca. 395 CE), Basil of Caesarea (ca. 330–379 CE), John Chrysostom (ca. 347–407), Severian of Jabalah (dates unknown, contemporary of John Chrysostom),[74] Severus of Antioch (ca. 465–538 CE), and Constantine of Assiut (dates unknown, consecrated bishop between 578 and 604 CE).

Although it is possible that the eleventh-/twelfth-century scribe who copied the codex was also its compiler, the headings of the texts provide clues that it is more likely that he was copying an existing compilation. Some of the texts identified as part of the codex are now acephalous fragments, but the headings of eleven texts are still in place. These headings use terminology that points to a date of compilation in the late sixth or early seventh century. First, the headings all seem to have been composed by the same person, who uses the word *likewise* at least four times to link the headings to each other. For example, in the manuscript containing *On Love and Self-Control* (BL Or. 8802), the text of *On Love and Self-Control* ends on line 24 of folio 4 verso; the heading of the next text, a letter of Severus of Antioch to Theognostus, begins on the next line with the words, "Likewise,

[74] The sermons of Severian of Jabalah were often transmitted under the name of John Chrysostom. In MONB.CP the folio containing the heading of Severian's sermon is missing, so it is impossible to see whether the scribe attributed the work to Severian or to Chrysostom.

an epistle." Certain phrases are repeated in the headings as well, such as "A word of [Name] that he preached," and "our holy father esteemed in every aspect."

Each extant heading names the author of the text it introduces. The scribe uses the title of *archbishop* to refer to Liberius of Rome, Athanasius of Alexandria, and John Chrysostom of Constantinople. Bishops of Alexandria, such as Athanasius, came to be called archbishop only from the turn of the fourth to the fifth century, after Athanasius's lifetime and after the original composition of *On Love and Self-Control*. The fact that the heading in MONB.CP refers to Athanasius as archbishop indicates that it was not part of the original mid-fourth-century text of *On Love and Self-Control* but was added later. In introducing works by Severus of Antioch the scribe consistently gives him the title *the holy patriarch and archbishop of Antioch*. Severus of Antioch is the only bishop who receives the title of *patriarch* in the extant headings of MONB.CP. The fact that this title is not applied to Athanasius in MONB.CP suggests that the headings were probably composed before the seventh century, because the title of *patriarch* was not applied to bishops of Alexandria until the late sixth or seventh century.[75]

The late sixth or early seventh century is the earliest time that the compilation could have been made. It includes a discourse by Constantine of Assiut. The exact years of Constantine's life

[75] Harmless, *Desert Christians*, 16; and Maged S. A. Mikhail, "Egypt from Late Antiquity to Early Islam: Copts, Melkites, and Muslims Shaping a New Society," PhD dissertation, The University of California, Los Angeles, 2004, 109, 278.

are not known, but he was consecrated bishop between 578 and 604 by Archbishop Damian of Alexandria (576–605 CE), who greatly admired him.[76] No author after Constantine's time is represented in MONB.CP, at least insofar as it has been reconstructed.

Damian's episcopate was a fruitful era for Coptic literature, characterized by a focus on uniquely Egyptian theology and the needs of the Egyptian church in the post-Chalcedonian environment. Tito Orlandi says that this focus included "an effort to identify the old leading personalities, especially Athanasius, as the founders of the Coptic church, which is now identified as the Egyptian church as a whole."[77] "The old leading personalities" certainly included the authors of the texts in MONB. CP, Athanasius among them. This may be the era in which a scribe put together this anthology, and it is very likely that the work was done in the *scriptorium* of the Monastery of Saint Shenoute of Atripe. The texts would have been at hand there, since during Shenoute's lifetime the library of his monastery was acquiring works by Athanasius,

[76] Basil Evetts, *History of the Patriarchs of the Coptic Church of Alexandria II: Peter I to Benjamin I (661)*, PO 4, tome I, fasc. 4, ed. René Graffin and François Nau (Paris: Firmin-Didot, 1907), 477; and Gérard Garitte, "Constantin, évêque d'Assiout," in *Coptic Studies in Honor of Walter Ewing Crum*, Bulletin of the Byzantine Institute 2 (Boston: The Byzantine Institute, 1950), 287–304.

[77] Tito Orlandi, "Coptic Literature," in *The Roots of Egyptian Christianity*, ed. Birger A. Pearson and James E. Goehring, Studies in Antiquity & Christianity (Philadelphia: Fortress, 1986), 75; see also Tito Orlandi, "Atanasio di Alessandria: 0014," in *Corpus dei manoscritti copti letterari*, http://www.cmcl.it/ (accessed January 2, 2012).

Basil of Caesarea, and Gregory of Nyssa, among others.[78] Shenoute's successor, Besa, reveals that the library had a work of Athanasius that was later included in MONB.CP when he explicitly quotes from "the beloved of God, Apa Athanasius," citing a paragraph from the *Fragments on the Moral Life* preserved in Manchester, J. Rylands Lib. 62 [Crawford 25], fol. 2.[79] Perhaps the scribe compiling MONB.CP was working during the lifetime or shortly after the death of Constantine of Assiut. He gives Constantine's discourse the following heading: "A word of our holy father, esteemed in every aspect, *Apa* Constantine, the bishop of the city of Assiut, that he preached in the presence of fathers of a faithful monastery, very reverent,

[78] Stephen Emmel, *Shenoute's Literary Corpus*, vol. 2, CSCO 600, Subsidia 112 (Louvain: Peeters, 2004), 607–8; and Tito Orlandi, "Gregorio di Nissa nella letteratura copta," *Vetera christianorum* 18 (1981): 335–38. Gregory of Nyssa's works may have been already translated for them from Greek into Sahidic in the fifth century by pro-Origenist Pachomians. See Tito Orlandi, "Gregorio di Nissa nella letteratura copta," 339; and Tito Orlandi, "Gregorio di Nissa: 0052," in *Corpus dei manoscritti copti letterari*, http://www.cmcl.it/ (accessed January 2, 2012).

[79] For Besa's quotation, see *Letters and Sermons of Besa*, ed. K. H. Kuhn, CSCO 157 (Coptic), and CSCO 158 (English) (Louvain: L. Durbecq, 1956), 157:82, 158:79. For the Athanasian original, see Lefort, *S. Athanase*, CSCO 150, pp. XXXI–XXXIII, 153, and CSCO 151, pp. 103–4; and Brakke, *Fragments on the Moral Life*, appendix in *Athanasius and Asceticism*, 315–16. See also Walter Ewing Crum, *Catalogue of the Coptic Manuscripts in the Collection of the John Rylands Library, Manchester* (Manchester: The University Press; London: Bernard Quaritch, and Sherratt and Hughes, 1909), 24–25. It is on the basis of Besa's witness that the text, which has lost its heading, is attributed to Athanasius.

chosen people and worshipers of God." The monastery he mentions could have been the Monastery of al-Hanadah in Assiut, where Constantine lived and which had ties with the Monastery of Shenoute of Atripe.[80]

In introducing a book about handwritten codices in the Middle Ages, Stephen Kelly and John Johnson write that a "manuscript book is often . . . constitutive of a community's sense of itself: of the narratives, discourses, grammars, and metaphors with which a community will give an account of itself."[81] If MONB.CP is one example of an Egyptian monastic community's accounting of itself, then the discourses included in MONB.CP, like *On Love and Self-Control*, must have expressed its values. If this anthology was indeed compiled at a time when the anti-Chalcedonian Egyptian church was at odds with its Byzantine rulers, then even the language in which the monks chose to express their values in MONB.CP is significant. They chose Sahidic rather than Greek, in spite of the fact that many of the texts in the codex are translations

[80] *The Coptic Encyclopedia*, vol. 2, s.v. "Constantine: History," by René-Georges Coquin; Coquin, "Saint Constantin, évêque d'Asyut," *Studia orientalia christiana collectanea* 16 (1981): 151–70; Émile Amélineau, *La Géographie de l'Égypte à l'époque copte* (Paris: Imprimerie nationale, 1893), 499–500; René Basset, *Le Synaxaire arabe jacobite (rédaction copte) II: Les Mois de Hatour et de Kihak*, PO 13, tome III, fasc. 3, 321–23; and Forget, *Synaxarium alexandrinum* I.3, CSCO 49, Scriptores arabici 5, ٣٠٥; and Forget, *Synaxarium alexandrinum* I, CSCO 78, Scriptores arabici 12, pp. 143–44.

[81] Stephen Kelly and John J. Johnson, *Imagining the Book*, Medieval Texts and Cultures of Northern Europe (Turnhout: Brepols, 2005), 9.

from Greek. The authors whose work the monks selected for their anthology and the language in which they presented that work may say something about the community's self-understanding as southern Egyptians in an anti-Chalcedonian church seeking to establish an identity as the true successor of the pre-Chalcedonian church.

Issues of Authorship

Attribution to Athanasius

The heading affixed to *On Love and Self-Control*, from which the English title comes, leads to questions about the author of the text. The heading says, "A letter of our holy father, esteemed in every aspect, *apa* Athanasius, the Archbishop of Alexandria, about love and self-control. In peace."[82] This heading thus explicitly attributes the work to Athanasius, the Bishop of Alexandria from 328–373 CE, and there is no reason to doubt that the scribe believed it was by Athanasius. The other works in the codex are correctly ascribed to their authors, and there are features of the discourse *On Love and Self-Control* that are compatible with Athanasian thought and style; these are summarized below. But there are also weighty features of the discourse that are incompatible with Athanasian thought and style. A review of these leads to the conclusion that Athanasius was probably not the author of the discourse *On Love and Self-Control*.

[82] Lantschoot, "Lettre de saint Athanase," 267; Lefort, "Sur la charité et la tempérance," CSCO 150, p. 110, and CSCO 151, p. 88.

Affinities between Athanasian Writings and On Love and Self-Control

A sixth- or seventh-century scribe of the Monastery of Shenoute encountering the text of *On Love and Self-Control* would have had good reasons to think it was Athanasian.[83] Theologically, the treatise does evoke themes found in Athanasius's works with by far the majority of these thematic elements found in Athanasius's *Festal Letters*, his annual open letters to the Egyptian church announcing the date of Easter and reflecting on the significance of the feast, along with other theological and practical matters. Some of the Athanasian themes in *On Love and Self-Control* also appear in the *Life of Antony* and in Athanasius's correspondence with monks, such as his letter to Dracontius, a monk seeking to avoid ordination by Athanasius as bishop of Hermopolis Parva; his two letters to Alexandrian female virgins; his treatise on virginity, and fragments of a treatise on the moral life. This last text is especially significant because Athanasius's treatise on the moral life is one of the other texts the scribe chose to include in MONB.CP. A theme echoing *On Love and Self-Control* also sounds in Athanasius's second brief letter to Horsiesios when Horsiesios was *Apa* of the Pachomian community.

In his examination of the authenticity of *On Love and Self-Control* as an Athanasian work, David Brakke identified three connections between *On Love and Self-Control* and Athanasius's writings:

[83] It is impossible to know whether the text that the scribe was copying was anonymous or was already attributed to Athanasius.

the use of nautical imagery to describe the Christian life, the cautionary example of the five virgins denied entry into the kingdom of heaven,* and the allowance for moderation in drinking wine instead of complete prohibition.[84] First, the use of nautical imagery relates to the predilection for the word ⲣ̄ϩⲙ̄ⲙⲉ (guide or pilot) in *On Love and Self-Control* in passages where by means of Christ's virtues, especially humility, God pilots a Christian through the stormy waves of life safely to the harbor of the holy ones. In his *Festal Letter* 19 (for the year 347), Athanasius calls the Lord, or the Word of God incarnate, the pilot who steers the Christian safely through the waves of affliction and temptation.[85] In his correspondence with female virgins in Alexandria, Athanasius tells them they need to attend to their vows in order to stay on course.[86] In his *Letter to Virgins Who Went and Prayed in Jerusalem and Returned*, Athanasius compares the virgins to sailors who pilot their crafts with fear and watchfulness through a storm, not with levity and laughter.[87] The *Lives* of Pachomius record the contents of a letter

*Matt 25:1-12

[84] Brakke, "The Authenticity of the Ascetic Athanasiana," 35–36.

[85] Archibald Robertson, *Select Writings and Letters of Athanasius, Bishop of Alexandria*, NPNF, 2nd series, ed. Philip Schaff and Henry Wace, repr. edition (Grand Rapids, MI: Wm. B. Eerdmans, 1987), 4:547, §7; and Alberto Camplani, *Atanasio di Alessandria: Lettere festali, Anonimo: Indice delle Lettere festali*, Letture cristiane del primo millennio 34 (Milan: Paoline, 2003), 426.

[86] Brakke cites Athanasius's *(First) Letter to Virgins*, which he has translated into English in *Athanasius and Asceticism* (see §33, p. 285) from Lefort, *S. Athanase*, CSCO 150, p. 90.

[87] Brakke, *Athanasius and Asceticism*, 296.

that Athanasius wrote to Horsiesios after Theodore died in which Athanasius sought to comfort the Pachomian community by painting in their minds the image of Theodore mooring his boat happily in the harbor where trials are no more.[88]

*Matt 25:1-12

A second thematic element, the parable of the five wise and five foolish virgins,* appears twice in Athanasius's seventh *Festal Letter*. He first puts it together with its parallel in Luke 13:25, as does *On Love and Self-Control*. Then he uses it to urge his hearers to purify themselves, not only in preparation for the feast of the resurrection, but their whole lives long.[89] Even more intriguing is Athanasius's use of this biblical passage in his treatise *On Virginity*, where the Lord tells the five foolish virgins that purity does not consist of fasting and celibacy alone but also of the other virtues mentioned in the Beatitudes: meekness, peacemaking, mercy, poverty of spirit, and purity of heart.[90] This is very similar to the way Jesus' parable is used at the end of *On Love and Self-Control*, which puts it in the context of this call: "We promised virginity to God. Let us give it to him sound, not merely a bodily virginity but a virginity erased of every sin."[91]

A third shared theme has to do with the drinking of wine. While *On Love and Self-Control* speaks

[88] Veilleux, *Pachomian Koinoina*, 1:265 (SBo 210) and 406–7 (G[1] 150); Lefort, *S. Pachomii vita bohairice scripta*, CSCO 89, pp. 214–15; and Halkin, *Sancti Pachomii vitae graecae*, 95–96.

[89] See NPNF, 2nd series, 4:524, §2, and 527, §10; and Camplani, *Atanasio di Alessandria: Lettere Festali*, 305–6, 317.

[90] Brakke, *Athanasius and Asceticism*, 307.

[91] Lantschoot, "Lettre de saint Athanase," 278; and Lefort, *S. Athanase*, CSCO 150, p. 120.

against an excess of wine, it does not forbid its use entirely. Similarly in his *Fragments on the Moral Life*, Athanasius condemns drunkenness but affirms drinking wine in moderation:

> Flee the burnings of the flesh's ease: I am talking about the excess of wine at the dinner-parties in the drinking places; I am not saying that you should withdraw from everything entirely. For this is a bodily thing and a good symbol of the person bodily: that he drink a little should he need it, but not so that you make the abundant Spirit a stranger to the soul (cf. 1 Tim. 5:23).[92]

[92] Brakke, *Athanasius and Asceticism*, 316; and Lefort, *S. Athanase*, CSCO 150, pp. 124–25. These fragments are in the parchment manuscript in Manchester, England, catalogued as J. Rylands Lib. 62 [Crawford 25], fol. 5. This manuscript is included in the codex that also contains *On Love and Self-Control*.

In a Sahidic text attributed to "the holy Athanasius" but classed under "dubia" in the *Clavis patrum graecorum*, ambivalence about wine is expressed. See Maurice Geerard, "#2187: Homilia adversus Arium, de s. genetrice dei Maria," in *Clavis patrum graecorum*, vol. 2: *Ab Athanasio ad Chrysostomum* (Turnhout: Brepols, 1974), 37. This is a late seventh-century manuscript in the collection at Turin. See Francesco Rossi, *I Papiri copti del museo Egizio di Torino*, vol. 2, fasc. 1 (Turin: Ermanno Loescher, 1888), 5–54 (Coptic) and 77–98 (Italian), especially 46, 95. For a study of the manuscript in Turin, see Louis-Théophile Lefort, "L'Homélie de s. Athanase des papyrus de Turin," *Le Muséon* 71 (1958): 5–50 (Coptic) and 209–39 (French), especially 45–46, 234–35.The section regarding drunkenness and fornication (discussed in that order, which is the reverse of the order in the Turin manuscript) is found among the papyri and ostraca of the Monastery of Epiphanius from the sixth and early seventh centuries. See Walter Ewing Crum and Hugh G. Evelyn-White, *The Monastery of Epiphanius at Thebes*, Part II: *Coptic Ostraca and Papyri, Greek Ostraca and*

In addition to the similar use of nautical imagery, the parable of the five wise and five foolish virgins, and cautions about wine, *On Love and Self-Control* and Athanasius's writings contain other similarities around other themes. To begin with, *On Love and Self-Control* uses Jesus' comment in Matthew 22:40 that the Law and the Prophets hang on loving God and neighbor to set the tone for the whole sermon. Similarly Athanasius uses it to sum up his *Festal Letter* for the year 330, the year of his first tour of Upper Egypt as bishop, during which he visited Pachomius's community: "Let us remember the poor and not forget hospitality; rather, let us clothe the naked and welcome those who have no homes into our houses. Before everything, let us have love for God and our neighbor
Matt 22:40 and so fulfil the Law and the Prophets and inherit the blessing through the only-begotten, our Lord Jesus Christ."[93] Both Athanasius and the author of

---

Papyri, The Metropolitan Museum of Art Egyptian Exhibition (New York: The Metropolitan Museum of Art, 1926), 11–12 (Coptic) and 162–63 (English). Although sections of the text are missing, the message is clear: Wine in moderation "is a physic," but "passion and all passions come from drunkenness, [. . . . .] is drunkenness, anger is drunkenness, [. . . . .] is drunkenness, much-speaking [is drunkenness], misanthropy is drunkenness, hypocrisy is drunkenness, [speaking] idle words is [drunkenness], wine-bibbing is drunkenness" (Crum and Evelyn-White, *The Monastery of Epiphanius at Thebes*, Part II, 11–12 [Coptic] and 162–63 [English]). Especially notable in connection with *On Love and Self-Control* is the linkage between wine and hateful or angry speech.

[93] Brakke, *Athanasius and Asceticism*, 323; Lefort, *S. Athanase*, CSCO 150, p. 42; and Camplani, *Atanasio di Alessandria: Lettere festali*, 246. This letter has traditionally been numbered 24, and Brakke retains this numbering. However, like most modern

On Love and Self-Control lift up Joseph* as an example of someone who loved others, even those who hated him, and was therefore honored by God.[94] Both authors draw on Romans 13:14 to call such an exercise of virtue "putting on Christ."[95]

*Gen 41:39-45; 45:5; 50:15-21

Again, Athanasius's *Festal Letters* and *On Love and Self-Control* both make a contrast between the true offering of one's life and body "as a holy sacrifice pleasing to God"*[96] and improper, hypocritical fasting that touches the body only and lets the sin of the heart remain.*[97] Both authors assert that God has given Jesus' followers the power to

*Rom 12:1-2

*Isa 1:13-14; 58:4-6, 9; 65:24

scholars of the *Festal Letters*, he thinks it is actually Athanasius's second letter and that the letter usually numbered 2 is actually the 24th (for the year 352). The rearrangement of the numbering is based on the fact that some letters announce only a Holy Week fast and some a full forty-day fast, a practice initiated in Egypt in 339 to bring it into harmony with churches elsewhere. Thus letters announcing a Holy Week fast are pre-339, and letters announcing a forty-day fast are post-339. See Carlton Mills Badger, Jr., "The New Man Created in God: Christology, Congregation and Asceticism in Athanasius of Alexandria," PhD diss., Duke University, 1990, 277. For a chonological chart, see Camplani, *Atanasio di Alessandria: Lettere festali*, 613–14.

[94] See *Festal Letter* 10 (for the year 338), §4, and *Festal Letter* 29 (for the year 357), in NPNF, 2nd series, 4:529; Brakke, *Athanasius and Asceticism*, 324; Lefort, *S. Athanase*, CSCO 150, p. 53; Camplani, *Atanasio di Alessandria: Lettere festali*, 331, 476.

[95] See *Festal Letter* 4 (for the year 332), §3, in NPNF, 2nd series, 4:516; and Camplani, *Atanasio di Alessandria: Lettere festali*, 264.

[96] See *Festal Letter* 25 (for the year 353) and *Festal Letter* 43 (for the year 371), in Camplani, *Atanasio di Alessandria: Lettere festali*, 452, 552; and Lefort, *S. Athanase*, CSCO 150, pp. 13–14, 34–35 (Codex B).

[97] See *Festal Letter* 1 (for the year 329), §4, and *Festal Letter* 19 (for the year 347), §2, in NPNF, 2nd series, 4:507–8, 545; Camplani, *Atanasio di Alessandria: Lettere festali*, 229, 418–19;

trample on the enemy, the devil, and his temptation.*[98] So, like *On Love and Self-Control*, Athanasius uses Jesus' parable of the servants entrusted with their master's money to maintain that God has high standards and expects to receive back with interest what he has first given.*[99] Fiery hell and the gnashing of teeth are the grisly consequences of failure to live a life productive of virtue.*[100]

*Luke 10:19

*Matt 25:27

*Matt 13:41-42, 49-50; 24:51; 25:30, 41

Reasons to Question an Athanasian Origin for On Love and Self-Control

In spite of the thematic similarities at points between *On Love and Self-Control* and the authentic

and Lefort, *S. Athanase*, CSCO 150, p. 4. See also *On Virginity* 9 and 16, in Brakke, *Athanasius and Asceticism*, 305–8.

[98] See *Festal Letter* 4 (for the year 332), §3, and *Festal Letter* 10 (for the year 338), §7, in NPNF, 2nd series, 4:516 and 530; Camplani, *Atanasio di Alessandria: Lettere festali*, 264, 335. See also Robert C. Gregg, *Athanasius: The Life of Antony and the Letter to Marcellinus*, The Classics of Western Spirituality (Mahwah, NJ: Paulist, 1980), §30, page 54; and Gérard Garitte, *S. Antonii vitae, Versio sahidica*, CSCO 117 (Paris: E typographeo republicae, 1949), 37–38.

[99] See *Ad Dracontium* §2, in NPNF, 2nd series, 4:558; *Athanasius Werke*, vol. 2, no. 8, ed. Hans Christof Brennecke, Uta Heil, and Annette von Stockhausen (Berlin and New York: Walter de Gruyter, 2006), 315–16; and in *Festal Letter* 3 (14), §2 (for the year 342), and *Festal Letter* 6, §5 (for the year 334). See NPNF, 2nd series, 4:513, 521; and Camplani, *Atanasio di Alessandria*, 398–99, 288. As with letters 2 and 24, letters 3 (traditionally dated for the year 331) and 14 (traditionally dated for the year 342) have been transposed. See Camplani, *Atanasio di Alessandria*, 613–14.

[100] See *Festal Letter* 3 (14) (for the year 342), §4, and *Festal Letter* 6 (for the year 334), §5, in NPNF, 2nd series, 4:514, 521; and Camplani, *Atanasio di Alessandria*, 402, 288.

writings of Athanasius, there are at least four significant reasons to question an Athanasian origin for *On Love and Self-Control*. They concern the relationship between speaker and audience implied in the text, the language in which the text was written (Sahidic), the use of a monastic title (ⲁⲡⲟⲧⲁⲕⲧⲓⲕⲟⲥ) that Athanasius does otherwise not use at all, and the repeated references to human beings as the image of God in a way that contradicts Athanasius's theological anthropology as expressed in his authentic writings.

The scribe who wrote the heading to *On Love and Self-Control* calls it a "letter," but it does not conform to the standard epistolary structure of its time. It lacks an introductory greeting identifying the sender and the recipient, and it lacks a conclusion with further greetings and blessings.[101] In genre, *On Love and Self-Control* is more like an instruction or sermon, addressing its unspecified hearers on a particular theological and moral theme. Although there is no recorded Athanasian discourse to the Pachomians to compare with *On Love and Self-Control*, there are records of Athanasian letters to the Pachomians. These make use of the standard elements of a letter in Late Antiquity. For example, Athanasius's second letter to Horsiesios begins, "Athanasius to Abba Horsiesios, father of monks, and to all those who practice with him the monastic life and are established in the faith of God; dearly beloved brothers, greetings in the Lord."[102] It

[101] The style of letters in antiquity is described in McNary-Zak, *Letters and Asceticism in Fourth-Century Egypt*, 107.

[102] Veilleux, *Pachomian Koinonia* 1:406 (G^1 150); Halkin, *Sancti Pachomii vitae graecae*, 95. (The Bohairic version of the letter is in

ends, "Greet all those who fear the Lord. Those who are with me greet you. I pray that you may have strength in the Lord, dear and beloved brothers."[103]

The scribe seems to have mistaken the genre of *On Love and Self-Control* by labeling it a letter instead of a discourse. Thus no conclusions about Athanasian authorship of *On Love and Self-Control* can be based on comparison of the style of the discourse with the style of Athanasius's other letters; the letters and the discourse represent two different genres. But there is something to be gained by comparing the tone of the Athanasian letters to the Pachomians with the tone of *On Love and Self-Control*. Athanasius's letters reveal a different kind of relationship between writer and recipients than the one reflected in *On Love and Self-Control*.

The Pachomian *koinonia* and Athanasius had a great deal of admiration and respect for each other, and Athanasius's communications with the Pachomians were certainly cordial, but they were also formal. Athanasius did not write directly to the Pachomian monks, as he wrote to the virgins of Alexandria and the monks of Lower Egypt, but rather he wrote officially to the *Apa*. His letters display none of the intimacy found in *On Love and Self-Control*. Even when Athanasius intervenes in the life of the *koinonia*, as in his letters to Horsiesios, he does so indirectly, without a discussion of the

---

Veilleux, *Pachomian Koinonia*, 1:264–66; and Lefort, *S. Pachomii vita bohairice scripta*, CSCO 89, pp. 214–15.) In the Greek version, the term for "monastic life" is μονήρη βίος, a term that does not appear in the Coptic version.

[103] Veilleux, *Pachomian Koinonia* 1:407 (G^1 150); Halkin, *Sancti Pachomii vitae graecae*, 96.

internal dynamics of the community. Everywhere in the Pachomian literature it is the *apas* themselves who address troubles in the community. It is they who help the monks to deal with feelings of hatred toward each other. Nowhere is an outsider, such as a bishop, invited to repair these rocky relationships in the way that *On Love and Self-Control* seeks to do. Thus, in terms of style, *On Love and Self-Control* is not characteristic of Athanasius and does not reflect the nature of his relationship and communications with the Pachomian community.[104]

Turning from issues of tone to issues of specific vocabulary in the text can start with the word ⲁⲡⲟⲧⲁⲕⲧⲓⲕⲟⲥ. As was seen before, *On Love and Self-Control* uses the threefold monastic language of virgins (ϩⲉⲛⲡⲁⲣⲑⲉⲛⲟⲥ), renunciants (ϩⲉⲛⲁⲡⲟⲧⲁⲕⲧⲓⲕⲟⲥ), and anchorites (ⲁⲛⲁⲭⲱⲣⲏⲧⲏⲥ) that was appropriate to the timespan of Athanasius's life in the fourth century. But, as Malcolm Choat has observed, Athanasius himself would not have used the term ⲁⲡⲟⲧⲁⲕⲧⲓⲕⲟⲥ (renouncer) in listing various types of monks. Athanasius avoided the word ἀποτακτικος as a monastic title entirely, maybe because he was aware of the disdain for the "renouncers" among many outside of Egypt, including the Emperor Julian, who mocked the ἀποτακτικοί as hypocrites.[105] Instead, Athanasius's

[104] An account of Athanasius's contacts with the Pachomians can be found in Leslie W. Barnard, "Athanasius and the Pachomians," in *Papers Presented at the Twelfth International Conference on Patristic Studies, held in Oxford 1995*, ed. Elizabeth Livingstone, Studia Patristica 32 (Louvain: Peeters, 1997), 3–11.

[105] Malcolm Choat, "Athanasius, Pachomius, and the 'Letter on Charity and Temperance,'" in *Egyptian Culture and Society,*

favorite terms for a male monk were μοναζον, which he used before 350 to refer to urban monks, and μοναχός, which he used after 350 to refer to

---

1:99; Badger, "The New Man Created in God," 175; Julian, "To the Cynic Heracleios," in *The Works of the Emperor Julian*, trans. Wilmer Cave Wright, 6 vols, The Loeb Classical Library, ed. T. E. Page and W. H. D. Rouse (London: William Heinemann; and New York: Macmillan, 1913), 2:122–23. Emperor Julian was no friend of Athanasius's. In 362, he issued two edicts against Athanasius in two letters to the Alexandrians and one to Ecdicius, the Prefect of Egypt. The first edict ordered that Athanasius leave Alexandria, as he did. The second edict banished him from Egypt, but he hid in Egypt instead until Julian's death in 363. See *The Works of the Emperor Julian*, trans. Wilmer Cave Wright, 6 vols., The Loeb Classical Library, ed. E. Capps, T. E. Page, and W. H. D. Rouse (London: William Heinemann; and New York: G. P. Putnam's Sons, 1923), 3:74–77, 140–51. Shortly after Athanasius's death (in 373) Basil of Caesarea wrote his second canonical letter (Ep 199, from 374–75 AD), in which he says that *apotaktikoi* who wish to join the mainstream church should be rebaptized because the *apotaktikoi* reject marriage and wine "and say that the creature of God is defiled" (Roy Defferari, trans., *Saint Basil: The Letters*, 4 vols. The Loeb Classical Library 243 (Cambridge, MA: Harvard University Press, 1952), 3:133. In around 376, Epiphanius included a section in his *Panarion* (Sect. 61, "Against Apostolics") against a group of *apotaktikoi* in Phrygia, Cilicia, and Pamphylia because they rejected marriage. See Frank Williams, *The Panarion of Epiphanius of Salamis: Books II and III* (Sects. 47–80, De Fide), Nag Hammadi and Manichaean Studies 36 (Leiden, New York, and Cologne: Brill, 1994), 114–21. See also James Goehring, *Ascetics*, 69. The pilgrim Egeria (404–17), however, speaks with respect of the *aputactitae* she sees on her pilgrimage through the lands of the biblical stories. See *Egeria: Diary of a Pilgrimage*, trans. George E. Gingres, Ancient Christian Writers 38 (New York and Ramsey, NJ: Newman Press, 1970), 213n255; *Itinerarium Egeriae*, in *Itineraria et alia Geographica*, CCSL 175 (Turnhout: Brepols, 1965), 37–90.

monks who had withdrawn from society.[106] For example, in the Greek version of the *Life of Pachomius* Athanasius calls Horsiesios πατρὶ μοναχῶν ("father of monks") in the letter that he wrote to Horsiesios in 368 to console him at the death of Theodore and to confirm him in his role as *Apa*.[107] If Athanasius wrote *On Love and Self-Control,* his reference to some monks as ϩⲉⲛⲁⲡⲟⲧⲁⲕⲧⲓⲕⲟⲥ is uncharacteristic.

The next issue is the understanding of humans as the image of God in *On Love and Self-Control.* In its most eloquent passages, *On Love and Self-Control* calls human beings "the image of God" (ⲑⲓⲕⲱⲛ ⲙ̄ⲡⲛⲟⲩⲧⲉ).[108] The very reason that the discourse calls its hearers to love and self-control is that their neighbor "is God"[109] and a child of God. Thus, "the one who is reconciled to his brother is reconciled to God, and the one who is separated from his brother is separated from God."[110] But Athanasius would not have described a human being as the image of God in such an unqualified way.

Scholars of Athanasius's works have long noted that he carefully and consistently reserves the unembellished term *image of God* for the Word and Son of God alone, who became incarnate.

[106] Brakke, *Athanasius and Asceticism*, 9.

[107] Badger, "The New Man Created in God," 233; Veilleux, *Pachomian Koinonia*, 1:406 (G[1] 150); and Halkin, *Sancti Pachomii vitae graecae*, 95.

[108] Lantschoot, "Lettre de saint Athanase," 271, 273, 278; and Lefort, *S. Athanase*, CSCO 150, pp. 114, 115, and 120.

[109] Lantschoot, "Lettre de saint Athanase," 269; and Lefort, *S. Athanase*, CSCO 150, p. 112.

[110] Lantschoot, "Lettre de saint Athanase," 271; Lefort, *S. Athanase*, CSCO 150, pp. 113–14.

With regard to anyone else, the phrase is qualified. Other human beings are made *according to* the image of this eternal Son of God, or they conform to and participate in the image of the incarnate Son of God by faith.[111] For Athanasius, the image of God is only a true image if it reflects the eternity and stability of God's essence. Only the uncreated Word and Son of God does that.[112] Thus, Athanasius writes, "to sum it all up, He [the Savior, Offspring, Power, Wisdom, and Word] is the wholly perfect Fruit of the Father, and is alone the Son, and unchanging Image of the Father."[113] Athanasius is so wary of calling human beings the image of God

[111] See A.-G. Hamman, *L'Homme, Image de Dieu*, Relais-études 2 (Paris: Desclée, 1987), 164–66; J. Roldanus, *Le Christ et l'homme dans la théologie d'Athanase d'Alexandrie*, Studies in the History of Christian Thought 4 (Leiden: E. J. Brill, 1968), 39; Régis Bernard, *L'Image de Dieu d'aprés saint Athanase*, Théologie 25 (Paris: Aubier, Éditions Montaigne, 1952), 104, 132–40; and Badger, "The New Man Created in God," 36–37.

[112] See *Contra Gentes* §41, in NPNF, 2nd series, 4:26; *S.P.N. Athanasii, archiepiscopi Alexandrini, opera omnia*, PG 25:81–83; *Defense of the Nicene Definition* §17, in NPNF, 2nd series, 4:161; *Athanasius Werke*, vol. 2, pt. 1, no. 2, ed. Hans-Georg Opitz (Berlin and Leipzig: Walter de Gruyter, 1935), 14–15; PG 25:452–53; *Contra Arianos* 1 §§20–22, 36, and 51–52, in NPNF, 2nd series, 4:318–19, 327, 336–37; *Athanasius Werke*, vol. 1, pt. 1, no. 2, ed. Karin Metzler and Kyriakos Savvidis (Berlin and New York: Walter de Gruyter, 1998), 129–32, 145–46, and 161–63; PG 26:53–60; *Contra Arianos* 2 §§2 and 43, in NPNF, 2nd series, 4:349, 371; *Athanasius Werke*, vol. 1, pt. 1, no. 2, pp. 178–79 and 219–20; PG 26:149–52, 237–40; and *Contra Arianos* 3 §§5–6, in NPNF, 2nd series, 4:396; *Athanasius Werke*, vol. 1, pt. 1, no. 3, ed. Karin Metzler and Kyriakos Savvidis (Berlin and New York: Walter de Gruyter, 2000), 310–13; and Migne, PG 26:329–33.

[113] See *Contra Gentes* §46, in NPNF, 2nd series, 4:29; and Migne, PG 25:92–93.

that in most cases where he cites Genesis 1:26, he cuts the verse short to "Let us make humankind," leaving off the phrase "in our image."[114] Athanasius asserts that in the beginning God delighted in creating human beings according to God's image so that, through participation in the image, they might come to know and love their maker.[115] But because of sin, humankind, by nature alterable, has lost the image in which it was made. In order to reunite humanity with the image of God, the true and full image of God became flesh.[116] Thus, through union with Christ humans bear the image of the Savior[117] and may be called God's image only

[114] See *Contra Arianos* 2 §§31 and 59, NPNF, 2nd series, 4:365, 381; *Athanasius Werke*, vol. 1, pt. 1, no. 2, pp. 207–8, 235–37; PG 26:212–13, 272–73; *Contra Arianos* 3 §§29, 61, NPNF, 2nd series, 4:410, 427; *Athanasius Werke*, vol. 1, pt. 1, no. 3, pp. 340, 373–75; and PG 26:385–88, 452–53. An exception is in *Fragments on the Moral Life* 9, in Brakke, *Athanasius and Asceticism*, 318; and Lefort, *S. Athanase*, CSCO 150, p. 127.

[115] See *Contra Gentes* §34, NPNF, 2nd series, 4:22; and PG 25:68–69; *De Incarnatione* §11, in NPNF, 2nd series, 4:42; and PG 25:113–16; *Contra Arianos* 1 §49, in NPNF, 2nd series, 4:335; and PG 26:113–16; *Contra Arianos* 2 §§48–49, 82, NPNF, 2nd series, 4:375, 393; *Athanasius Werke*, vol. 1, pt. 1, no. 2, pp. 159, 224–26, and 259–60; PG 26:248–52, 320–21; *Festal Letter* 2 (24) (for the year 352), §2, NPNF, 2nd series, 4:510; Lefort, *S. Athanase*, CSCO 150, pp. 8–9; and Camplani, *Atanasio di Alessandria*, 442–43.

[116] See *Letter to Virgins who Went and Prayed in Jerusalem and Returned*, in Brakke, *Athanasius and Asceticism*, 292; *De Incarnatione* §13, in NPNF, 2nd series, 4:43; PG 25:117–20; and *Contra Arianos* 1 §41, in NPNF, 2nd series, 4:330; *Athanasius Werke*, vol. 1, pt. 1, no. 2, pp. 150–52; PG 26:96–97.

[117] See *Festal Letter* 2 (24) (for the year 352) §5, in NPNF, 2nd series, 4:511; Lefort, *S. Athanase*, CSCO 150, pp. 9–10; Camplani, *Atanasio di Alessandria*, 446.

on his account: "For though we have been made after the image, and called both image and glory of God, yet not on our own account still, but for that image and true glory of God inhabiting us, which is His Word, who was for us afterwards made flesh, have we this grace of our designation."[118] Athanasius never calls humanity in itself "the image of God" in the straightforward manner that *On Love and Self-Control* calls human beings the image of God. Thus, if he wrote *On Love and Self-Control*, he would have been departing from his normal word usage with regard to a matter reaching deeply into the core of his theology.

Last, the text is in Sahidic, the language of southern Egypt at that time. It is unlikely that Athanasius knew Sahidic or any dialect of Coptic. In 1933 Louis-Théophile Lefort had questioned the assumption that Coptic letters to monks and ascetic treatises ascribed to Athanasius were translations from Greek, and he called for a reexamination of the texts.[119] In 1994 David Brakke reexamined the texts and found that indeed most of this ascetic literature ascribed to Athanasius was originally written in Greek, even if it survives only in translations into Coptic and other languages. But Brakke concluded that *On Love and Self-Control* seems to have been written originally in Coptic.[120] If *On Love and Self-Control* was written by Athanasius in Coptic, it would be an unlikely exception. There is evi-

[118] See *Contra Arianos* 3 §10, in NPNF, 2nd series, 4:399; *Athanasius Werke*, vol. 1, pt. 1, no. 3, pp. 316–18; PG 26:341–44.

[119] Lefort, "S. Athanase écrivain copte," 29–33.

[120] Brakke, "The Authenticity of the Ascetic Athanasiana," 17–56.

dence in the Pachomian literature that Athanasius wrote to the Pachomian community in Greek. The Bohairic version of the *Life of Pachomius* records that when Theodore was the *Apa* of the Pachomian community, he rejoiced over Athanasius's thirty-ninth *Festal Letter*, in which Athanasius listed the acceptable sacred scriptures. The fact that the community received this *Festal Letter* in Greek is revealed by Theodore's request that it be translated from Greek into Sahidic for the monks who did not know Greek.[121]

A Possible Origin for On Love and Self-Control *among the Pachomians*

The previous section shows that certain features of *On Love and Self-Control* call into question an Athanasian origin for the discourse. The style and tone of the discourse, the way in which it uses the terms ⲁⲡⲟⲧⲁⲕⲧⲓⲕⲟⲥ and *the image of God*, and the fact that it was composed in Sahidic are all uncharacteristic of genuine Athanasian material. However, the very features of the text that are uncharacteristic of Athanasius are characteristic of the Pachomians, the community in which *On Love and Self-Control* was in use. Furthermore, the themes in *On Love and Self-Control* that do have parallels in other Athanasian texts have parallels in Pachomian texts as well. The process of uncovering these Pachomian parallels reveals that most of them are in the writings of one Pachomian in particular, Horsiesios. This finding raises the

[121] Veilleux, *Pachomian Koinonia* 1:230–32; Lefort, *S. Pachomii vita bohairice scripta*, CSCO 89, pp. 177–78.

possibility that Horsiesios may be the one who first delivered the discourse *On Love and Self-Control*, although that cannot be proven definitively.

To begin with the Sahidic language of *On Love and Self-Control*, Sahidic was the native language of most of the Pachomians. The first Pachomian monasteries were located in southern or Upper Egypt, the region in which Sahidic was spoken in the fourth century. The Pachomian *Apas* originally wrote their letters, instructions, and rules in Sahidic, although some of these texts have survived only in translations. While Athanasius would have had to study Sahidic in order to deliver the discourse *On Love and Self-Control*, it would have been natural for a Pachomian *Apa* to deliver this discourse in Sahidic. Likewise, regarding the style of the text, it has already been shown that the speaker's disregard for formal literary structure and his familiarity with the relational dynamics of the Pachomian monks suggests that *On Love and Self-Control* was an inside job, not the work of an occasional visitor of note, like the bishop of Alexandria.

Moving from observations about the Pachomian nature of the text of *On Love and Self-Control* as a whole to observations about the Pachomian nature of some of its particulars, we begin with a look at the word ⲁⲡⲟⲧⲁⲕⲧⲓⲕⲟⲥ, a word that Athanasius never used. Malcolm Choat notes that although the term was also avoided "in the Greek and Latin Pachomian *Lives* of Pachomius, Pachomian texts in Coptic and in contemporary papyri show that *apotaktikos* was in fact a regular self-designation for the monks in the Pachomian *koinonia.*"[122] It was not only a self-designation but also a term by which Pachomian monks were known to others, even officially. A record of taxes paid in the Hermopolite Nome, for instance, notes the receipt of tax payments on uncultivated agricultural land in 367/368 from a Tabennesiote ἀποτακτικος named Anoubion.[123] If *On Love and Self-Control* "originated in a Pachomian milieu," as Choat suggests,[124] then it would not be unusual to find in this Coptic text a reference to monks as ϩⲉⲛⲁⲡⲟⲧⲁⲕⲧⲓⲕⲟⲥ (renunciants).

With regard to the use of the phrase *image of God* (ⲑⲓⲕⲱⲛ ⲙ̄ⲡⲛⲟⲩⲧⲉ), we have already seen that the discourse's use of *image of God* as a synonym

[122] Choat, "Athanasius, Pachomius, and the 'Letter on Charity and Temperance,'" 101. James Goehring explains that the word ἀποτακτικος was not used in the Greek and Latin Pachomiana because these literary productions were intended for a broad readership not limited to Egypt. Like Athanasius, the Pachomian authors were aware of the negative connotations of the term ἀποτακτικος abroad. See Goehring, *Ascetics*, 69.

[123] Malcolm Choat, "Property Ownership and Tax-Payment in Fourth-Century Monasticism," in *Monastic Estates in Late Antiquity and Early Islamic Egypt: Ostraca, Papyri, and Essays in Memory of Sarah Clackson* (*P. Clackson*), ed. Anne Boud'hors, James Clackson, Catherine Louis, and Petra Sijpesteijn, American Studies in Papyrology 46, ed. Ann Ellis Hanson (Cincinnati, OH: The American Society of Papyrologists, 2009), 130–33. On the basis of his reading of the papyrus, Choat argues that Anoubion was not paying taxes for the Tabennesiotes but was transporting the villagers' taxes for them in a boat of the Tabennesiotes. For a different reading, see Wipszycka, "Les Terres de la congrégation pachômienne dans une liste de payments pour les apora," 625–36.

[124] Choat, "Athanasius, Pachomius, and the 'Letter on Charity and Temperance,'" 101.

for "human being" was not part of Athanasius's theological anthropology but was a very important part of Pachomian theological anthropology. It came to the fore in the monastic dispute of 399–400 over whether sin had destroyed the image of God in humanity. The way that *On Love and Self-Control* was integrated with *Instruction concerning a Spiteful Monk* and a third discourse into a new compilation focusing on forgiving one's neighbor provides a clue that the Pachomians were not untouched by the controversy. The fact that in this compilation the neighbor, although in need of forgiveness, is explicitly called the image of God shows that it mattered to at least some of the Pachomians to assert that human beings were still the image of God in spite of sin.

Alongside these differences between *On Love and Self-Control* and the genuine Athanasiana, however, the two also have some very real similarities. But closer inspection reveals that these similarities extend also to the genuine Pachomiana. Athanasius and the Pachomians shared some theological and ethical commitments. Comparing Pachomian writings with *On Love and Self-Control* reveals that the common themes between this discourse and Athanasius's works (particularly nautical imagery, the example of the wise and foolish virgins, and teachings about drinking wine in moderation) are also common to Pachomian literature.[125]

First, nautical imagery among the Pachomians. The image of a boat coming to moor safely in the

[125] Nautical imagery for the struggle of the soul was used not only by Athanasius and the Pachomians but generally by writers of ascetic literature at this time. See Goehring, "The Ship of the Pachomian Federation," 291.

harbor after sailing rough seas is primarily used by Pachomius and by Horsiesios.[126] In an instruction by Pachomius on the six days of the Passover, a Pachomian equivalent of an episcopal festal letter, Pachomius urges the monks to steadfast observance of fasting and prayer during the week leading up to "the Sunday of the Holy Resurrection" so that all might come "safe to the shore."* [127] In a letter to the monastery at Thmoushons, Pachomius told the monks that knowing God and God's wisdom piloted Noah through the flood and blessed his family.[128] Later, Horsiesios urged the Pachomian community to remember and follow what Pachomius had taught them, since he "showed a harbor of peace to those on a storm-tossed sea."[129] Horsiesios reminded the heads of the individual houses in particular that they would be held accountable for all that had been entrusted to them. If they neglected any, then "when you have left the body and have been freed from the turmoil of this

*Acts 27:44

[126] The Bohairic version of the *Life of Pachomius* records one occasion on which Theodore also used nautical imagery. It tells a story about Theodore weeping over Pachomius's grave and praying to God about the serious state of the monasteries since they had acquired many possessions. He says, "Indeed, we are like those at sea in the time of a storm because we pay no attention to the proper behavior which your servant, our holy father, enjoined upon us." See Veilleux, *Pachomian Koinonia*, 1:246 (SBo 198); Lefort, *S. Pachomii vita bohairice scripta*, CSCO 89, p. 193.

[127] Veilleux, *Pachomian Koinonia*, 3:48; Lefort, *Oeuvres de s. Pachôme*, CSCO 159, p. 25.

[128] Veilleux, *Pachomian Koinonia*, 3:55, 57 (Letter 3.8, 10); Hans Quecke, *Die Briefe Pachoms*, 103, 105; Boon, *Pachomiana latina*, 82–83.

[129] Veilleux, *Pachomian Koinonia*, 3:206 (*Testament* 47); Boon, *Pachomiana latina*, 140.

world, you may think you have entered the harbor of tranquility only to meet with the shipwreck of injustice."[130]

Moving next to the issue of wine, *On Love and Self-Control* insists that it is all right for sick people to drink wine (as the "great ascetic Timothy," Paul's coworker, did, it points out) but that in healthy people wine is a "greedy pleasure" that leads to "lack of restraint." This is consistent with the Pachomian attitude toward wine and its use in the community. Among the Pachomians wine was a special item reserved for the sick, not to be sought except out of need; otherwise it would signal one's desire for special treatment in the community.[131] Horsiesios assured the monks that the rule against seeking "wine or special food" had nothing to do with an unreasonable or arbitrary abuse of power, for "if all the brothers need a bit of beer or any other food that accords with the law of the *Koinonia*, the superior of the community will grant this to them generously and gladly."[132] The key phrase for Horsiesios was "all the brothers." Horsiesios insisted that everyone should have the same amount of the same things. Otherwise, "one is hungry and the other is drunk," as 1 Corinthians 11:34 says.[133]

[130] Veilleux, *Pachomian Koinonia*, 3:181 (*Testament* 16); Boon, *Pachomiana latina*, 118.

[131] Veilleux, *Pachomian Koinonia*, 2:152 (*Precepts* 45); Boon, *Pachomiana latina*, 24.

[132] Veilleux, *Pachomian Koinonia*, 2:215 (*Regulations of Horsiesios* 49); Lefort, *Oeuvres de s. Pachôme*, CSCO 159, p. 96.

[133] Veilleux, *Pachomian Koinonia*, 3:194 (*Testament* 29); Boon, *Pachomiana latina*, 130. Wine may even have contributed to the trouble between *Apa* Horsiesios and the monks at Thmoushons following the deaths of Pachomius and Petronius, which has

Drunkenness was prohibited to all Pachomians. Therefore the monks, especially those in charge of

---

been identified as a possible context for the delivery of the discourse *On Love and Self-Control*. With the expansion of the monastic federation, the Greek *Life of Pachomius* says that the *apa* at Thmoushons began to acquire extra supplies for the monastery, for which he wished not to be accountable to the Great Steward at Pbow. It is possible that some of the extra supplies gathered at Thmoushons included wine. From Pachomius's third letter, written to the previous *apa* at Thmoushons, it seems that the issue of wine had come up at Thmoushons before. The letter makes frequent mention of wine and drunkenness and links these with the problems of negligence in caring for the monks and bad stewardship of monastic property. Pachomius's communications are hard to understand, partly because in them he used a code written in letters of the Greek alphabet. Christoph Joest suggests that these ciphers are the first letters of Greek words that represent semantic domains, so, for example, in Pachomius's third letter, θ could stand for "God" (Θεός) and ε could stand for "desert or wilderness" (ἔρημός). (See Christoph Joest, "Die Pachom-Briefe 1 und 2: Auflösung der Geheimbuchstaben und Entdeckungen zu den Briefüberschriften," *Journal of Coptic Studies* 4 [2002]: 25–98, especially 52–56 and 61.)

> Keep θ, lest you receive the reproach made to the one to whom it was said, *Give me the account of your stewardship* [Luke 16:2]; or the reproach made to the one *eating and drinking with drunkards* [Matt 24:49], because he did not give *himself to digging* [Luke 16:3] or *to giving food at the proper time* [Matt 24:45]. Because of that, the same was done to him, because he forgot the law of his God and *did not visit the sick* [Matt 25:43]. Therefore he became *tossed about* [Isa 47:20], without bread, like the *pretentious* [Sir 10:27] and the arrogant [Prov 21:24], who *did not build the house* [1 Chr 17:6] ε. O man, know their conscience; the battle of the Lord is in their hands, and they have been charged with dominating their own flesh.
>
> . . .

others, were told not to "sit in the lower places, by the monastery vessels," that is, in the wine cellar.[134] The low place of drunkenness was contrasted with the high place of wisdom (paradoxically the place of humility). In Pachomius's third letter, the divine wisdom that guides people like a pilot is to be found only in the "high place," where there is a sober lack of desire for more than what one's neighbor has.[135] Pachomius's *Institutes* likewise bring up humility in connection with wine: No one shall "get drunk with wine; he shall have humility joined with truth."[136]

In use of Jesus' parable of the five wise and
Matt 25:1-12 five foolish virgins in the Pachomian literature, an intriguing pattern begins to emerge. This passage

---

> *Do not drug yourself with strong wine* [Eph 5:18], from which come beggary and people walking naked.
>
> . . .
>
> A drunken man does not help another drunken man.
>
> . . .
>
> It is written indeed, *You shall not covet* [Exod 20:17], and again, *You shall not get drunk* [Eph 5:18]. Covetousness is not one thing, and drunkenness is not one thing (Veilleux, *Pachomian Koinonia*, 3:53–59; Quecke, *Die Briefe Pachoms*, 100–107; Boon, *Pachomiana latina*, 79–81).

[134] Veilleux, *Pachomian Koinonia*, 2:172 (*Institutes* 18); Boon, *Pachomiana latina*, 58.

[135] Veilleux, *Pachomian Koinonia*, 3:54–55 (Pachomius, Letter 3.4–7); Boon, *Pachomiana latina*, 80–81; Quecke, *Die Briefe Pachoms*, 101–2. In a very fragmentary letter, Horsiesios also seems to be addressing the problem of drunkenness. See Veilleux, *Pachomian Koinonia*, 3:162–63 (Horsiesios, Letter 4.4).

[136] Veilleux, *Pachomian Koinonia*, 2:174 (*Institutes* 18); Boon, *Pachomiana latina*, 61.

was a special favorite of Horsiesios. He cited it in every genre associated with his name: his letters, his *Testament*, and his *Regulations*. Except for *Instruction concerning a Spiteful Monk*, no other extant Pachomian writing uses this parable.[137] When Theodore was dying, Horsiesios referred to the parable in his worried letters to the monks to spur them to acts of virtue done in the fear of God. In his *Regulations*, Horsiesios notes that only the wise virgins were admitted to the wedding banquet in Matthew 25:1-12; the foolish virgins were left out, just like the man in another parable, who was thrown out of the wedding banquet for lack of an appropriate garment into the place where there is "weeping and grinding of teeth."[138]* References to these two parables are also placed side by side in *On Love and Self-Control*. In all of Horsiesios's writings the tale is told for the same purpose: to urge imitation of the five virgins who kept their lamps trimmed and supplied with oil (good works) in order to avoid the words of divine rejection, "I do not know you," spoken to the five virgins who came to the wedding banquet unprepared.

*Matt 22:13

[137] In the *Instruction concerning a Spiteful Monk*, the single reference to this parable has been influenced by *On Love and Self-Control*. The two discourses have the last line, where the parable is mentioned, in common. See Veilleux, *Pachomian Koinonia* 3:37; Budge, *Coptic Apocrypha*, 170, 377; Lefort, *Oeuvres de s. Pachôme*, CSCO 159, p. 20, and CSCO 160, p. 22; Lantschoot, "Lettre de saint Athanase," 278; Lefort, "Sur la charité et la tempérance," CSCO 150, p. 119, and CSCO 151, p. 98.

[138] Veilleux, *Pachomian Koinonia*, 2:197–98 (*Regulations* 3); Lefort, *Oeuvres de s. Pachôme*, CSCO 159, pp. 82–83.

Horsiesios and On Love and Self-Control

The frequency with which *On Love and Self-Control* cites biblical passages that appear only in the writings of Horsiesios among the Pachomians is striking. In most cases these passages appear specifically in Horsiesios's *Testament*. The *Testament* or *Liber* of Horsiesios, which exists only in a Latin translation made by Jerome, was written at the end of Horsiesios's life as a call to the community to return to the ideals of its founder, Pachomius.[139] A number of key scriptural parallels between *On Love and Self-Control* and the writings of Horsiesios open the possibility that Horsiesios may have composed *On Love and Self-Control*.

Some biblical passages that occur only in *On Love and Self-Control* and in Horsiesios's *Testament* revolve around the major theme of *On Love and Self-Control*: loving one's neighbor, which Joest has called the ground rule of the Pachomian *koinonia*.[140] In chapter 9 of the *Testament* Horsiesios sets the tone, saying, "And be especially careful not to love one and hate another. Show an equal attitude to all, lest the one whom you love God hate, and the one whom you hate God love."[141] He reiterates this idea in chapter 16: "I will say it again and again and will repeat it: Take care not to love some and hate others."[142] Horsiesios tells his community to

[139] Heinrich Bacht made two good studies of the *Liber*: "Studien zum 'Liber Orsiesii,'" *Historisches Jahrbuch* 77 (1958): 98–124; and *Das Vermächtnis des Ursprungs*.

[140] Joest, "Die Pachom-Briefe 1 und 2," 67.

[141] Veilleux, *Pachomian Koinonia*, 3:176; Boon, *Pachomiana latina*, 113.

[142] Veilleux, *Pachomian Koinonia*, 3:181; Boon, *Pachomiana latina*, 118.

be "mindful of that precept, *You must not bear hatred for your brother in your heart.*"[143]* For just as God entrusted a deposit to Timothy and he was commanded to guard it,* so "God has also entrusted a deposit to us: the brothers' way of life."[144] The positive content of that way of life is the precept that "our Lord and Savior gave his apostles . . . [:] *I give you a new commandment: Love one another as I have loved you.*"[145]* Horsiesios turns to Matthew to urge the monks to wake up and love God and one another, because "on these two commandments the whole law and the prophets depend."[146]*

*Lev 19:17

*1 Tim 6:20

*John 13:34

*Matt 22:40

At several points in the *Testament*, Horsiesios quotes from the book of Malachi; he is the only Pachomian writer to use the book of Malachi.[147] Two of the passages he uses from Malachi are common to the *Testament* and *On Love and Self-Control*. When, in the *Testament*, Horsiesios calls on all the brothers to be equal, he cites Malachi 2:10-11 ("Did one God not create [all of] you? Have you not all one father? Why has each of you abandoned his brother,

[143] Veilleux, *Pachomian Koinonia*, 3:177 (*Testament* 9); Boon, *Pachomiana latina*, 113–14.

[144] Veilleux, *Pachomian Koinonia*, 3:178 (*Testament* 11); Boon, *Pachomiana latina*, 116.

[145] Veilleux, *Pachomian Koinonia*, 3:188 (*Testament* 23); Boon, *Pachomiana latina*, 124–25.

[146] Veilleux, *Pachomian Koinonia*, 3:199 (*Testament* 38); Boon, *Pachomiana latina*, 134.

[147] There is a reference to Malachi 1:6 in *Instruction concerning a Spiteful Monk*, but it is in the section in common with *On Love and Self-Control* and has been influenced by that text. See Veilleux, *Pachomian Koinonia* 3:32; Budge, *Coptic Apocrypha*, 166, 372; Lefort, *Oeuvres de s. Pachôme*, CSCO 159, p. 17, and CSCO 160, p. 17; Lantschoot, "Lettre de saint Athanase," 274; and Lefort, "Sur la charité et la tempérance," CSCO 150, p. 116, and CSCO 151, p. 94.

thus profaning the covenant of your fathers?").[148] He quotes Malachi 1:6 to urge the community to continue living in the "bonds of charity" that they learned from Pachomius, "lest it be said of us, *A son honors his father, and a servant his master. If I am a father, where is my honor? If I am a master, where is my fear?*"[149]

Horsiesios is also alone in the Pachomian community to cite Ecclesiastes 12:13-14 (although not uniquely in the *Testament*); it appears to have been a favorite of his. In his *Testament*, while addressing the housemasters in particular, Horsiesios warns that if the leaders ignore the monks in their care (apparently by sitting in the wine cellar) and leave them to be consumed by hatred and anger, they will be held accountable not only for their own sins but also for the sins of their brothers and sisters. "We cannot plead ignorance," Horsiesios insists, "for it is written, 'God will bring every deed to judgment, in everything that was neglected,
Eccl 12:14 whether good or evil.'"[150] At the close of the *Testament*, Horsiesios repeats Ecclesiastes 12:13-14 as a final incentive to fear God and obey his commandments.[151] The same selection from Ecclesiastes appears in Horsiesios's first letter. This letter is about keeping God's commandments, and it ends with the warning from Ecclesiastes: "for God will cause every creature to appear before him in

[148] Veilleux, *Pachomian Koinonia*, 3:188 (*Testament* 23); Boon, *Pachomiana latina*, 124–25.

[149] Veilleux, *Pachomian Koinonia*, 3:207 (*Testament* 47); Boon, *Pachomiana latina*, 140.

[150] Veilleux, *Pachomian Koinonia*, 3:177 (*Testament* 10); Boon, *Pachomiana latina*, 115.

[151] Veilleux, *Pachomian Koinonia*, 3:215 (*Testament* 56); Boon, *Pachomiana latina*, 147.

order to judge it for every act in which it has been forgetful, either for good or for evil."[152]

The significant number of scriptural citations in *On Love and Self-Control* that Horsiesios alone uses in the Pachomian literature suggests that he may be the author, or better, the original speaker of *On Love and Self-Control*. But one difficulty with this conclusion must be dealt with. If Horsiesios is the one who gave this discourse on love and self-control, then it seems to be the only work of his that uses the significant phrase "image of God." In the Pachomian literature reference to humans as the image of God is attributed almost exclusively to Pachomius himself, and only in the Coptic sources, not the Greek sources. A look at the related discourse, *Instruction concerning a Spiteful Monk*, may help to unravel this difficulty.

The Pachomian *Instruction concerning a Spiteful Monk* in its present form is a compilation of three parts, not all by Pachomius himself. The first part contains the original instruction by Pachomius, the second part borrows heavily from *On Love and Self-Control*, and the third part maintains the same theme of the need for reconciliation. In the Pachomian literature, almost half the occurrences of the phrase *image of God* are in the *Instruction concerning a Spiteful Monk*. There the expression is used seven times, twice before the section in common with *On Love and Self-Control*, four times in the common section, and once in the last section.[153]

[152] Veilleux, *Pachomian Koinonia*, 3:156 (Letter 1.6); and Lefort, *Oeuvres de s. Pachôme*, CSCO 159, p. 65.

[153] Veilleux, *Pachomian Koinonia*, 3:21, 27, 30, 31, 33, 40 (§§22, 33, 36, 38 [twice], 41, 59); Lefort, *Oeuvres de s. Pachôme*, CSCO

Extensive study by Christoph Joest has demonstrated that the last part of the *Instruction concerning a Spiteful Monk* may be by Horsiesios. Joest has made careful stylistic comparisons between each of the three sections of *Instruction concerning a Spiteful Monk* and the letters of Pachomius, Theodore, and Horsiesios. He has compared the length of sentences, the average number of words in each sentence, the percentage of Greek loan words, differences in the use of the Greek vocabulary, the number of biblical quotations and allusions, the relative focus on particular biblical books, and the style of introduction of biblical material (whether it is simply merged into the text or explicitly cited as a quotation, and whether it is introduced generally or with a biblical author specified).[154] Using these comparisons, Joest has noted that the *Instruction concerning a Spiteful Monk* becomes stylistically less and less like the writings of Pachomius as it proceeds through its three distinct sections. Meanwhile it becomes progressively more like the writings of Theodore and especially Horsiesios, who use longer sentences and introduce their scriptural citations more explicitly.[155]

Significantly, Joest has noted that the last section of *Instruction concerning a Spiteful Monk* contains a biblical passage used only by Horsiesios

---

159, pp. 8, 13, 15, 16 (lines 4 and 6), 17, 23; Budge, *Coptic Apocrypha*, 155, 161, 163, 164, 166, 174.

[154] Joest, "Horsiese als Redaktor von Pachoms Katechese 1," 65–66; and Joest, "Pachoms Katechese 'an einen gröllenden Mönch,'" 93.

[155] Joest, "Pachoms Katechese 'an einen gröllenden Mönch,'" 94.

among the Pachomians, Genesis 14:23: "I will act like Abraham, I will raise [my hand] to God the Most High, who made heaven and earth; not to take anything that is yours, from a thread to a shoe lace."[156] Elsewhere Horsiesios uses this verse consistently to support the ideal of monastic poverty.[157] In the third part of the *Instruction concerning a Spiteful Monk*, this verse is directed at the problems of greed and possessions, suggesting that the

[156] Veilleux, *Pachomian Koinonia*, 3:37 (*Instruction concerning a Spiteful Monk* 53); Budge, *Coptic Apocrypha*, 171; Lefort, *Oeuvres de s. Pachôme*, CSCO 159, p. 21. See also Veilleux, *Pachomian Koinonia*, 2:208 (*Regulations of Horsiesios* 30) and 3:186 (*Testament* 21); Lefort, *Oeuvres de s. Pachôme*, CSCO 159, p. 90; and Boon, *Pachomiana latina*, 122.

[157] Joest, "Die sog. 'Règlements' als Werk des Pachomianers Horsiese († nach 386)," *Vigiliae christianae* 63 (2009): 489–90; Joest, "Pachoms Katechese 'an einen gröllenden Mönch,'" 96; and Joest, "Horsiese als Redaktor von Pachoms Katechese 1," 83–84. Joest asserts that Horsiesios is the only one in all monastic literature, east or west, to use Genesis 14:23. But it is found in some of Shenoute's canons and in later references to these rules by Besa, Shenoute's successor. Three of Shenoute's canons (Book 1, rule 18; Book 3, rule 90; Book 9, rule 467) indicate that the house leaders had charge of all items needed for craftwork and that monks who stole anything, including a cord or sandal-thong, were cursed. See Bentley Layton, *The Canons of Our Fathers: Monastic Rules of Shenoute*, Oxford Early Christian Studies (Oxford: Oxford University Press, 2014), 97, 125, 293. Besa makes allusions to Genesis 14:23 in two writings ("Reproofs and Monastic Rules" and "To Thieving Nuns"), both dealing specifically with the problem of theft in the monasteries. He cites "our father" (Shenoute) in both documents to curse anyone who steals "anything anywhere in these communities, from a cord to a shoestrap" (*Letters and Sermons of Besa*, ed. Kuhn, CSCO 157 [Coptic], pp. 30, 34–35, 72; and CSCO 158 [English], pp. 28, 33, 69). (These citations of Shenoute by Besa are also in Layton, *The Canons of Our Fathers*, 337, 339.)

third part of the *Instruction concerning a Spiteful Monk* may have come from the same conflicted context as *On Love and Self-Control*, in which greed and possessions were at issue.[158] It is possible that not only *On Love and Self-Control* but also the third part of *Instruction concerning a Spiteful Monk* is by Horsiesios.

If that is the case, then the phrase *image of God* may not be as uncharacteristic of Horsiesios as it first seems. It occurs three times in *On Love and Self-Control* and once in the final section of *Instruction concerning a Spiteful Monk*, two Pachomian texts that have not been associated with Horsiesios in the past but that cannot be ruled out as Horsiesian in light of this recent scholarship.[159] Horsiesios may have adopted the language of the *image of God* from Pachomius. Joest posits that Pachomius's original instruction, delivered to a spiteful monk from the monastery at Sheneset in the presence of others early in the life of the community, was recorded and became a local tradition at Sheneset, where it

[158] Rousseau, *Pachomius*, 157.

[159] On the three occurences of the phrase in *On Love and Self-Control*, see Lantschoot, "Lettre de saint Athanase," 271, 273, 278; and Lefort, *S. Athanase*, CSCO 150, pp. 114, 115, 120. In the last section of the *Instruction concerning a Spiteful Monk*, the *Apa* invites the monk to imagine that someone has spoken painful words to him or has received what he considers undeserved praise. He advises the monk not to be spiteful about it but to remember his own sin, to think of the cruel treatment that Christ suffered "because of you," to pray, "Forgive me, Lord, for I have made your image suffer," and to run and be reconciled. See Veilleux, *Pachomian Koinonia*, 3:40; Budge, *Coptic Apocrypha*, 174; Lefort, *Oeuvres de s. Pachôme*, CSCO 159, pp. 23–24.

was recycled in various forms as circumstances required.[160] Horsiesios, as a later *apa* of the monastery of Sheneset, would have been very familiar with the ideas contained in the *Instruction*.[161]

The Use of the Discourse *On Love and Self-Control* Beyond the Seventh Century

Fading in and out of the historical record over the centuries, *On Love and Self-Control* seems to become visible during moments of conflict, which is perhaps not surprising for a discourse urging a fractured community to love and self-control. But "every unhappy moment is unhappy in its own way" (to paraphrase Leo Tolstoy).[162] As the focus of the conflicts varied, the uses of *On Love and Self-Control* seemed to vary as well. A summary of the way the text was used up to the start of the seventh century may serve as an example.

On Love and Self-Control was originally delivered to the Pachomian community when it was experiencing internal conflict, prescribing the fruits of the Holy Spirit of Christ so that the community could be reconciled. The focal point of the text appears to have been the call to reconciliation. *On Love and Self-Control* next showed up as a paraphrased selection forming part of the *Instruction concerning a Spiteful Monk*. This Pachomian

[160] Joest, "Pachoms Katechese 'an einen gröllenden Mönch,'" 97–98, 129.

[161] Joest, "Horsiese als Redaktor von Pachoms Katechese 1," 62.

[162] Leo Tolstoy, *Anna Karenina* (New York: Random House, 1993), 3.

compilation seems to have been created during an Egyptian phase of the Origenist controversy in 399–400, when the question at issue was whether sinful humans retained the image of God. The focal point of the compilation appeared to have been the phrase *the image of God*; the editor's careful choice of selections to splice together may have been designed to reassure the readers that God recognized his image even in sinful humans and sent Christ to rescue and heal them. The next probable context in which *On Love and Self-Control* emerged was the turn of the sixth and seventh centuries, when Egyptian supporters and opponents of the Council of Chalcedon each claimed continuity with the great church leaders of the past. *On Love and Self-Control* was attributed to Athanasius in an anti-Chalcedonian codex and thus lifted up as part of that valuable heritage for the opponents of the Council of Chalcedon. The focal point of the text appears to have been its author and his place in the honorable theological and ethical tradition represented by the collection of texts.

On Love and Self-Control continued to be used beyond the seventh century, still in conflicted circumstances, and its use continued to vary with each shift of unhappy moments. It appears next in the historical record in the tenth, eleventh, and twelfth centuries on three occasions. The first was at the end of the tenth century, when the *Instruction concerning a Spiteful Monk* with its paraphrased selection from *On Love and Self-Control* was copied as part of a codex commissioned as a gift to the Upper Egyptian monastery of St. Mercurius at Edfu. The second was in the eleventh century, when the section about wine, common to *On Love and Self-Control* and *Instruction concerning a Spiteful Monk*, was inserted into a text titled *The Apocalypse of Samuel of Qalamun*. The third was at the end of the eleventh century or the beginning of the twelfth, when the codex MONB.CP itself was copied, containing what has become the only surviving manuscript of *On Love and Self-Control*. Each of these occasions will be discussed within its historical context so that some hints may be discerned about what may have been the focal point of the text for its community on each occasion.

Events Affecting the Church in Egypt from the Seventh to Tenth Centuries

In the seventh century (619–629 CE), the Persians temporarily drove the Chalcedonian Byzantine government out of Egypt,[163] and then the Arabs drove it out permanently (641 CE). The first Muslim governor, 'Amr ibn al-'As, summoned the non-Chalcedonian Patriarch Benjamin I to a meeting in Alexandria in 644 and there established the new role of the church leader in relation to the Muslim rulers. *History of the Patriarchs* records that 'Amr told Benjamin to "administer the affairs of

[163] During their invasion of Egypt, Persian troops attacked many monasteries in order to appropriate their wealth. Shenoute's monastery was among those attacked; it is likely that its great church was burned at this time. Reconstruction and renovation of the building took place from then until the thirteenth century. *History of the Patriarchs*, ed. Basil Evetts, PO 4, tome I, fasc. 4, 484–86; and Caroline T. Schroeder, "'A Suitable Abode for Christ': The Church Building as Symbol of Ascetic Renunciation in Early Monasticism," *Church History: Studies in Christianity & Culture* 73, no. 3 (2004): 476–83.

his church and the government of his nation."[164] The patriarch, as the administrator of the Egyptian Christian community, became the official representative of that community, both in spiritual and in practical matters.

As *dhimmī* (protected people), Egyptian Christians paid a land tax (*kharaj*) and a head tax (*jizya*). These taxes were received through the patriarchal office.[165] At the turn of the seventh to the eighth century, the governor of Egypt, 'Abd al-'Aziz, was charged by the caliph with the task of carrying out a census and land surveys in Egypt in order to facilitate more careful accounting and taxation. Taxes were paid with new coins that bore Islamic statements of faith in Arabic. Arabic was declared the official administrative language, and Christian administrators began to be replaced by Muslim Arabs.[166] When Qurrah ibn Sharik was governor (709–714), travelers had to carry a paper of identification in order to prevent tax evasion by flight.[167]

[164] Evetts, *History of the Patriarchs*, PO 4, tome I, fasc. 4, 496.

[165] Mark Swanson, *The Coptic Papacy in Islamic Egypt, 641–1517*, The Popes of Egypt 2 (Cairo: The American University of Cairo Press, 2010), 4–8.

[166] Petra M. Sijpesteijn and Sarah Clackson, "*P. Clackson* 45–46: A Mid-Eighth Century Trilingual Tax Demand Related to the Monastery of Apa Apollo at Bawit," in *Monastic Estates in Late Antiquity and Early Islamic Egypt*, ed. Boud'hors, Clackson, Louis, and Sijpesteijn, 104; Leslie S. B. MacCoull, *Coptic Perspectives on Late Antiquity*, Variorum Collected Studies (Aldershot, Hampshire, UK, and Brookfield, Vermont: Variorum, 1993), 63; Swanson, *The Coptic Papacy in Islamic Egypt*, 16.

[167] Hugh Kennedy, "Egypt as a Province in the Islamic Caliphate, 641–868," in *Islamic Egypt, 640–1517*, ed. Carl F. Petry, vol. 1 of *The Cambridge History of Egypt*, ed. M. W. Daly (Cambridge: Cambridge University Press, 1998), 73.

The rates of taxation increased as a result of these measures, especially for Christians.

These changes signaled to the Copts (as Egyptian Christians came to be known) that the Islamic government was not going to be temporary. The responses evoked included conversion, accommodation, resistance, rebellion, and a theological turn toward apocalyptic literature. Coptic Christians interpreted the events of their time as symptomatic of the last days, and apocalyptic literature, with its urgent call for repentance and preparedness, flourished. Harald Suermann notes that a special characteristic of Egyptian apocalypses is that they are paranetic. They appeal to the Copts to lead a moral and God-pleasing life, not faltering under pressure or converting to Islam. In these apocalypses Muslim rule is depicted as a punishment for Christian faithlessness.[168]

A Tenth-Century Reception of On Love and Self-Control *by way of* Instruction concerning a Spiteful Monk

In this context and in a spirit of repentance, Chael, a man from a rural area just north of Sne (Esna) in southern Egypt, commissioned a codex containing a copy of the *Instruction concerning a Spiteful Monk*, with its inserted selection from *On Love and Self-Control.* This Sahidic copy of the

[168] Harald Suermann, "Koptische arabische Apokalypsen," in *Studies on the Christian Arabic Heritage in Honor of Father Prof. Dr. Samir Khalil Samir S.I. at the Occasion of His Sixty-Fifth Birthday*, ed. Rifaat Ebied and Herman Teule, Eastern Christian Studies 5 (Louvain: Peeters, 2004), 42–43.

Instruction concerning a Spiteful Monk is the one Coptic manuscript that is still extant; two later Arabic translations are also extant.[169] The Coptic codex has a colophon at the end from the scribe. A colophon is an appendix written by the copyist, usually naming the scribe, the *scriptorium*, and the date the work was completed. If the manuscript or codex was intended as a gift, the donor and destination were also named. The colophon of the codex that contains the *Instruction concerning a Spiteful Monk* (with its heading attributing it to Pachomius) along with a sermon on John the Baptist reveals that for its donor repentance in the fear of the Lord may have been the focal point: a valuable, if bracing, prescription for health that he found directly in the *Instruction concerning a Spiteful Monk* and thus indirectly in *On Love and Self-Control*. The colophon says, "I, Theopistos, the insignificant deacon," in the city of Sne (Esna), "wrote this book with my hand" for Chael, who was giving it to the Monastery of Saint Mercurius at Edfu "for the salvation of his soul." Chael asked Mercurius, John the Baptist, and Pachomius to beg Christ for his blessings

[169] The manuscript is in the British Library, catalogued as Or. 7024. The Coptic text is published in Budge, *Coptic Apocrypha*, 145–77, with an English translation on pages 352–82; and Lefort, *Oeuvres de s. Pachôme*, CSCO 159, pp. 1–24 (Coptic) and CSCO 160, pp. 1–26 (French). A modern English translation is in Veilleux, *Pachomian Koinonia*, 3:2–3, 13–46. The Arabic translations are discussed in K. Samir, "Témoins arabes de la catéchèse de Pachôme 'A propos d'un moine rancunier' (CPG 2354.1)," *OCP* 42 (1976): 494–508. In "S. Athanase écrivain copte," 1–33, Lefort put the corresponding passages from *On Love and Self-Control* and *Instruction concerning a Spiteful Monk* in parallel columns for easy comparison.

in this world and for his salvation "from all the snares of the devil and wicked people" and for his "assistance in every good work" so that Chael might receive forgiveness of his sins and "an inheritance with all the saints." The colophon says that the book was completed on the date equivalent to February 10, 987 CE.[170]

The codex containing *Instruction concerning a Spiteful Monk* was not the only work that Chael commissioned from Theopistos for the Monastery of St. Mercurius at Edfu. Five years earlier, Chael, the same donor, had commissioned a copy of the story of Abbaton, the angel of death, from the same scribe for the same monastery.[171] The theme of this distinctively Upper Egyptian story points again to the emphasis that Chael seems to have placed on repentance. Abbaton was the same angel who brought God the clay from which to form humanity in God's image (on the 13th of the Coptic month of Hatur), in spite of his consciousness that humanity would bring sin into the world. Afterward God tasked Abbaton with terrifying humanity in order to bring them to fear and repentance and thus to save them. Only those who observed Abbaton's

[170] Budge, *Coptic Apocrypha*, 175–76 (my translation). The colophon is also published and described in Arnold van Lantschoot, *Les Colophons coptes des manuscrits sahidiques*, vol. 1 of *Recueil des colophons des manuscrits chrétiens d'Égypte* (Louvain: J.-B. Istas, 1929), fasc. 1, pp. 189–90, and fasc. 2, pp. 77–78. See also Lefort, "S. Athanase écrivain copte," 1, and Lefort, *Oeuvres de s. Pachôme*, CSCO 159, p. VI.

[171] London, BL Or. 7025. See Lantschoot, *Les Colophons coptes des manuscrits sahidiques*, 187; and Budge, *Coptic Martyrdoms, &c., in the Dialect of Upper Egypt*, vol. 4 of *Coptic Texts* (London: British Museum, 1914), xxii–xxiii, lxviii–lxxii, 225–49, and 474–96.

day (the 13th of Hatur) in repentance with charity and almsgiving would see Abbaton in gentle form at their deaths, when Abbaton would bear them tenderly to the kingdom of God; all others would see Abbaton in horrifying form as they died.[172] The theme of living in virtuous preparation for one's entry into God's kingdom ties together the texts of the *Discourse on Abbaton* and *Instruction concerning a Spiteful Monk*, and the section of *On Love and Self-Control* contained in the latter.

On Love and Self-Control *in the Eleventh-Century* Apocalypse of Samuel of Qalamun

The next appearance of *On Love and Self-Control* was apocalyptic; its focal point was the section of the text regarding wine. Understanding its context requires a look at the mid-ninth century, when the Abbasid caliph al-Mutawakkil came to power and instituted a conservative Sunni religious agenda that had an impact upon Christians as he sought to make clear distinctions between Muslims and *dhimmīs*. In order to do this,

[172] Budge, *Coptic Martyrdoms*, 225–49 (Coptic) and 474–96 (English). The account of creation in this story highlights the Upper Egyptian focus on humanity as the image of God in spite of sin. After God formed the clay into a human body, God hesitated to give it life because of the suffering it would cause and experience. But, when Jesus (who is telling the story to his disciples) promised to be humanity's advocate in spite of the cost, the Father "breathed into [the man's] nostrils the breath of life three times, saying, 'Live! Live! Live! according to the type of My Divinity.' And the man lived straightway, and became a living soul, according to the image and likeness of God" (Budge, *Coptic Martyrdoms*, 234, 483).

al-Mutawakkil used an eighth-century document called *The Pact of 'Umar*, which summed up the principles of the treatment of *dhimmīs*. Although not always enforced, the pact created a stricter standard than had applied before its time.[173] The drinking of wine was one of the practices prohibited to Muslims as a mark of distinction. In a letter that al-Mutawakkil wrote to the district governors in 850, he reminded Muslims of the Qur'anic prohibition against wine (al-Qur'an 5:90–92), a drink that he associated with Christians: "God thereby forbids Muslims . . . to imbibe the drink of theirs that most arouses enmity and hatred and that most impedes mentioning God's name and praying."[174]

Many of the measures that al-Mutawakkil imposed in the ninth century were reinstated by the Shi'ite caliph al-Hakim bi-Amr Allah in the eleventh century (996–1021) as al-Hakim began a campaign against *dhimmīs* and Sunnis that lasted from around 1004 until around 1019. During these years of persecution, many churches and monasteries were destroyed, as were wine and the ingredients to make it.[175]

[173] Milka Levy-Rubin, "The Pact of 'Umar," in *Christian-Muslim Relations: A Bibliographic History*, ed. David Thomas and Barbara Roggema, vol. 1 (600–900), History of Christian-Muslim Relations 11 (Leiden and Boston: Brill, 2009), 360–64.

[174] Joel L. Kraemer, trans., *Incipient Decline*, vol. 34 of *The History of Al-Tabari*, Bibliotheca Persica, Series in Near Eastern Studies (Albany: SUNY Press, 1989), 92.

[175] Aziz Suryal Atiya, Yassa 'Abd al-Masih, and O. H. E. Khs-Burmester, *History of the Patriarchs of the Egyptian Church, Known as the History of the Holy Church, by Sawīrus ibn al-Muḳaffaʿ, Bishop of al-Ašmūnīn*, vol. 2, part 2: *Khaël III-Shenouti II (A.D. 880–1066)*, Textes et Documents (Cairo: La Société

In this period of al-Hakim's rule, conversion to Islam accelerated. Many conversions were coerced either directly or indirectly. As the percentage of Egyptians who were Muslim increased, so did the use of Arabic, even among Egyptians who remained Christian. But toward 1020 al-Hakim had a change of heart. He relaxed restrictions on Christians, allowing them to worship again and to rebuild churches, and permitting forced converts to revert to Christianity.[176] Al-Hakim treated Muslims, however, with increasing violence until he disappeared on a solitary walk at night in 1021.[177]

---

d'Archéologie Copte, 1948), 187–92 (English), ١٢٦-١٢٤ (Arabic). See also Otto F. Meinardus, *Two Thousand Years of Coptic Christianity* (Cairo and New York: The American University in Cairo Press, 1999), 65; Swanson, *The Coptic Papacy in Islamic Egypt*, 54–55, 174n67; and Werthmuller, *Coptic Identity and Ayyubid Politics in Egypt*, 34–35. When the Coptic priest Abu al-Makarim Sa'adallah ibn Jirjis ibn Mas'ud wrote an account of the churches and monasteries of Egypt in the twelfth century, he noted that Pbow had been ruined by al-Hakim. It is more likely that Pbow had already fallen into ruin; perhaps under al-Hakim it was looted for whatever of value was left. See Evetts, *The Churches and Monasteries of Egypt*, 281–82; Werthmuller, *Coptic Identity and Ayyubid Politics in Egypt*, 23–25; Goehring, *Ascetics*, 86; and *The Coptic Enclyclopedia*, s.v. "Pbow: Archaeology," by Peter Grossmann. Al-Hakim also closed down the *scriptorium* in the Fayyum that had supplied the library of the Monastery of Shenoute of Atripe with many of its manuscripts in the tenth century. See Takla, "Biblical Manuscripts of the Monastery of St. Shenoute the Archimandrite," in *Christianity and Monasticism in Upper Egypt*, ed. Gabra and Takla, 1:160.

[176] Atiya,'Abd al-Masih, and Burmester, *History of the Patriarchs of the Egyptian Church*, vol. 2, part 2, pp. 205, 208 (English), ١٣٧, ١٣٥ (Arabic).

[177] Stanley Lane-Poole, *A History of Egypt in the Middle Ages*, 2nd rev. ed. (London: Methuen, 1914; repr. Karachi, Pakistan: S. M. Mir, 1977), 132–33; Werthmuller, *Coptic Identity and Ayyu-*

Strong opposition to the Arabization of Egyptian Christianity came from the monasteries, particularly those in Upper Egypt, far away from the capital city.[178] A clear example is provided by the *Apocalypse of Samuel*, written in Coptic by an unknown monk, probably from the Monastery of Samuel of Qalamun in the Fayyum. It exists today only in an Arabic translation made in 1606.[179] In

---

bid Politics in Egypt, 35–38; and Swanson, *The Coptic Papacy in Islamic Egypt*, 55–56.

[178] Papaconstantinou, "'They Shall Speak the Arabic Language,'" 292; Paul Maiberger, *"Das Buch der kostbaren Perle" von Severus ibn al-Muqaffa': Einleitung und arabischer Text (Kapitel 1–5)*, Akademie der Wissenschaften und der Literatur, Veröffentlichungen der orientalischen Kommission 28 (Wiesbaden: Franz Steiner, 1972), 68; and MacCoull, *Coptic Perspectives on Late Antiquity*, 37.

[179] The manuscript is Paris, BnF, arabe 150 (fol. 20–30). The text can be found with a French translation in J. Ziadeh, with a note by F. Nau, "L'Apocalypse de Samuel, supérieur de Deir-el-Qalamoun," *Revue de l'Orient chrétien* 20 (1915–1917): 374–407. For an English translation of the French, see Roger Pearse, "Apocalypse of Samuel, Superior of Deir-el-Qalamoun," April 17, 2009, www.roger-pearse.com/weblog/2009/04/17/the-apocalypse-of-samuel-of-kalamoun-now-online/ (acc. Aug. 18, 2016). Jos van Lent's comment that Egyptian apocalyptic texts are notoriously difficult to date is especially applicable to *The Apocalypse of Samuel*. See Jos van Lent, "Les Apocalypses coptes de l'époque arabe: Quelques réflexions," in *Études coptes V: Sixième journée d'études, Limoges 18–20 juin 1993 et septième journée d'études, Neuchâtel 18–20 mai 1995*, ed. M. Rassart-Debergh, Cahiers de la Bibliothèque copte 10 (Paris and Louvain: Peeters, 1998), 186–87. While earlier scholars dated the *Apocalypse of Samuel* to the early eighth century, recent scholarship has moved the date to later centuries, both because of the *Apocalypse*'s reliance on earlier apocalyptic texts and because its content reflects a situation in which Arabic was being used more extensively by Christians than it had been in the early eighth

writing his apocalypse the monk found occasion to quote the passage about wine that *On Love and Self-Control* and *Instruction concerning a Spiteful Monk* have in common.

In this work the apocalypse is placed anachronistically in the mouth of Samuel, the seventh-century superior of the monastery of Qalamun, a large, wealthy monastery in the Fayyum, north of the Monastery of Saint Shenoute of Atripe. Samuel is asked about the future of the church under Islam. After describing the spread of the Arab people and their influence, Samuel says regretfully that many Christians will adopt their ways. One of the behav-

---

century. Maged Mikhail points out that the use of Arabic in the liturgy, which is criticized in the *Apocalypse*, cannot be verified earlier than the tenth century (Mikhail, "Egypt from Late Antiquity to Early Islam," 161). There is a growing consensus that the text seems best to fit local conditions in the Fayyum in the second half of the eleventh century, when the Coptic culture and language were still predominant there but the Arabic language and Muslim customs were starting to make inroads. On the eighth-century dating, see F. Nau, "Note sur l'Apocalypse de Samuel," *Revue de l'Orient chrétien* 20 (1915–1917): 405–7; and MacCoull, *Coptic Perspectives on Late Antiquity*, 70n35. On the later dating, see John Iskander, "Islamization in Medieval Egypt: The Copto-Arabic 'Apocalypse of Samuel' as a Source for the Social and Religious History of Medieval Copts," *Medieval Encounters* 4, no. 3 (1998): 219–27; Papaconstantinou, "'They Shall Speak the Arabic Language and Take Pride in It,'" 282–84; Lent, "The Apocalypse of Samuel," in *Christian-Muslim Relations: A Bibliographical History*, ed. David Thomas and Alex Mallett, vol. 2 (900–1050), History of Christian-Muslim Relations 14 (Leiden and Boston: Brill, 2010), 746–47; Lent, "The Apocalypse of Samuel of Qalamun Reconsidered," paper presented at the Tenth International Congress of Coptic Studies, Rome, September 17–22, 2012; and Jason Zaborowski, "From Coptic to Arabic in Medieval Egypt," *Medieval Encounters* 14 (2008): 15–40.

iors he decries is the way these former Christians will represent humans, the image of God. They will call them pigs, dogs, and donkeys.[180] They will take

[180] Ziadeh, "L'Apocalypse de Samuel," 377 (Arabic) and 394 (French). Cf. Émile Amélineau, *Vie de Schnoudi*, in *Monuments pour servir à l'histoire de l'Égypte chrétienne*, Mémoires publiés par les membres de la mission archéologique française au Caire, tome 4, fasc. 1 (Paris: Ernest Leroux, 1888), 333. In the *Qur'an*, Surat Al-Mā'idah (V): 60, people of the book who are disobedient to God are warned about being turned into apes and pigs and slaves of idols. In times of conflict between Jewish and Christian subjects and their Muslim rulers in Spain and North Africa, Jews were depicted as apes and Christians as pigs. In the ninth-century Aghlabid dynasty of Ifriqiya, under the *kadi* of Kairouan, Ahmad ibn Talib, Jews were required to wear a shoulder patch of an ape and to hang a picture of an ape on their doors. Christians were required to wear a shoulder patch of a pig and to hang a picture of a pig on their doors. (See *Encyclopédie de l'Islam*, new edition, s.v. "Kird," by F. Viré.) In Egypt, under the caliph al-Mutawakkil, the placard of a demonic dog was sometimes required to be hung on the door of a Coptic home (Lane-Poole, *A History of Egypt*, 39). Perhaps these bestial associations are the source of the complaints in Egyptian Christian apocalyptic writings of this time about calling the image of God pigs and dogs. Maybe the addition of *donkeys* in the *Apocalypse of Samuel* (not present in a similar passage from the seventh-century Arabic *Life of Shenoute*) is connected with the later requirement that Christians ride only donkeys, not horses. For the Arabic *Life of Shenoute*, see Amélineau, *Vie de Schnoudi*, 331–33. Note that in the *Apocalypse of Samuel* it is Christians who are accused of using such degrading language about human beings. Muslims used the word *dog* as a term of derision for other Muslims too. For example, in his *Dictionary of Men of Letters*, the Muslim historical geographer Yaqut al-Hamawi tells about a meeting he had in 1197/98 with an Islamic scholar whom he found eminent but arrogant because he referred to other Islamic scholars as dogs and refuse. (See the Foundation for Science, Technology, and Civilization, Limited, "Yaqut al-Hamawi," 11 May 2007, http://www

the modes of expression and the language itself of the Arabs, leaving behind "the beautiful Coptic language, in which the Holy Spirit has often spoken through the mouths of our spiritual fathers," Samuel laments.[181] They will no longer worship and will no longer understand the Gospel because they will have forgotten their language. This is because the clergy will be negligent and unprepared for their duties. No one will read or take care of the Coptic books anymore, says Samuel. He recognizes that some Christians, specifically those in Upper Egypt, will still speak Coptic, but he foresees that they will be scorned by Arabic-speaking Christians.[182]

Samuel predicts that Christians will compete for status, leaving humility behind along with the language of their ancestors, but he warns his listeners to be vigilant in resisting temptation and in practicing virtues.[183] One of the practices he recommends for Christians, as Caliph al-Mutawakkil had recommended for Muslims for similar reasons, is abstention from wine. At this point Samuel's speech seems to borrow from a passage common to *On Love and Self-Control* and *Instruction concerning a Spiteful Monk*:

> It is only at the cost of great humiliation that our fathers accomplished their course,

---

.muslimheritage.com/topics/default.cfm?ArticleID=694 [accessed 2 February 2013].)

[181] Papaconstantinou, "'They Shall Speak the Arabic Language and Take Pride in It,'" 275; Ziadeh, "L'Apocalypse de Samuel," 379 (Arabic), 395 (French).

[182] Ziadeh, "L'Apocalypse de Samuel," 380 (Arabic), 395 (French).

[183] Ziadeh, "L'Apocalypse de Samuel," 382–84 (Arabic), 397–98 (French).

> suffering hunger and thirst, and abstaining completely from drinking any kind of wine, for the troubles of concupiscence arise in the human members through the excessive use of wine: wine excites concupiscence, rendering it improper, and it is what breaks the flesh of the body. In general, excessive use of wine grieves the Holy Spirit, and our fathers knew the numerous sorrows caused by wine from the beginning. Therefore, abstain. But, in small amounts, it could be used with bodily illnesses; for if the great ascetic Timothy was authorized to take a little wine because of his stomach and his numerous weaknesses, what will I do, then, for those who are in the effervescence of youth and who are often subject to great suffering? Truly, my children, it is good to be reserved in everything, and there is no greater profit than humiliation; for the one who humbles his soul saves it and sends it to the harbor of salvation and will be filled with the good things of the heavenly Jerusalem.[184]

The author is probably using *Instruction concerning a Spiteful Monk* here. Most of the second half of this excerpt from the *Apocalypse of Samuel* is more closely related to *Instruction concerning a Spiteful Monk* than it is to *On Love and Self-Control*

[184] Ziadeh, "L'Apocalypse de Samuel," 386 (Arabic), 400 (French). (My translation is from the French.) See *On Love and Self-Control* in Coptic at Lantschoot, "Lettre de saint Athanase," 276–77; and Lefort, CSCO 150, pp. 118–19. See *Instruction concerning a Spiteful Monk* in Veilleux, *Pachomian Koinonia*, 3:34–35 (§§45–47); in Coptic at Lefort, *Oeuvres de s. Pachôme*, CSCO 159, pp. 18–19, and in Budge, *Coptic Apocrypha*, 168–69.

(see Appendix A for a comparison). In the absence of a Coptic version of *The Apocalypse of Samuel* it is difficult to reach a definitive conclusion about whether the scribe was copying from *On Love and Self-Control* or *Instruction concerning a Spiteful Monk*, but whichever discourse was his source, the author of the *Apocalypse* is either abridging it or using an abridged copy, leaving out several biblical allusions and quotations.[185]

[185] *On Love and Self-Control* seems never to have been translated into Arabic, but Arabic translations of *Instruction concerning a Spiteful Monk* are available. I was able to view an image of Sbath 1018, a manuscript of the Melkite Greek-Catholic Archbishopric of Aleppo, provided by the Hill Museum and Manuscript Library at Saint John's University in Collegeville, Minnesota, where it is catalogued as GAMS 01018. The relevant pages are 218–20. Sbath 1018 is a faithful rendering into Arabic of the Coptic original of *Instruction concerning a Spiteful Monk*. It does not exactly match the Arabic text of the *Apocalypse of Samuel of Qalamun*, but it is difficult to evaluate the divergences because the author of the *Apocalypse* was writing in Coptic and surely consulting a Coptic source for this section about wine. Paris, BnF, Syriac 239 is an Arabic manuscript of *Instruction concerning a Spiteful Monk* written in the Syriac script. Lefort used this manuscript in a literal translation supplied for him by Lantschoot to check against the Coptic as he made his edition of *Instruction concerning a Spiteful Monk* (Lefort, *Oeuvres de s. Pachôme*, CSCO 159, pp. VI–VII). Lefort did not add any notes referring to the Arabic text to the section of *Instruction concerning a Spiteful Monk* regarding wine. Samir, "Témoins arabes de la catéchèse de Pachôme," 494–508, discusses the Arabic versions of *Instruction concerning a Spiteful Monk*, mentioning Lefort's use of Paris, BnF, Syriac 239 on pages 498–99, and indicating on pages 501–2 that Paris, BnF, Syriac 239 seems to be a much looser translation than Sbath 1018. Although Samir notes that some Arabic versions of the *Life of Pachomius* are expanded to include excerpts from the Pachomian *Instructions*, the Arabic *Life of Pachomius* from BL

Through Samuel's words the author paints a picture of a Coptic community that had absorbed a sense of inferiority based on its distinction from the Muslim community. The Copts of Samuel's speech no longer recognized the image of God in one another. Even the Coptic language in which such theology had been expressed was experienced as inferior, for example. Furthermore, the Coptic community seems to have been marked as a community lacking in self-control because of the distinctive association of Christians with wine. Although the author does not tell his readers about his source, he uses a text in the Coptic language to remind Christians that they, too, have a heritage of abstention from wine for the sake of self-control. They are no less disciplined than their neighbors. What the author of the *Apocalypse of Samuel* seems to find valuable for the health of his community in his selection of the passage about wine, originally from *On Love and Self-Control,* is the text's recommendation for the exercise of discipline, or self-control, as a traditionally Coptic mark of dignity and worth.

Or. 4523, in Amélineau, *Monuments pour server à l'histoire de l'Égypte chrétienne au IV*[e] *siècle: Histoire de saint Pakhôme et de ses communautés,* Annales du Musée Guimet 17 (Paris: Ernest Leroux, 1889), does not include the section of *Instruction concerning a Spiteful Monk* that deals with wine. On the Pachomian corpus in Arabic, see Georg Graf, *Geschichte der christlichen arabischen Literatur,* vol. 1, Studi e testi 118 (Vatican: Biblioteca apostolica vaticana, 1944), 459–61; and Graf, *Catalogue de manuscrits arabes chrétiens conserves au Caire,* Studi e testi 63 (Vatican: Biblioteca apostolica vaticana, 1934), 117–18, 190, 202 (nos. 321 II, 495, 536).

The Copying of On Love and Self-Control *in the Eleventh or Twelfth Century*

It was probably shortly after the production of the *Apocalypse of Samuel* that the codex MONB.CP containing *On Love and Self-Control* was copied at the Monastery of Saint Shenoute of Atripe. A large number of Sahidic manuscripts were copied in this *scriptorium* between the ninth and thirteenth centuries as the community sought to convert its papyrus holdings to parchment.[186] The scribe who

[186] Hany Takla, "Biblical Manuscripts of the Monastery of St. Shenoute the Archimandrite," in *Christianity and Monasticism in Upper Egypt*, ed. Gabra and Takla, 1:156, 160.

It may have been at this time of scribal activity, around the same time that MONB.CP was copied, that the Sahidic inscriptions listing books were made on the walls of the north *pastophorium* of the church at the monastery and signed by Papa Klaute. This may be the same Klaute (or Claudius) who is named in the colophon of a manuscript copied in 1091 as the superior of the monastery. See Paris, Copte 132^{1}, fol. 66, in Lantschoot, *Les Colophons coptes des manuscrits sahidiques*, 127–31; and *The Coptic Encyclopedia*, s.v. "Dayr Anbā Shinūdah: History," by René-Georges Coquin and Maurice Martin, 763. On the north wall, Klaute wrote, ⲡⲓϩⲏⲕⲉ ⲡⲡⲁ ⲕⲗⲁⲩⲧⲉ ⲩⲩ ⲡⲁⲗⲉⲩ ⲕⲟⲩ ⲛⲁⲓ ⲉⲃⲟⲗ, "the poor Papa Claudius, son of Paleu, forgive me." On the east wall, he wrote, ⲁⲣⲓ ⲡⲁⲙⲉⲩⲉ ⲛⲁⲕⲁⲡⲉ ⲡⲓϩⲏⲕⲉ ⲡ̅ⲡ̅ⲁ ⲕⲗⲁⲩⲧⲉ ⲩⲩ ⲡⲁⲗⲏⲩ ⲙⲓⲥϫⲓⲛ, "Remember me in love, the poor Papa Claudius, the son of Paleu the Poor [ⲙⲓⲥϫⲓⲛ]." On the west wall he signed his name ⲕⲗⲁⲩⲧⲉ ⲩⲩ ⲙⲙⲓⲥϫⲓⲛ (Claudius, son of the Poor One) and asked for forgiveness (Crum, "Inscriptions from Shenoute's Monastery," 564–65). Crum suggests that ⲙⲓⲥϫⲓⲛ was either the grandfather of Klaute or another name for his father, Paleu (Crum, "Inscriptions from Shenoute's Monastery," 564–65), while Stefan Timm suggests that ⲙⲓⲥϫⲓⲛ might be the nephew of Klaute or Paleu (Timm, *Das christlich-koptisch Ägypten in arabischer Zeit*, 621). I have followed Crum's suggestion that ⲙⲓⲥϫⲓⲛ is part of Paleu's name, like a title, and my translation of ⲙⲓⲥϫⲓⲛ as "the poor one" makes it a Coptic trans-

copied the sole manuscript of *On Love and Self-Control* wrote with dark ink and hasty handwriting sloping slightly to the right and fully covering seven pages at fifty to sixty lines per page. The verso of folio 4 is shared with the beginning of a letter from Severus of Antioch to Theognostus. There are no columns and no ornamentation in the manuscript. The text is the top layer of parchment palimpsests with the underlying tenth-century documents showing through as well.[187]

Unfortunately, MONB.CP does not seem to end with a colophon that would state the precise date on which it was copied. Catherine Louis suggests that an acephalous sermon on the moral life attributed to Athanasius might be the last manuscript in the codex because its text ends at the top of a page with the rest of the page left blank.[188]

---

literation of the Arabic word المسكين. Thus, even these names are a sign of the times. The monk Klaute the (Coptic) poor is the son of Paleu (presumably a layperson) the (Arabic) poor.

[187] Layton, *Catalogue of Coptic Literary Manuscripts in the British Library*, #174, pp. 215–16 and plate 23. Arnold van Lantschoot published a study of the erased texts of this palimpsest in "Les Textes palimpsestes de B.M., Or. 8802," *Le Muséon* 41 (1928): 225–47. A page from another codex by the same hand as one of the erased texts contains a note from the scribe, who dated his work. The date corresponds to 990 CE. See Alin Suciu, "À propos de la datation du manuscript contenant de Grand Euchologe du Monastère Blanc," *Vigiliae Christianae* 65 (2011): 189–98.

[188] Catherine Louis, *Catalogue raisonné des manuscrits littéraires coptes conservés à l'IFAO du Caire* (L'Institut français d'archéologie orientale, forthcoming). Athanasius's sermon is translated into English as "Fragments on the Moral Life," in Brakke, *Athanasius and Asceticism*, 314–19. See also Lefort, *S. Athanase*, CSCO 150, pp. XXXI–XXXIII, 123, and CSCO 151, pp. 103–4; Crum, *Catalogue of the Coptic Manuscripts in the Collection of the John*

There is otherwise no blank space in this codex. The texts follow one another directly with only a line drawn across the page to separate them. The apparent lack of a colophon may suggest that the community copied this book from its own library and for its own use.

The lack of a colophon giving a clear date complicates the process of determining the time at which a manuscript was copied. But in the case of *On Love and Self-Control* scholarly consensus on the dating of the manuscript has been achieved on other grounds. On the basis of paleography, on the Sahidic language of the text, and on the fact that it is part of an anthology, scholars date the existing copy of *On Love and Self-Control* to the late eleventh or early twelfth century. Thus its historical context is the same as that of the *Apocalypse of Samuel of Qalamun,* and the fact that it was chosen to be copied and preserved may mean that it spoke to some of the concerns of the Coptic monastic community at that time.

Lefort and Lantschoot dated the copying of BL Or. 8802, the manuscript of *On Love and Self-Control,* to the eleventh or twelfth century on paleographic grounds.[189] This range also makes sense historically. In the eleventh century the Sahidic language had not yet been replaced by Bohairic or Arabic at the Monastery of Saint Shenoute of Atripe, although both were making inroads. A tenth-/

Rylands Library, 24–25; and Kuhn, *Letters and Sermons of Besa,* CSCO 157, p. 82; and CSCO 158, p. 79.

[189] Lantschoot, "Lettre de Saint Athanase," 265; and Lefort, *S. Athanase,* CSCO 150, p. XXIX.

eleventh-century Sahidic copy of the *Great Euchologion* used in worship at that monastery attests to the fact that at that time the community still used Sahidic.[190] But in the twelfth century the liturgy came to be sung in Bohairic, even in Upper Egypt.[191] A sign of the shifting linguistic situation appears in the ritual for a pilgrimage to the Monastery of Shenoute "on the Monday of the Second Week of the Holy Forty Days," which possibly took place from as early as the sixth century until around 1200. A copy of this ritual survives in a fifteenth-/sixteenth-century manuscript (Paris, FR-BN Copte 68) that is mostly in Sahidic but has some sections in Bohairic, Greek, and Arabic.[192] Heinzgard Brakmann, who works extensively on the Coptic liturgy, points out that, although it is impossible to pinpoint exactly when Bohairic

[190] Lanne, *Le grand euchologe du Monastère Blanc*, PO 135, tome XXVIII, fasc. 2.

[191] Lanne, *Le grand euchologe du Monastère Blanc*, 273; Zanetti, "Bohairic Liturgical Manuscripts," 67; Brakmann, "Fragmenta graeco-copto-thebaicq," 136.

[192] Hans Quecke, *Untersuchungen zum koptischen Stundengebet*, Publications de l'Institut orientaliste de Louvain 3 (Louvain: Institut orientaliste, Université catholique de Louvain, 1970), 488–505; Janet Timbie, "A Liturgical Procession in the Desert of Apa Shenoute," in *Pilgrimage and Holy Space in Late Antique Egypt*, ed. David Frankfurter, Religions in the Graeco-Roman World 134 (Leiden, Boston, and Cologne: Brill, 1998), 417; and Janet Timbie, "Once More into the Desert of Apa Shenoute," in *Christianity and Monasticism in Upper Egypt*, ed. Gabra and Takla, 1:169–78. A small section of the rite is in MS. Insinger, N° 44, in Leiden. See Willem Pleyte and Pieter Adrian Aart Boeser, *Manuscrits coptes du Musée d'antiquités des Pays-Bas à Leide publiés d'apres les orders du gouvernement* (Leiden: Brill, 1897), 244–46.

replaced Sahidic at the White Monastery, by 1361 the installation of Bishop Philotheos of Panopolis and Lycopolis (the diocese of the Monastery of Shenoute of Atripe) was recorded in Bohairic.[193]

Another feature of BL Or. 8802 that fits well into the eleventh or early twelfth century is the fact that it is part of an anthology. There was a trend toward that genre in the Coptic literature of the late ninth to eleventh centuries. These centuries were characterized by a monastic reappropriation of earlier literature, including the copying and production of anthologies, like MONB.CP.[194] The copy of MONB.CP was made in the same historical context as *The Apocalypse of Samuel of Qalamun*, which is to say that it was made at a time when the Christian population in Egypt was declining, along with its traditional language, even in Upper Egypt. Keeping in mind the feelings expressed in *The Apocalypse of Samuel*, it seems that one response to such a situation was for the community to cling to the Christian identity it had received from its heritage.[195] This heritage was well represented in

[193] Brakmann, "Fragmenta graeco-copto-thebaicq," 136n70.

[194] Tito Orlandi, "Coptic Literature," in *The Roots of Egyptian Christianity*, ed. Pearson and Goehring, 75–81; and *The Coptic Encyclopedia*, vol. 5, s.v. "Literature, Coptic," by Tito Orlandi.

[195] In our own time, the same response to a similar situation can be seen in a field study done by Loren Lybarger among Palestinian Christians in the Occupied Palestinian Territories in the late 1990s and early 2000s, after the first *intifada* and the disappointment of the Oslo Accords (Loren D. Lybarger, "For Church or Nation? Islamism, Secular Nationalism, and the Transformation of Christian Identities in Palestine," *Journal of the American Academy of Religion* 75, no. 4 [2007]: 777–813). The Palestinian Christian population was greatly reduced in

MONB.CP, and it was expressed in the traditional language of Sahidic.

The Dismemberment of the Codex in the Nineteenth Century and Its Current Reconstruction

We have tracked *On Love and Self-Control* from the situation that elicited this discourse through its use in other situations, its merger with other texts, its ascription to Athanasius, and its recopying over the centuries. Now *On Love and Self-Control* exists as a fragment from an anthology of texts by different authors that once were drawn together into a codex, a book. But no Coptic codex survived the nineteenth century whole. Today the various documents from MONB.CP are scattered in several libraries because of a string of events that began in the mid-eighteenth century. But the story does not end there. Presently, efforts are being made to reconstruct the codex by identifying the various manuscripts that once belonged together and determining as accurately as possible the sequence in which they once appeared in the book. Below I provide a list of all the contents of MONB.CP as

---

the twentieth century, and Palestinian Christians headed into the twenty-first century with a heightened sense of vulnerability, a fear of extinction, and a "search for alternative identity orientations in the face of a wrenching crisis" (Lybarger, "For Church or Nation," 792). Lybarger examined emerging Christian approaches to dealing with the stress of these fears and with the political and religious pressures experienced under ongoing occupation by Israel and increasingly powerful Islamic movements within Palestinian society. One approach taken by Palestinians was to reappropriate the long Christian heritage of their past.

they have been reconstructed so far. (The content is summarized in Appendix B.) But the sequencing of *On Love and Self-Control* has not yet become possible. The work is ongoing; one day the place of *On Love and Self-Control* in its codex may become clear.

The historical record is silent about *On Love and Self-Control* from the twelfth century to the nineteenth. Then, gradually, the text reemerged. The story picks up in 1742, when Charles Perry, a visitor to the Monastery of St. Shenoute of Atripe, noted the presence there of a large number of parchment manuscripts; however, he did not see the repository in which in 1883 so many manuscripts were found. Starting in 1778, many of the manuscripts from that monastery and from other libraries in Egypt began to trickle into Europe through the hands of antiquities dealers, but no one knew their exact source.[196] In one early purchase of the 1780s, the orientalist and librarian Charles Woide bought a batch of folios from Upper Egypt through a British agent there; these folios included two that were later determined to be from the same codex as *On Love and Self-Control*.[197]

[196] Stephen Emmel, *Shenoute's Literary Corpus*, CSCO 599, 1:19.

[197] They are now Oxford, Cl. Pr. b. 25, fols. 1–2. Folio 1 contains part of a sermon by Severien of Jabalah on Jesus' washing of his disciples' feet. Folio 2 contains part of Severus of Antioch's homily 28 on Thomas. See Henri Hyvernat, "Catalogue of the Clarendon Press Sahidic Fragments Deposed in the Bodleian Library" (unpublished manuscript, Oxford, 1886–1887), 59–60. Woide later donated his collection to the Clarendon Press, and it now resides in the Bodleian Library in Oxford, where Hyvernat's catalogue is located in the Special Collections Reading Room at call number 2.Cat.2.

On Love and Self-Control itself comes from the collection of Robert Curzon. Fascinated by the history of writing, Curzon journeyed from England to Egypt in 1833–1834 and again in 1838–1839 to collect manuscripts.[198] Some of his purchases were made for him after his second trip by Rudolph Theophilus Lieder, an Anglican missionary who lived in Cairo. A few months after Curzon left in 1839, Coptic scholar Henry Tattam and his stepdaughter and assistant Eliza Platt arrived in Egypt from England, intending to collect Coptic biblical manuscripts. Lieder entrusted to them a box of manuscripts to deliver to Curzon. Curzon received the box from them after their return to England later the same year; among other texts, it contained *On Love and Self-Control*. In studying this process of transmission Stephen Emmel writes that Lieder "had access to some channel through which White Monastery manuscripts were moving downstream from Upper Egypt," although "how the manuscripts made their way down the Nile from the White Monastery to Lieder remains unknown."[199]

[198] Stephen Emmel, "Robert Curzon's Acquisition of White Monastery Manuscripts," in *Actes du IVe congrés copte, Louvain-la-Neuve, 5–10 septembre 1988*, ed. Marguerite Rassart-Debergh and Julien Ries, vol. 2, Publications de l'Institut orientaliste de Louvain 41 (Louvain-la-Neuve: Université catholique de Louvain, Institut orientaliste, 1992), 224–31. In Emmel's article, Or. 8802 (which was donated to the British Museum in 1917) is called La. 175 (with the erased text of the palimpsest called La. 174), the number given to it in Layton, *Catalogue of Coptic Literary Manuscripts in the British Library*, 216–18.

[199] Emmel, "Robert Curzon's Acquisition of White Monastery Manuscripts," 2:231. Emmel's study is important because in Curzon's published account of his travels, he mentions

Sometime before 1868, Lord Lindsay, Earl of Crawford, purchased several folios (some perhaps from Lieder) that are now known to be from the same codex as *On Love and Self-Control*,[200] but it was not until 1882 that Gaston Maspero, Director of the Egyptian Antiquities Service, was able to trace some Sahidic fragments then for sale in Cairo to the White Monastery and to learn of many more fragments still there. It was determined that the entire collection would be bought for the Bibliothèque Nationale in Paris, but confusion over who was authorized to make the purchase, Gaston Maspero or Émile Amélineau, led to a prolongation of the process, during which the prices were jacked up, purchased fragments went missing from their boxes, and individual pieces were sold to antiquities dealers.[201] The dealers passed them

acquiring manuscripts only at the Syrian monastery in Wadi al-Natrun, plus one leaf that he took from the Monastery of al-Baramus. See William Cureton, "British Museum—MSS. From the Egyptian Monasteries," *Quarterly Review* 77 (1845–1846): 52–55; and Robert Curzon, *Visits to Monasteries in the Levant* (London: John Murray, 1849), 72, 75–91. This has left scholars to puzzle over how manuscripts from the Monastery of St. Shenoute of Atripe, such as *On Love and Self-Control*, ended up in the Syrian Monastery. Emmel shows that Curzon did not acquire them at the Syrian Monastery.

[200] Crum, *Catalogue of the Coptic Manuscripts in the Collection of the John Rylands Library, Manchester*, vii. The Crawford collection was purchased by Mrs. Rylands in 1901; the folios mentioned are Manchester, J. Rylands Lib. 25, fols. 1–6 (John Chrysostom, *Homilies 4 and 5 on the Epistle to the Hebrews*; Athanasius, *Fragments on the Moral Life*; Basil of Caesarea, *Preface to the Longer Rules*). See entry #62 in Crum's *Catalogue*, on pages 24–26.

[201] Catherine Louis, "The Fate of the White Monastery Library," in *Christianity and Monasticism in Upper Egypt*, ed. Gabra and Takla, 1:83–90. See also Paul Devos, Introduction

on to form smaller collections, such as the one at the Hofbibliothek (now the Österreichische Nationalbibliothek) in Vienna, purchased in 1884, which contained one folio later connected to the codex of *On Love and Self-Control.*[202] Several folios from the White Monastery (some from MONB. CP)[203] were given by Émile Amélineau to the Institut Français d'Archéologie Orientale in Cairo in 1885. The Pierpont Morgan Library in New York got its collection from Henri Hyvernat in 1912, including an as-yet-unidentified manuscript now known to be also from the codex of *On Love and Self-Control.*[204] By 1887, however, the Bibliothèque

to Lucchesi, *Répertoire des manuscrits coptes (sahidiques), publiés de la Bibliothèque nationale de Paris*, Cahiers d'orientalisme 1 (Geneva: Patrick Cramer, 1981), 9; Gaston Maspero, *Fragments de manuscrits coptes-thébains provenant de la bibliothèque du deir Amba-Schenoudah*, Mémoires publiés par les membres de la mission archéologique française au Caire, tome 6, fasc. 1 (Paris: Ernest Leroux, 1892), 1–2; Émile Amélineau, *Oeuvres de Schenoudi: Texte copte et traduction française* (Paris: Ernest Leroux, 1907), I:I; Henri Hyvernat, Introduction to Èmile Porcher, "Analyse des manuscrits coptes 131^{1-8} de la Bibliothèque nationale, avec indication des textes bibliques," *Revue d'égyptologie* 1 (1933): 107–9; and Tito Orlandi, "The Library of the Monastery of Saint Shenoute at Atripe," 212.

[202] K 9170 (part of John Chrysostom, *Homily Seven on the Epistle to the Hebrews*).

[203] IFAO 171 (part of John Chrysostom, *Homily 7 on the Epistle to the Hebrews*); IFAO 172 and 212A (part of Severus of Antioch, *Homily 14 on the Virgin Mary*); IFAO 173 (part of Liberius of Rome, *On the Fast*); IFAO 174 (part of Severus of Antioch, *Homily 14 on the Virgin Mary,* and part of Constantine of Assiut, *Homily on Isaiah 14:18*); IFAO 301 (part of the end of an unidentified letter and part of Liberius of Rome, *On the Fast*).

[204] The manuscript is M664B (40/2). See Hyvernat, Introduction to Porcher, "Analyse des manuscrits coptes 131^{1-8} de la

Nationale possessed 3,500 sheets and fragments of manuscripts from the White Monastery, more than any other library. Among them were seven folios belonging to the same codex as *On Love and Self-Control*.[205]

The discovery of the source of these manuscripts was important because it meant that the harm from dismemberment of codices and their piecemeal sale could be mitigated, at least. Material consciously acquired from the White Monastery could now be used to locate other material from the same source among the scattered fragments and to indicate which fragments were originally bound together. This is done by sequencing of pages (where page numbers exist, or where comparison of the text to a different manuscript of the same text is possible to ascertain the flow of the text), and comparison of handwriting, page dimensions, number of lines per page, ink used, style of punctuation and decoration, and subject

Bibliothèque nationale," 107–10; and René-Georges Coquin, "Le Fonds copte de l'Institut français d'archéologie orientale du Caire," in *Écritures et traditions dans la littérature copte: Journée d'études coptes, Strasbourg 28 mai 1982*, Cahiers de la Bibliothèque copte 1 (Louvain: Éditions Peeters, 1983), 9–10.

[205] Louis, "The Fate of the White Monastery Library," in *Christianity and Monasticism in Upper Egypt*, ed. Gabra and Takla, 1:89. The folios are BnF 131[1], fol. 37 (part of John Chrysostom, *Homily 31 on the Gospel of Matthew*); BnF 131[1], fol. 67 (part of Severus of Antioch, *Homily 14, on the Virgin Mary*); BnF 131[4], fol. 162 (part of Gregory of Nyssa, *First Panegyric of Stephen the Protomartyr*); BnF 131[4], fol. 163 (part of John Chrysostom, *Homily 31 on the Gospel of Matthew*); BnF 132[3], fols. 252 and 269 (unidentified); and BnF 132[4], fol. 346 (Severian of Jabalah, *The Washing of the Feet*).

matter, among other factors. This work is not yet finished.

One major effort in reconstructing Coptic codices was begun in 1969 by Tito Orlandi when he initiated the *Corpus dei Manoscritti Copti Letterari* (CMCL) that now serves as a web-based tool and resource for scholars.[206] In CMCL the codex that contained *On Love and Self-Control* was given the label MONB.CP. Catherine Louis has had occasion to present most fully the present state of the reconstruction of MONB.CP in the course of preparing a catalogue of the Coptic literary manuscripts in the Institut Français d'Archéologie Orientale in Cairo (IFAO).[207] Along with Enzo Lucchesi she has even been able to put some of the contents in sequence, although some texts cannot yet be sequenced, and some have not yet been identified.[208] They have reasonably surmised the order of the seven sequenced texts from surviving page numbers, continuity of text, or, in the case of the fragment of Athanasius's acephalous sermon on the moral life,

[206] See *Corpus dei manoscritti copti letterari*, http://rmcisadu.let.uniroma1.it/~cmcl. See also Orlandi, "The Library of the Monastery of Saint Shenoute at Atripe," 230–31.

[207] Louis, *Catalogue raisonné des manuscrits littéraires coptes conserves à l'IFAO du Caire*. In the draft copy that Catherine Louis graciously sent me, this information was contained in entry #98, pages 44–48.

[208] On the sequencing and identification of these works, see also Enzo Lucchesi, "L'Homélie XIV de Sévère d'Antioche: Un second témoin copte," *Aegyptus* 86 (2006): 199–205; Lucchesi, "Un fragment sahidique du premier panégyrique d'Étienne le protomartyr par Grégoire de Nysse," An Boll 124 (2006): 11–13; and Lucchesi, "Un temoin copte de l'homélie de Sévérien de Gabala sur le lavement des pieds," An Boll 127 (2009): 299–308.

a long blank space at the end, hinting that nothing followed it. Because the manuscript BL Or. 8802, which contains *On Love and Self-Control*, bears no ancient pagination, no way has yet been found to determine the place of *On Love and Self-Control* in its codex. If it and the other remaining eight identified texts and three unidentified texts of MONB. CP are to be fully ordered, it will need to be on the basis of yet undiscovered paginated fragments or fragments that complete the currently incomplete texts in the codex.

Following is a listing of all the texts known to be from MONB.CP, arranged in order, from the sequenced texts to the identified but not yet sequenced texts to the still unidentified texts. The notes supply information about the catalogue in which the manuscript is described; the published edition of the text, if there is one; and any available translations. Summaries of the content of the texts in MONB.CP can be found in Appendix B.

The texts that can be sequenced are as follows:

Page numbers in the codex	*Manuscripts*	*Authors and Texts*
17–18	Paris, BnF, copte 131[4], fol. 162	Gregory of Nyssa, *First Panegyric of Stephen the Protomartyr*[209]
55–56	Paris, BnF copte 131[1], fol. 67	Severus of Antioch, *Homily 14, on the Virgin Mary*[210]
57–58	Cairo, IFAO, copte 172+212A	Severus of Antioch, *Homily 14, on the Virgin Mary*[211]

[209] The manuscript is catalogued in Porcher, "Analyse des manuscrits coptes 131[1-8] de la Bibliothèque nationale," 240. It was identified by Lucchesi in "Un Fragment sahidique du premier panégyrique d'Étienne le protomartyr," 12. The parts of the Coptic that survive correspond to the following section of the Greek versions: Otto Lendle, *Gregorius Nyssenus, Encomium in sanctam Stephanum protomartyrem* (Leiden: Brill, 1968), 26 (line 6)–30 (line 14); and J.-P. Migne, *S.P.N. Gregorii, episcopi Nysseni, Opera omnia*, PG 46:712 D (line 2)–713 D (line 9). Gregory of Nyssa's panegyric on Stephen was probably not the first text in MONB.CP. Its beginning is missing and the extant pages are numbered 17 and 18. But unless the beginning of the Coptic text was much longer than the beginning of the Greek text, it would not require sixteen pages.

[210] Émile Amélineau, "Catalogue des manuscrits coptes de la Bibliothèque nationale" (unpublished), 139; Enzo Lucchesi, *Répertoire des manuscrits coptes (sahidiques), publiés de la Bibliothèque nationale de Paris*, Cahiers d'orientalisme 1 (Geneva: Patrick Cramer, 1981), 70; Porcher, "Analyse des manuscrits coptes 131[1-8] de la Bibliothèque nationale," 132; Porcher, "Sévère d'Antioche dans la literature copte," *Revue de l'Orient chrétien* 12 (1907): 119–24. The Coptic text with a French translation is in Porcher, "Un Discours sur la sainte Vierge par Sévère d'Antioche," *Revue de l'Orient chrétien* 10, no. 20 (1915): 416–23. There is an English translation of the Syriac version of this sermon in Pauline Allen and C. T. R. Hayward, *Severus of Antioch*, The Early Church Fathers, ed. Carol Harrison (London and New York: Routledge, 2004), 111–18. However, the Syriac represents a manuscript tradition that differs from the Coptic manuscript.

[211] Lucchesi, "L'Homélie XIV de Sévère d'Antioche," 199–205; and Louis, *Catalogue raisonné des manuscrits littéraires coptes conserves à l'IFAO du Caire*, draft pages 44-48. The Coptic with an English translation are in Youhanna Nessim Youssef, "The Coptic Marian Homilies of Severus of Antioch," *Bulletin de la Société d'archéologie copte* 43 (2004): 132–38.

Page numbers in the codex	*Manuscripts*	*Authors and Texts*
59	Cairo, IFAO, copte 174 r°, lines 1–34	Severus of Antioch, *Homily 14, on the Virgin Mary*[212]
59–60	Cairo, IFAO, copte 174 r°, line 35–174 v° end	Constantine of Assiut, *Homily on Isaiah 14:18*[213]
	London, BL Or. 3581A(13) r°, lines 1–32 + Cairo, IFAO, copte 301 r°	End of an unidentified letter[214]
	London, BL Or. 3581A(13) r°, lines 33–48	Severus of Antioch, *Letter to Probus the General*[215]

[212] IFAO 174 and IFAO 173 are a bifolio but not the central bifolio in their gathering of eight. The content of IFAO 174 comes before the content of IFAO 173 in the codex. No other bifolia from this codex remain connected to each other, and the scribe is not consistent in placing hair sides and flesh sides of the parchment, so it is not possible to piece together the whole gathering. It is Lucchesi who identified Cairo, IFAO, copte 174 r°, lines 1–34, as Severus of Antioch's *Homily 14, on the Virgin Mary* in "L'Homélie XIV de Sévère d'Antioche," 199–205; it is catalogued in Louis, *Catalogue raisonné des manuscrits littéraires coptes conserves à l'IFAO du Caire*, draft pages 44–48. There is no published edition of this manuscript. For access to this and the other manuscripts from this codex in the archives at IFAO, I especially thank Nadine Cherpion, Responsable des archives scientifique, L'Institut français d'archéologie orientale, Cairo.

[213] Louis, *Catalogue raisonné des manuscrits littéraires coptes conserves à l'IFAO du Caire*, draft pages 44–48. Louis translates the last lines into French on draft page 47. There is no published edition.

[214] London, BL Or. 3581A(13) r°, lines 1–32, is catalogued in Walter Ewing Crum, *Catalogue of the Coptic Manuscripts in the British Museum* (London: The British Museum, 1905), #185, pp. 73–74. Cairo, IFAO, copte 301, is a small corner-piece catalogued in Louis, *Catalogue raisonné des manuscrits littéraires coptes conserves à l'IFAO du Caire*, draft pages 44–45. There is no published edition.

[215] Crum, *Catalogue of the Coptic Manuscripts in the British Museum*, #185, pages 73–74. There is no published edition. On Probus the General, see F. J. Hamilton and E. W. Brooks, trans., *The Syriac Chronicle Known as that of Zachariah of Mitylene* (London: Methuen, 1899), 5, 179–80 (book VII, chapter X), and 329–30 (book XII, chapter VII).

Page numbers in the codex	*Manuscripts*	*Authors and Texts*
	London, BL Or. 3581A(13) v° + Cairo, IFAO, copte 301 v°	Liberius of Rome, *On the Fast*[216]
75–76	Cairo, IFAO, copte 173	Liberius of Rome, *On the Fast*[217]
Last page	Manchester, J. Rylands Lib. 25, fols. 2, 5, 6	Athanasius, *Fragments on the Moral Life*[218]

Some texts are identified but are lacking page numbers or other clues to their sequence within the codex. These include *On Love and Self-Control*. The texts that cannot yet be sequenced are as follows:

[216] Crum, *Catalogue of the Coptic Manuscripts in the British Museum*, #185, pp. 73–74; Louis, *Catalogue raisonné des manuscrits littéraires coptes conserves à l'IFAO du Caire*, draft pages 44–45. Liberius's Coptic sermon on the Lenten fast preserved in MONB.CP has an equivalent (also from the Monastery of Shenoute of Atripe and also in Coptic) in Paris, BnF, copte 131², fols. 120, 118 (in that order), followed by Naples, B.N., IB. 15.29–31 [= Zoega CCXCIX, fols. 3–5]. See Louis-Théophile Lefort, "Homélie inédite du Pape Libère sur le jeûne," *Le Muséon*, n.s., 12 (1911): 1–22; George Zoega, *Catalogus codicum copticorum manuscriptorum*, rev. ed. (Leipzig: J. C. Hinrichs'sche, 1903), 636; Paola Buzi, *Catalogo dei manuscritti copti borgiani conservati presso la Biblioteca nazionale "Vittorio Emanuele III" di Napoli*, Atti della Accademia nazionale dei Lincei: Memorie, Ser. IX, vol. XXV, fasc. 1 (Rome: Scienze e lettere editore commerciale, 2009–2010), 311–12; and Paul Devos and Enzo Lucchesi, "Un corpus basilien en copte," An Boll 99 (1981): 88–89.

[217] Louis, *Catalogue raisonné des manuscrits littéraires coptes conserves à l'IFAO du Caire*, draft pages 44–48. There is no published edition of this manuscript.

[218] Crum, *Catalogue of the Coptic Manuscripts in the Collection of the John Rylands Library, Manchester*, #62, pp. 24–25. The text was edited and translated into French by Lefort in *S. Athanase*, CSCO 150, pp. 121–29 (Coptic), CSCO 151, pp. 99–109 (French). It was translated into English by Brakke under the title "Fragments on the Moral Life," in *Athanasius and Asceticism*, 314–19.

Manuscripts	*Authors and texts*
London, BL Or. 8802, fols. 1–4 v°, line 24	Athanasius (?), *On Love and Self-Control*[219]
London, BL Or. 8802, fol. 4 v°, line 25, 6 r°, line 20	Severus of Antioch, *Letter to Theognostus*[220]
London, BL Or. 8802, fol. 6 r°, line 21 - 6 v°	Severus of Antioch, *Letter to Caesaria*[221]
Manchester, J. Rylands Lib. 25, fol. 3	Basil of Caesarea, *Proemium in regulas fusius tractatas (Preface to the Longer Rules)*[222]

[219] Lantschoot, "Lettre de saint Athanase," 265–92; and Lefort, "Sur la charité et la tempérance," in *S. Athanase*, CSCO 150, pp. 110–20. (Lefort provides a French translation in CSCO 151, pp. 88–98.)

[220] Layton, *Catalogue of Coptic Literary Manuscripts in the British Library*, #175, pp. 216–18. The full text of Or. 8802, fol. 4 v°, line 25–fol. 6 r°, line 20, is edited and translated into French by Arnold van Lantschoot in "Une Lettre de Sévère d'Antioche à Théognoste," *Le Muséon* 59 (1946): 470–77.

[221] Layton, *Catalogue of Coptic Literary Manuscripts in the British Library*, #175, pp. 216–18. On Caesaria's life, see François Nau, "La Patrice Césaria, correspondante de Sévère d'Antioche (VIe siècle)," *Revue de l'orient chrétien* 6 (1901): 470–73. On Severus's other extant letters to Caesaria, see E. W. Brooks, *A Collection of Letters of Severus of Antioch from Numerous Syriac Manuscripts*, PO 58, tome XII, fasc. 2, 170, and PO 67, tome XIV, fasc. 1 (Paris: Firmin-Didot, 1919–1920), 194–259; and Brooks, *The Sixth Book of the Select Letters of Severus Patriarch of Antioch in the Syriac Version of Athanasius of Nisibis*, vol. 1 (text), part 2, Works issued by the Text and Translation Society (London and Oxford: Williams and Norgate, 1902), 277–82, 306–9, 504–11, and vol. 2 (translation), part 2, Works issued by the Text and Translation Society (London: Williams and Norgate, 1904), 244–49, 272–75, and 448–55. Fragments of some of Severus's letters to Caesaria survive also in Greek, as do quotations from the letters to Caesaria in Greek commentaries on the Scriptures. See #7071 in Geerard, *Clavis patrum graecorum*, 3:336, and Supplement, 404.

[222] Crum, *Catalogue of the Coptic Manuscripts in the Collection of the John Rylands Library*, #62, pp. 24–25. Although it is missing the first paragraph, the Coptic corresponds closely to the Greek in J.-P. Migne, *S.P.N. Basilii, Caesareae Cappadociae archiepiscopi, Opera Omnia*, PG 31:889B, line 2–896B, line 6. An English translation of this work was made by E. F. Morison in *St. Basil and His Rule: A Study in Early Monasticism*, S. Deiniol's Series III (London: Oxford University Press, 1912), 137–44, and slightly revised in W. K. L. Clarke, *The Ascetic Works of*

Manuscripts	*Authors and texts*
Paris, BnF, copte 131[1], fol. 37	John Chrysostom, *Homily 31 on the Gospel of Matthew*[223]
Paris, BnF, copte 131[4], fol. 163	John Chrysostom, *Homily 31 on the Gospel of Matthew*[224]
Manchester, J. Rylands Lib. 25, fol. 4	John Chrysostom, *Homilies 4 and 5 on the Epistle to the Hebrews*[225]

Saint Basil, Translations of Christian Literature, Series 1, Greek Texts (London: Society for Promoting Christian Knowledge, 1925), 145–51. There is another English translation in *St. Basil: Ascetical Works*, trans. M. Monica Wagner, The Fathers of the Church 9 (Washington, DC: Catholic University of America Press, 1962), 223–31.

[223] Amélineau, "Catalogue des Manuscrits coptes de la Bibliothèque nationale," 138; Porcher, "Analyse des manuscrits coptes 131[1-8] de la Bibliothèque nationale," 126. Although the bottom of fol. 37 is missing, Paris, BnF, copte 131[1], fol. 37, corresponds roughly to J.-P. Migne, *S.P.N. Joannis Chrysostomi, archiepiscopi Constantinopolitani, Opera Omnia*, PG 57:373.17–375.4. However, the Coptic version of Chrysostom's sermons on the Gospel of Matthew seems to have been made from a Greek original that was not the same at all points as the Greek version presented in Migne (Enzo Lucchesi, "Deux commentaires coptes sur l'évangile de Matthieu," *Le Muséon* 123, nos. 1-2 [2010]: 34–35). There is an English translation of the Greek by George Prevost in *Saint Chrysostom: Homilies on the Gospel of Saint Matthew*, ed. Philip Schaff, NPNF (New York: The Christian Literature Company, 1888), 10:205–10. The part corresponding to Paris, BnF, copte 131[1], fol. 37, is on pages 207, §3–208, §5.

[224] Lucchesi, "Un Fragment sahidique du premier panégyrique d'Étienne le protomartyr," 12–13; Porcher, "Analyse des manuscrits coptes 131[1-8] de la Bibliothèque nationale," 240. This folio follows immediately after Paris, BnF, copte 131[1], fol. 37, although the top of the page is missing. The section of the homily in Paris, BnF, copte 131[4], fol. 163, corresponds roughly to PG 57:375.5–376.24. The corresponding English translation of the Greek by Prevost in *Saint Chrysostom: Homilies on the Gospel of Saint Matthew*, NPNF, vol. 10, is on pages 208, §5–209, §6.

[225] Crum, *Catalogue of the Coptic Manuscripts in the Collection of the John Rylands Library*, #62, pp. 25–26; and Louis, *Catalogue raisonné des manuscrits littéraires coptes conserves à l'IFAO du Caire*, draft page 45. Like Chrysostom's sermons on Matthew in Coptic, his sermons on Hebrews in Coptic seem to be translated from a Greek source that differs from any extant Greek version.

Manuscripts	*Authors and texts*
Manchester, J. Rylands Lib. 25, fol. 1	John Chrysostom, *Homilies 4 and 5 on the Epistle to the Hebrews*[226]
Vienna, K 9170	John Chrysostom, *Homily 7 on the Epistle to the Hebrews*[227]
Cairo, IFAO, copte 171	John Chrysostom, *Homily 7 on the Epistle to the Hebrews*[228]

For a discussion of problems associated with John Chrysostom's homilies on Hebrews in Coptic, see Tito Orlandi, "Giovanni Crisostomo *In ep. Ad Hebreos* = clavis 0169 (CG 4440)," in *Corpus dei manoscritti copti letterari,* http://www.cmcl.it/ (accessed Jan. 2, 2012); Lucchesi, "Deux commentaires coptes sur l'évangile de Matthieu," 36.

[226] Crum, *Catalogue of the Coptic Manuscripts in the Collection of the John Rylands Library*, #62, p. 26. Crum hints that this homily is in Chrysostom's style, and I have been able to confirm that it is by Chrysostom. It is the continuation of Homily 5 on the Epistle to the Hebrews and follows immediately after Manchester, J. Rylands Lib. 25, fol. 4. On the recto, it corresponds closely to J.-P. Migne, *S.P.N. Joannis Chrysostomi, archiepiscopi Constantinopolitani, Opera Omnia*, PG 63:51.33–52.42. In the English, this is NPNF 14, top of p. 392 to six lines before §8. On the verso, the Coptic and Greek are still discussing the same theme but not in the same way. The words match only occasionally, but with increasing frequency as both texts draw to their close.

[227] Louis, *Catalogue raisonné des manuscrits littéraires coptes conserves à l'IFAO du Caire*, draft page 45. This Coptic homily corresponds to John Chrysostom's Homily 7 on the letter to the Hebrews in the Greek version, but it is impossible to determine how closely. Vienna, K 9170 is a very badly damaged fragment. Its text seems to begin with a correspondence to PG 63:63, around line 18. In English, this is in NPNF 14:399, at the beginning of §5.

[228] Louis, *Catalogue raisonné des manuscrits littéraires coptes conserves à l'IFAO du Caire*, draft pages 44–47. The Coptic is very close to the Greek text in PG 63:64.3.3–66.7. In English, the text is in NPNF 14:400.7.6–401, at the end of §8. There is an image of Cairo, IFAO, copte 171 r° at Alin Suciu, "The Homilies on the Epistle to the Hebrews by John Chrysostom: A Complement to the Coptic Version," July 12, 2011, http://alinsuciu.com/2011/07/12/the-homilies-on-the-epistle-to-the-hebrews-by-john-chrysostom-a-complement-to-the-coptic-version/ (accessed July 6, 2013).

Manuscripts	*Authors and texts*
Paris, BnF, copte 132[4], fol. 346	Severian of Jabalah, *The Washing of the Feet*[229]
Oxford, Cl. Pr. b. 25, fols. 1-2 r°, line 15	Severian of Jabalah, *The Washing of the Feet*[230]
Oxford, Cl. Pr. b. 25, fol. 2 r°, line 16–2 v°	Severus of Antioch, *Homily 28, on Thomas*[231]
Strasbourg, BNU, Kopt. 100 [b]	Severus of Antioch, *Homily 28, on Thomas*[232]

[229] Lucchesi, "Un témoin copte de l'homélie de Sévérien de Gabala sur le lavement des pieds," 306. Severian's sermons were often transmitted under the name of John Chrysostom. Even the scribe who copied Severian's sermon on the washing of the feet for MONB.CP may have thought he was copying a work of John Chrysostom's. But, as of now, the folio that bears the heading of this manuscript has not been uncovered, so we cannot know to whom the scribe attributed it. Severian of Jabalah's authorship of the sermon has only recently been established. See Antoine Wenger, "Une homélie inédite de Sévérien de Gabala sur le lavement des pieds," *Revue des études byzantines* 25 (1967): 219–34; and S. J. Voicu, "L'Omelia *In lotionem pedum* (CPG 4216) di Severiano di Gabala: Due note," *Le Muséon* 107 (1994): 349–65.

[230] Lucchesi, "Un témoin copte de l'homélie de Sévérien de Gabala sur le lavement des pieds," 301, 306; and Henri Hyvernat, "Catalogue of the Clarendon Press Sahidic Fragments," 59–60.

[231] Hyvernat, "Catalogue of the Clarendon Press Sahidic Fragments," 59–60; Lucchesi, "Un témoin copte de l'homélie de Sévérien de Gabala sur le lavement des pieds," 301–2. The text is in Youhanna Nessim Youssef, "A Coptic Version of the Homily 28 of Severus of Antioch," *Bulletin de la Société d'archéologie copte* 43 (2009): 121–26. The Coptic version is close to the Syriac version, which is in Maurice Brière and René Graffin, *Les Homiliae cathedrales de Sévère d'Antioche, Traduction syriaque de Jacques d'Édesse*, PO 170, tome XXXVI, fasc. 4 (Turnhout: Brepols, 1974), 574–87, with the Syriac on the even pages and a French translation on the odd pages.

[232] Lucchesi, "Un témoin copte de l'homélie de Sévérien de Gabala sur le lavement des pieds," 301–2; Anne Boud'hors, *Catalogue des fragments coptes de la Bibliothèque nationale et universitaire de Strasbourg, I. Fragments bibliques*, CSCO 571, Subsidia 99 (Louvain: Peeters, 1998), 123–24 (bottom fragment).

Some remaining works belong to the codex but are not yet identified:

Paris, BnF, copte 132^3, fol. 252
Paris, BnF, copte 132^3, fol. 269
New York, Pierpont Morgan Library, M664B (40/2).[233]

Conclusion

In the first centuries of Christian monasticism, pilgrims and disciples would seek out a famous anchorite or *apa* and beg, "Give me a word." They would then be taught something about how to live. *On Love and Self-Control* was a word from an *apa* first addressed to a specific situation within a certain monastic community, where hatred of one's neighbor had become a problem. Seven hundred years later this word of wisdom was being used as part of an anthology of letters and "words" (homilies) by highly respected church leaders around the broad theme of living an ascetic life and developing the spiritual virtues. It had become part of a host of words forming a grand tradition for Egyptian Christians.

In a study of the current Coptic Church, Sana Hasan concludes that even today this community creatively draws upon its past, understood mythically, to shape its identity in the present. The community finds strength in that heritage, particularly in its insistence upon self-control. Hasan explores the tradition of self-control in the Coptic Church, particularly in the monastic communities from which its leadership comes. In interviewing Bishop

[233] Leo Depuydt, *Catalogue of Coptic Manuscripts in the Pierpont Morgan Library*, vol. 1, Corpus of Illuminated Manuscripts 4, Oriental Series 1 (Louvain: Peeters, 1993), #194, 375–76.

Arsanios of Minya in Upper Egypt, she learned that superiors in the monasteries train novices to suffer humiliation, even unreasonable humiliation, without loss of control. This training has not only personal ramifications but also political ones:

> Later, when some of these monks were selected to be bishops, they would be called upon not only to ease the suffering of members of their community but also to right their wrongs vis-à-vis a discriminatory state, without letting themselves fall prey to feelings of hatred toward the Muslims. This serenity, which bishops had to radiate in public life, was to be painfully acquired through an internal war with private anger.
>
> To achieve this kind of utter self-control, to be able to make such a terrible demand on himself, the Orthodox would-be saint had to engage in a perpetual battle with Satan, who was known to use every trick to bring about [his] downfall.[234]

So it seems that the issues raised on *On Love and Self-Control* do not go away but are perpetual. In various ways and with varying points of accent, *On Love and Self-Control* has been treasured over the centuries as a prescription of the "medicines" of the Holy Spirit that are an antidote to hatred (faith, knowledge, intelligence, wisdom, fasting, self-control, purity, caution, love, peace, patience, gentleness, joy, generosity, kindness, prayer, steadfastness, modesty, simplicity, silence, the withholding of judgment, difficulty, injustice, and humility).

[234] Hasan, *Christians versus Muslims in Modern Egypt*, 65–66.

Apart from the spiritual meaning of *On Love and Self-Control*, and in spite of the differences of accent that may have been heard in *On Love and Self-Control* at different times, there has also been a basic stability to the text. First, it was always rooted in a monastic milieu, even when monks copied it for laypeople also to hear when they worshiped at the monastery's church. Second, it remained in its original language, Sahidic. If a translation of the whole was ever made before modern times, it does not survive or has not yet been discovered. Only the altered section that was incorporated into the *Instruction concerning a Spiteful Monk* made its way into Arabic. Third, all of the layers of witnesses to the text are Middle or Upper Egyptian; there is no extant witness to *On Love and Self-Control* north of the Fayyum. When Sahidic was no longer in regular use, not even in Upper Egypt, *On Love and Self-Control* was simply guarded as part of a cherished past.

Today it is scholars who attend to the manuscript of *On Love and Self-Control*. Like the texts of the codex MONB.CP itself, their work is scattered, appearing in bits and pieces in various journals. Synthesized in this introduction, it provides a view of *On Love and Self-Control* from many angles in order to make the translation of the text as rich in significance as possible for readers.

This story of the discourse *On Love and Self-Control* began with an account of how it was born in the Pachomian community of Upper Egypt, suggesting that during the struggles over institutional development and continuity following the death of Pachomius, the discourse addressed the community's need for reconciliation in a time of bitterness. But there have been long-standing questions about whose discourse this really was. The heading of the text calls it a letter from Athanasius, "Archbishop" of Alexandria, but a close reading of the heading indicates that it was a later addition to the text. Furthermore, studies of two terms in the text, ⲁⲡⲟⲧⲁⲕⲧⲓⲕⲟⲥ (renouncer) and ⲑⲓⲕⲱⲛ ⲙ̄ⲡⲛⲟⲩⲧⲉ (image of God), reveal that the discourse sometimes speaks in ways that are not characteristic of Athanasius but that are characteristic of the Pachomians. Although studies of biblical passages in the text reveal that the text also sometimes speaks similarly to Athanasius, these similarities are found also among the Pachomians, particularly in the writings of Horsiesios, raising the possibility that Horsiesios, who was *Apa* of the community at the time of its troubles in the mid-fourth century, was the composer of *On Love and Self-Control*.

The life of the text can be traced past the fourth century through many permutations. It appeared as an oral discourse, a written discourse, a paraphrased selection inserted into another text, a whole text inserted into an anthology, a quoted text, a copied text, a text torn away from its codex, and, finally, a text awaiting the rediscovery of its place in the codex. The various forms that the text takes in the historical record mark different moments in the history of the Egyptian church, with each new context affecting the meaning that people seem to have drawn from the discourse.

Although this Introduction to *On Love and Self-Control* is intended to be as comprehensive as possible, it must leave the story of *On Love and Self-Control* unfinished, because the painstaking work of reconstructing the codex MONB.CP is not yet finished and may never be. Nevertheless, although its codex is not whole, *On Love and Self-Control* itself has been preserved whole and is now accessible in English so that a broader audience can encounter this beautiful example of a Coptic discourse originally meant for the spiritual care of a monastic community. Historically the discourse was reappropriated for a long time past its first occasion. It is worth a current reading.

On Love and Self-Control
A Translation

This English translation is based on the two modern editions of the text of *On Love and Self-Control* checked against an image of the single surviving manuscript, in London at the British Library, catalogued as Or. 8802, fols. 1–4 v°, line 24. Significant variants between the two modern editions are indicated in the footnotes along with an explanation of which variant has been chosen and why. The first modern edition of the text was by Arnold van Lantschoot, who published an edition in 1927 that added spaces between the words but otherwise left the spelling and minimal punctuation marks of the manuscript unchanged. He wrote what he saw. In 1955, Louis-Théophile Lefort published a second edition that standardized the spelling, added diacritical marks, and sought to clear up confusing words or phrases. Sometimes Lefort did this through comparison of *On Love and Self-Control* with *Instruction concerning a Spiteful Monk*, because the middle section of *Instruction concerning a Spiteful Monk* is very similar to the last two-thirds of *On Love and Self-Control*. At times the two are exactly alike, word for word.

In the present translation, notes in the margin indicate the location of the text at that point in the folios of the manuscript BL Or. 8802 and in both Lantschoot's and Lefort's editions. For ease of reading, these notes are in shortened form. The full references to Lantschoot's and Lefort's editions are

Arnold van Lantschoot, "Lettre de saint Athanase au sujet de l'amour et de la tempérance," *Le Muséon* 40 (1927): 265–92.

Louis-Théophile Lefort, "Sur la charité et la tempérance," in *S. Athanase: Lettres festales et pastorales en copte*, CSCO 150, Scriptores coptici 19 (Louvain: L. Durbecq, 1955), 110–20.

A word about biblical citations is needed, because *On Love and Self-Control* is saturated with them. In this translation quotation marks enclose only those biblical passages that are presented in the text as direct quotations from the Bible. Other biblical allusions are identified in the marginal notes, using the observations of Arnold van Lantschoot, Louis-Théophile Lefort, and Janet Timbie, as well as the translator's own.

The Text

*A letter of our holy father, esteemed in every aspect, *apa* Athanasius, the Archbishop of Alexandria, about love and self-control. In peace. [*fol. 1r (Lantschoot, 267–69; Lefort, 110–11)]

Now, above all, O my brothers, it is fitting for us always to give thanks to God for his grace and his love that he showed us, having reconciled us to himself through his beloved son* [*Rom 5:10; 2 Cor 5:18] and sealed us through his Holy Spirit# [#2 Cor 1:22] so that, since we have clothed ourselves with good zeal and obedience, we may be saved by his mercy in his kingdom forever. Because of this, in a multitude of forms* [*Heb 1:1] and with much encouragement, God has urged us in the Holy Scriptures, commanding us from the beginning until now to keep his commandments and to love one another,* [*John 13:34; 15:12, 17; 1 John 3:22-23] so that each of us might watch over his neighbor, in order not to make him angry,* [*Eph 6:4; Col 3:21] but to act with mercy and righteousness, each one toward his brother, just as he himself does who guides us lovingly and mercifully.

Sometimes he comforts us and encourages us with a strong entreaty to repent* [*Matt 4:17; Luke 13:3, 5; Acts 17:30] and fear him# [#1 Pet 2:17] so that he might give his inexpressible promises and eternal life to us. But also, sometimes, with a grieving heart, he testifies to us of the rejection and the punishment of the hell of fire and weeping,* [*Matt 25:41] of the gnashing of teeth* [*Matt 13:41-42, 49-50; 24:51] and eternal death# [#Matt 25:46] if we are disobedient to him and do not turn from our evil way.§ [§Jer 18:11; 25:5] Look at Nineve, who burned in a fire of such size because he did not remember to treat Lazarus, his brother, charitably.*[1] [*Luke 16:19-31] Look at Esau, how he was

[1] The rich man is named *Nineve* in the Sahidic New Testament. See Horner, *The Gospel of S. Luke*, in *The Coptic Version of*

deprived of the blessing of sonship, since he
Gen 27 hated his brother Jacob. Joseph, however, loved
his brothers, and God raised him up and honored
Gen 41:39-45; 45:5; 50:15-21 him in his time over all the earth. And Moses,
too, loved all his people with love and patience,
bearing with gentleness hard words from those
who rose up against him and those who were jeal-
Num 12; 16 ous of him. For this reason he saw God face to
face and spoke with him as one speaks with his
*Exod 33:11 friend.*If the law and the prophets hang on loving
Matt 22:40 your neighbor as yourself, then the gospels and
the apostles too are bound and confirmed in love
toward one another, so that each one might give
his life for the sake of one another. "There is no
Jesus love," he said, "greater than this, that each one lay
down his life for his friends. As for you, you are
John 15:13-15 my friends, and I will lay down my life for you
John 10:11, 15 as a shepherd lays down his life for his sheep."

So, look, O my beloved ones, you see the Scripture persuading us and compelling us to love one another and to walk in purity and dignity, giving glory to God, who entreats us through the mouth of his holy ones, just as Paul said, "I urge you, my brothers, by the mercies of God, to offer your bodies as a holy sacrifice pleasing to God so that you may discover what the will of God is that is

---

the New Testament in the Southern Dialect, 2:314–20. Bishop Peter of Alexandria (300–311 CE) preached a sermon on riches that included a full retelling of the story of Lazarus and Nineve, with emphasis upon the great fire in which Nineve was burning and thirsting. See Birger Pearson and Tim Vivian, *Two Coptic Homilies Attributed to Saint Peter of Alexandria: On Riches, On the Epiphany*, Unione accademica nazionale, Corpus dei manoscritti copti letterari (Rome: C.I.M., 1993), 49–53 (Sahidic) and 104–8 (English).

good and pleasing and perfect."* And he tells us *Rom 12:1-2
the will of God, saying, "Do not owe anyone anything except to love one another."[2] Elsewhere, he entreats us, saying, "I urge you, I who am bound in the Lord, to walk worthy of the call by which you were called, in all humility and gentle*ness, in pa- *fol. 1v (Lantschoot 269–70; Lefort 111–13)
tience, bearing with each other in love."# It is also #Eph 4:1-2
written in Acts, "With many other words he was testifying and entreating them, saying, 'Be saved from this perverse generation.'"* Peter entreats us *Acts 2:40
elsewhere, too, in his letter, saying, "I urge you, as strangers and sojourners, to withdraw from every fleshly desire that fights against your lives."* *1 Pet 2:11

You have seen how the Holy Spirit urges us in many ways so that we also may comfort each other with the comfort with which God has comforted us,* so that by steadfastness and the comfort of the *2 Cor 1:4
Scriptures we shall obtain hope for ourselves.* But *Rom 15:4
you also know, brothers, the contrasting threats of his wrath, which are written in fear and trembling because of the Judgment that will happen. For so it is written in the gospel: "Withdraw from me, those who are cursed, to the eternal fire that has been prepared for the devil and his angels. For I was hungry," he said, "and you did not feed me.[3] I was thirsty and you did not give me a drink. I was a stranger and you did not receive me. I was

[2] This biblical quotation follows Lantschoot's edition (268), which, faithful to the manuscript, reads as an exact quotation of Rom 13:8: ⲙⲡⲉⲣⲕⲁⲗⲁⲁⲩ ⲉⲣⲱⲧⲛ ⲛⲧⲛⲗⲁⲁⲩ ⲛⲥⲁⲡⲙⲉⲣⲉⲛⲉⲧⲛⲉⲣⲏⲩ. Lefort's edition (111) leaves out the words ⲉⲣⲱⲧⲛ ⲛⲧⲛⲗⲁⲁⲩ.

[3] The manuscript mistakenly has "and you fed me."

naked[4] and you did not clothe me. I was sick and
Matt 25:41-43 — in the prison and you did not look for me." It is
also written in another place, "You understand
this, that everyone who is sexually immoral and
unclean, covetous, that is, a worshiper of idols,
does not have a share in the kingdom of Christ and
Eph 5:5 — God." So, therefore, let us be afraid and put love
in our heart and pleasantness toward one another.

Is there not only one God over all of us? Why
has each of us left his brother behind to defile
Mal 2:10-11 — the covenant of life and peace that is with us?
Understand, then, that your brother, who is your
neighbor, is God and not merely a human. So if
your brother is God, he is also his son, whom he
bought at the price of the blood of his only son
when he gave him over into the hands of sinners.
Isa 53:6-7; Acts 8:32; 1 Cor 6:20 — They killed him as he kept silence, so that we, too,
having seen such love and grace that he has carried
out with us, might also turn around and love each
other and die for each other in humility and love,
each of us sparing his neighbor in fear of God and
Gal 5:13 — becoming servants to each other in his love, for
this is the will of God, and this is the way in which
he came to us. Therefore, let us be eager to bear
away these faults, according to what is written:
"If someone has a charge against another, just as
*Col 3:13 — Christ has forgiven us, you, too, act this way."*For
God does not hate anyone except those who are
set in evil. For it is written, "The one who hates

[4] The stative "naked" (ⲕⲏ ⲕⲁϩⲏⲩ) is from ⲕⲱ ⲕⲁϩⲏⲩ (strip), the term used in the Sahidic New Testament of Jesus' treatment prior to his execution (Matt 27:28-31).

his brother is a murderer, and we know that every murderer does not have life in him."* *1 John 3:15

So what will we do about these wicked, evil things, or how will we escape? Is it when we fast and clothe ourselves with a sackcloth of weeping and ashes?* *Dan 9:3 Our fasting is not acceptable. For the Lord has proclaimed through the mouth of Isaiah, "Why do you fast for me as today, to make me listen to your* *fol. 2r (Lantschoot, 270–72; Lefort, 113–14) voice in an outcry? This is not the fast that I have chosen, not even if you bend your neck like a reed and lay out sackcloth and ashes for yourself, you shall not call it 'the acceptable fast.' But unfasten every chain of violence; then you will cry out and God will listen to you. While you are still speaking, he will say, 'Look, it is I.'"* *Isa 58:4-6, 9; 65:24 Even our prayers and our sacrifices are not acceptable while these things are in us. For he also said, "If you bring me fine flour, it is useless, and incense is an abomination to me. You have become too much for me, and I will not forgive your sins.* *Isa 1:13-14 Take these evil things out of your hearts," he said, "away from in front of my eyes. Cease from your evil. Come and be reconciled with one another," says the Lord.*[5] *Isa 1:16, 18

So understand that the one who is reconciled to his brother is reconciled to God, and the one who is

[5] In verse 18, the author is exactly quoting the Sahidic Bible with the phrase "Come and be reconciled with one another" (ⲛ̄ⲧⲉⲧⲛ̄ⲉⲓ ⲛ̄ⲧⲉⲧⲛ̄ϩⲱⲧⲡ̄ ⲉⲛⲉⲧⲛ̄ⲉⲣⲏⲩ, Lefort, 113; Lantschoot, 270–71). See Amélineau, "Fragments de la version thébaine de L'Écriture (Ancien Testament)," 116. The Greek has instead "Come and let us converse" (Καὶ δεῦτε καὶ διελεγχθῶμεν, Alfred Rahlfs, ed., *Septuaginta*.

separated from his brother is separated from God:[6]
"For the one who does not love his brother, whom
he sees, cannot love God either, whom he does not
1 John 4:20 see." You have seen that there is nothing greater
than peace and simplicity, so that each one might
swallow the violence of his neighbor, whether in
Matt 5:39-41 his speech or in his action. "I walked," he said,
"in the simplicity of my heart in the middle of my
Ps 101:2 house." If the Lord has commanded us to love
our enemy and to bless those who curse us and to
Luke 6:27-28 do good to those who hate us, then what sort of
danger are we in if we hate our brothers, our holy
Eph 4:25 members and our coheirs, children of God,# cho-
#Rom 8:16-17 sen shoots of the true grapevine,° lost and scattered
°John 15:5 *Matt 18:12; 1 Pet 2:25 sheep,* to whom the only-begotten son of God
came forth! Having rescued them from the enemy,
Heb 7:27; 9:14, 28; 10:12 he offered himself up as a sacrifice for them. This
very form, namely the human being, the image
Gen 1:26 of God, this one for whom the living Word bore
these troubles, you hate because of jealousy and
empty glory or greatness, in which the enemy has
bound you so that he might make you a stranger
to the living God.

What, then, is the cure that will heal this kind
of wound, or whom will we visit so that he might
cure us quickly, before we come into the hands of
Heb 10:31 the living God? Paul, the trustworthy teacher, will
tell you about the cure, saying, "So now, brothers,
everything true, everything dignified, everything
just, everything holy, everything good, every bless-

[6] The parallels with *Instruction concerning a Spiteful Monk* begin with this sentence and go to the end of the penultimate paragraph of the document.

ing, every virtue, every honor—think about these
things, namely, the things that you have learned and
received and heard and seen through me. Do these
things, and the God of peace will be with you."* *Phil 4:8-9
He says also in another place, "Every violence,
every anger, every cry, and every blasphemy—
remove them from among you with every evil.
And be kind toward each other in mercy, forgiving
one another, as God has forgiven you in Christ."* *Eph 4:31-32
Peter, the foundation of the church,* also says, *Matt 16:18
"This is the word that was proclaimed to you, so
that, having put down every evil, every deceit,
every hypocrisy, every slander, and every insult,
like little children who have* just been born, you *fol. 2v (Lantschoot, 272–73; Lefort, 114–16)
may love the holy, spiritual milk in which there is
no deceit."#[7] #1 Pet 1:25–2:2

These are the living cures that the apostles have taught us, teaching us to pluck up the root of evil in us. They heard their teacher saying, "Do not judge so that you might not be judged; do not condemn so that you might not be condemned. Forgive and you will be forgiven."* Then, if you *Luke 6:37
will not forgive, understand that you will not be forgiven either. If you condemn, then you will be condemned. If you hold your brother liable for what he owes and you make him pay without restraint,* and you get revenge in this world, get *Matt 18:28-30

[7] Here the quotation is from the Sahidic New Testament, which contains a phrase lacking in the Septuagint: "in which there is no deceit" (ⲉⲧⲉⲙⲛ̄ⲕⲣⲟϥ ⲛ̄ϩⲏⲧϥ̄). See Horner, *The Catholic Epistles and the Apocalypse*, 7:16. This passage is not quoted in the corresponding section of *Instruction concerning a Spiteful Monk* (Veilleux, *Pachomian Koinonia*, 3:30; Budge, *Coptic Apocrypha*, 163–64; Lefort, *Oeuvres de s. Pachôme*, 15).

Rom 14:10, 12 ready also to give account of all that you owe, either in your words or your misdeeds. You will *Matt 12:36 repay them on the Day of Judgment,* while the whole world looks at you and the whole army of angels stands with all the holy ones standing confidently, asking you what you owe, while your mouth is shut. For God's creation is going to stand and be judged for everything that has been *Eccl 12:1 neglected.*

For how many wrongdoings will you be able to give account, O human? For the numerous and varied sexual immoralities, which are a cancer *Matt 6:19 and a moth for our souls?* The gaze of our eyes that is full of defiling desire, which distresses the Holy Spirit of God in us? The destruction that is many sins of the mouth? The tongue that speaks *Jas 3:6 great words that burn and defile the whole body?* The lie and the dishonesty? The joking and the bad amusements? The slander and the jealousy of your heart[8] that is full of disgrace? The desires of the belly, because of which you hate your neighbor? The secret passions that are a shame to speak of? The adulteries of the heart toward the image of God? The anger and the shamelessness? The empty disputes and impudence? The hypocrisy and the drunkenness?[9] They will ask you about all of these, about the chains in your heart that you have with regard to your neighbor, because you did not acquire kindness and love and humility in

[8] This follows the edition of Lantschoot (273); Lefort's edition leaves out the words "of your heart," ΜΠΕΚϨΗΤ (115).

[9] This list of vices is drawn from the various lists of vices in the Pauline literature, such as Rom 13:13; 1 Cor 6:9-10; 2 Cor 12:20-21; Gal 5:19-21; Eph 4:4-5; Col 3:5-9.

this world. Have you not heard that "mercy prides
itself over judgment"* and "love covers a multi- *Jas 2:13
tude of sins,"* and that "this is how my father who *1 Pet 4:8
is in heaven will act toward you if each one does
not forgive his brother in your hearts"?* *Matt 18:35

So, let us pay attention and take hold of the
fear of God, for in the fear of God everyone turns
away from what is evil.[10]* Struggle for purity with *Sir 1:21
all caution, since you are the house of God and the
resting place of the Holy Spirit.* Then let us not *fol. 3[r] (Lantschoot, 273–74; Lefort, 116–17)
defile his temple lest God destroy us.[#] We have
clothed ourselves with the good and human-
loving Christ:[§] let us not strip ourselves of him for #1 Cor 3:16-17; 6:19
the sake of defiling acts. We have promised God
virginity: let us not be caught in sexual immorality §Rom 13:14; Gal 3:27
and sink below every person. We have dedicated
ourselves as disciples of Christ: let us humble ourselves in every affliction so that sins do not make
us slaves.* We were appointed as illuminators of *John 8:34; Rom 6:6
the world:[#] let the world not stumble through us, #Matt 5:14; Acts 13:47
because of our slackening. The one who hates his
brother is in darkness and walks in darkness and
does not know where he is going because darkness
has closed his eyes.* Moses said, "You shall not *1 John 2:11
hate your brother in your heart."* But instead, let *Lev 19:17
us walk in tranquility and silence and be firm in
the faith of the gospel,* that is, the foundation of *Col 2:7
all your good acts, and do not participate in con-

[10] Extant Coptic translations of Sirach do not contain v. 21. Not even all recensions of the Greek translations do. It is in a Greek recension by Lucian and in the recension of the Hexapla made by a follower of Origen. See Joseph Ziegler, *Sapientia Iesu Filii Sirach*, Septuaginta 12/2 (Göttingen: Vandenhoeck & Ruprecht, 1965), 57–58, 64, 131.

versation with any heresy in argument, lest the inexpressible glory of divinity be blasphemed.[11] For a multitude of lives have been saved because of silence and freedom from anxiety, as the judgment is cast to the true judge, who has said, "Cast the
Rom 12:19 judgment to me and I myself will repay," and also,
Eccl 3:15 "God will seek the one being pursued."

1 Pet 5:8; 1 Thess 5:6, 8; 2 Tim 4:5 So be sober. It is God who has said it and not a person. For he is coming, and he destroys the disobedient, and the one who knows all will say to them,

> *Matt 25:12; Luke 13:25 "I do not know you."* Even if you are virgins [ϩⲉⲛⲡⲁⲣⲑⲉⲛⲟⲥ], even if you are renunciants [ϩⲉⲛⲁⲡⲟⲧⲁⲕⲧⲓⲕⲟⲥ] or anchorites [ⲁⲛⲁⲭⲱⲣⲏⲧⲏⲥ], "*Hand over what is mine with*
> *Matt 25:27 *its interest*.* Where is the garment of your
> *Matt 5:16; 25:1-13 works?[12] Where is the light of your lamp?* If
> #Mal 1:6 you are my servant, where is the fear of me?#
> *Rom 8:21 If you are my child, where is my glory?* For

[11] This could be a reference to the Arian controversy, which raged in Egypt through most of the fourth century. The Arians denied the divinity of the Word/the Son of God. In their literature the Pachomians present themselves as anti-Arian. To give just one example, when the Duke Artemios came to search for Athanasius at Pbow in 360, the monks would not pray with him because of his Arian connections. See Veilleux, *Pachomian Koinonia*, 1:220–24 (SBo 185) and 395–97 (G[1] 137–38); Lefort, *S. Pachomii vita bohairice scripta*, CSCO 89, Scriptores coptici 7, 164–68; and Halkin, *Sancti Pachomii vitae graecae*, 86–87.

[12] This translation agrees with Lefort, who has ⲑⲃ̄ⲥⲱ ("garment, clothing," 116). Lefort has amended the text by following *Instruction concerning a Spiteful Monk* in order to capture the biblical allusion to Matt 22:12 (Veilleux, *Pachomian Koinonia*, 3:32; Budge, *Coptic Apocrypha*, 166; Lefort, *Oeuvres de s. Pachôme*, 16). Lantschoot leaves the text unamended with ⲑⲉⲃ (274), which he translates as "product" (*produit*), based on the context (287).

> you have not spared me in this world. You
> have despised me and scorned me. You have
> shamed me. Because of this I am not at peace
> with you. I entrusted what is mine to your
> care,* and you destroyed it. You despised *1 Tim 6:20
> the poor,* you did not spare the wretched *Jas 2:6
> and the humble, that is, me. Did I change
> you at all toward me through the honor that
> I brought to the world for you? Did I not
> graciously give you the Holy Spirit?* Did I *Rom 5:5
> not give my body and my blood for you so
> that I might make you a brother and friend
> to me? Did I not give you the way and the
> authority to trample on the enemy and all his
> power?* Did I not give you many life-giving *Luke 10:19
> medicines of life by which you will be
> saved?* I have taught you about my powers *Sir 6:16
> and my virtues, which I wore in the world,
> the strong weapons of your warfare,* so that *2 Cor 10:4
> you might arm yourself with them and cast
> down the height of Goliath, that is, the boast-
> ing of the arrogance of the devil.* *Eph 6:11-13

So be acquainted with these weapons, O my beloved, that is, the virtues of the virgin Spirit of Christ, trustworthy supporters in the hour of need, helpers in the hour of the fall,* pilots in the middle of the bitter waves, ones who raise the soul from the dead. It is these that God has graciously given to us. *fol. 3v (Lantschoot, 274–76; Lefort, 117–18)

Now, first of all, we have been given faith and knowledge so that by them we might fight against unbelief and senselessness.[13] Next we have been

[13] The gifts of the Holy Spirit and the virtues listed in this paragraph are largely drawn (like the vice lists earlier) from the Pauline letters, such as Gal 5:22-23; Eph 4:2-3; and Col 3:12-14, as well as from 2 Pet 1:3-11.

given intelligence and wisdom so that we might understand the ones who are coming toward us and be alert so that they do not take away what is ours.[14] We have also been given fasting and self-control, which will give tranquility and calm

[14] Early Egyptian Christians regarded the soul as vulnerable to seizure by inimical spirits, especially with one's final exhalation at the time of death. The dying person would be able to see these horrifying demons approaching. The scene is vividly captured in the apocryphal *Life of Joseph the Carpenter*, especially chaps. 19, 21, and 23. There, Joseph, Jesus' father, lies on his deathbed, with Mary and the risen Jesus in attendance. Joseph's conscience is troubled because of a time that he scolded Jesus and pulled on his ear. He is stricken with terror when he sees what Jesus narrates: "Then I looked to the south of the door, and I saw Death. He came, Amente following him, who is the counselor and the villain, the devil from the beginning, many attendants of diverse aspects following him, all armed with fire, without number, brimstone and smoke of fire coming forth from their mouth. My father Joseph looked, and he saw those who came after him . . . and he wept." Joseph's soul sought in vain for a hiding place until Jesus rebuked the host of enemies, who then fled. Then "Michael and Gabriel and the choir of the angels came from heaven" and waited to take Joseph's soul away in a silk napkin. Meanwhile, Death cowered in fear until given permission by Jesus to do what Jesus' father had commanded (the English translation is from Forbes Robinson, *Coptic Apocryphal Gospels: Translations Together with the Texts of Some of Them*, Texts and Studies: Contributions to Biblical and Patristic Literature, ed. J. Armitage Robinson, vol. 4, no. 2 [Cambridge: Cambridge University Press, 1967], 157–58). This section of the Sahidic text is reproduced in Thomas O. Lambdin, *Introduction to Sahidic Coptic* (Macon, GA: Mercer University Press, 1983), 205–7, from Paul de Lagarde, *Aegyptiaca* (1883; repr. Osnabrück: Otto Zeller, 1972), 23–25. In *Die Geschichte von Joseph dem Zimmermann*, Texte und Untersuchungen zur Geschichte der altchristlichen Literatur 56, series V (Berlin: Akademie-Verlag, 1951), 1:60–71, Siegfried Morenz has demonstrated how closely the story of

to the passions of our body. We have been given purity and caution because of which God dwells in the person. For purity is the temple of God, and caution is his resting place. We have been given love and peace, these strengths in the battle that make you a friend to God. For the enemies are not able to approach the place where these things are. We have been given patience and gentleness. If we guard these, we will inherit the glory of all the holy ones.* We have been commanded about joy, so we shall fight against the grief of the world through it. For the grief of the world produces death.* We have been taught generosity and kindness so that we might find grace through them in the fruit of holy hands. We have been given prayer and steadfastness, which fill the eyes of the soul with light up to the place where God sits, so that we might gaze at the glory of the unseen one himself and fear before his unnameable fatherhood.[15] We have been given modesty and simplicity, which cause evil to cease and which take away the hatred of the evil powers of darkness.* Silence and the

*Col 1:12

*2 Cor 7:10

*Col 1:13

Joseph's death reflects the story of Osiris's death in traditional Egyptian religion.

[15] The ineffability of the divine Fatherhood is a Platonic idea that was widespread in Egyptian Christianity in antiquity. It is found in the works of figures as diverse as the Gnostic Valentinus, Origen, and Athanasius. In *Instruction concerning a Spiteful Monk* the reference to God's "unnameable Fatherhood" is deleted, and the sentence is shortened to "We have been given holy prayer and steadfastness, which fill the soul with light." Veilleux, *Pachomian Koinonia*, 3:34; Budge, *Coptic Apocrypha in the Dialect of Upper Egypt*, 218, 274; and Lefort, *Oeuvres de s. Pachôme*, CSCO 159, p. 18 (Coptic), and CSCO 160, p. 19.

withholding of judgment have been prescribed for
Rom 14:13 us so that we might be victorious over the lie, the
evil flaw[16] that is in the person, and be confident in
1 John 4:17 blamelessness on the Day of Judgment. We have
been given difficulty and injustice so that laziness does not cast us down and temporary contentment does not put us to shame, for the contentment of the body and the satisfaction of the flesh are the resting places of sexual immorality and the path of pollution.

For our fathers all completed their lives in grief and need and great pain and in hunger and thirst, and they became friends with purity. And all the more did they flee from drinking wine, which is full of every sort of harm. All the disturbances and disorders in the members are because of too much wine: the great madness of sin, the excess that makes the fruit fall. Greedy pleasure makes the reasoning foolish and makes you unashamed
Jas 3:2-5 and breaks the bridle of the tongue so that you
shall not spare anyone. The enthusiasm for wine
Eph 4:30 is a grief to the Holy Spirit. So let us withdraw
from the abundance of wine lest we be dazed with pleasure. "The priest and the prophet were dazed,"

[16] Lefort and Lantschoot divide the words differently here. This translation follows Lefort's word division (ⲉⲡϭⲟⲗ ⲡⲉϫⲃⲓⲛ ⲉⲑⲟⲟⲩ, "the lie, the evil blemish," 118) because, although the meaning Lantschoot's word division gives (ⲉⲡϭⲟⲗⲡ ⲉϫⲃⲓⲛ ⲉⲑⲟⲟⲩ, "the unveiling of the evil blemish," page 275) fits the context well, it is difficult to justify grammatically. Lefort's word division echoes *Instruction concerning a Spiteful Monk* (Veilleux, *Pachomian Koinonia*, 3:34; Budge, *Coptic Apocrypha*, 167; Lefort, *Oeuvres de s. Pachôme*, CSCO 159, p. 18).

he* said, because of too much wine.#[17] Moses said, *Isaiah #Isa 28:7
"If a person makes a promise to God, that person
or priest shall not drink wine all the days of his
promise, and he shall not eat anything that comes
from the grapevine,"* because he knows the lack *Num 6:2-4
of restraint in wine; if one gives himself to it, he
will not become wise,* and he will not preserve his *Prov 20:1
virginity stainless.

Wine is good if you drink within measure,[18] but
if you drink more you will be put to shame, and
you will show contempt for the nobility of your
soul. But it is profitable and is a great benefit for
everyone who has been prepared to become a dis-
ciple* of Jesus to withdraw from the excess of wine. *fol. 4r (Lantschoot, 276–78; Lefort, 118–20)
So, since our fathers understood the disturbances
and deficiencies that are in wine, therefore they
withdrew from it, drinking a little within measure.

[17] With the phrase "because of too much wine" (ⲉⲧⲃⲉⲡⲉϩⲟⲩⲉⲥⲉⲏⲣⲡ̄, Lefort, 118; Lantschoot, 276), *On Love and Self-Control* deviates from both the Sahidic version of Isaiah and the Septuagint, as well as from *Instruction concerning a Spiteful Monk*, all of which have simply "because of wine" (ⲉⲧⲃⲉ ⲡⲏⲣⲡ̄, Gaston Maspero, *Fragments de la version thébaine de l'Ancien Testament* [tome] 6, fasc. 2, 218; Veilleux, *Pachomian Koinonia*, 3:35; Budge, *Coptic Apocrypha*, 168; Lefort, *Oeuvres de s. Pachôme*, CSCO 159, p. 18) (διὰ τὸν οἶνον, Rahlfs, *Septuaginta*).

[18] Sir 31:27-28 (in most modern translations). There is considerable confusion in the ancient manuscripts of Sirach; the verses in chapters 31-36 are arranged variously. In Lagarde's edition of the Coptic version of Sirach (*Aegyptiaca*, 167), these verses are numbered 34:30-31. In Herbert Thompson, *The Coptic (Sahidic) Version of Certain books of the Old Testament from a Papyrus in the British Museum* (London: Oxford University Press, 1908), 180, they are numbered 34:27-28. In Ziegler's critical edition of the Greek Sirach (*Sapientia Iesu filii Sirach*, 273), these verses are numbered 31:32-36 or 34:27-28.

For if this great self-controlled one,[19] Timothy,
whose body had many ailments, was given a little
1 Tim 5:23 wine, then what will we say to the one who is
strong in the flesh and in the prime of his youth, on
whom are many great waves of pollution so that
Eph 4:14 he cannot keep his head up at all? I am afraid to
say, "Let him not drink at all," lest the one whose
pleasure in wine is great, who hates only the pilot,
grumble and slander. For this word is difficult for
many. Nevertheless, the caution and the pain itself
are good. If one maintains them he will bring his
boat safely without disturbance into the harbor of
the city of the holy ones.

And finally, after all these things, we have been given humility, the guardian and sentinel of all

[19] This biblical allusion (not a quotation) follows Lantschoot's edition, which is faithful to the manuscript by reproducing the word ⲉⲛⲉⲕⲣⲁⲧⲏⲥ ("self-controlled one," Lantschoot, 276), even though it is misspelled. Lefort corrects it by adopting the word ⲉⲣⲅⲁⲧⲏⲥ ("worker," Lefort, 119), which is used in the equivalent section of *Instruction concerning a Spiteful Monk* (Veilleux, *Pachomian Koinonia*, 3:35; Budge, *Coptic Apocrypha*, 168; Lefort, *Oeuvres de s. Pachôme*, CSCO 159, p. 19). Timothy is called a worker (ⲛ̄ⲟⲩⲉⲣⲅⲁⲧⲏⲥ) in 2 Timothy 2:15 in the Sahidic New Testament. See Herbert Thompson, *The Coptic Version of the Acts of the Apostles and the Pauline Epistles in the Sahidic Dialect* (Cambridge University Press, 1932), 241. However, ascribing self-control to Timothy rather than identifying him as a worker suits the theme of this sermon on love and self-control better. As can be seen in Appendix B, the eleventh-century *Apocalypse of Samuel of Qalamun* contains a paraphrase of this discussion of wine that likewise describes Timothy as a self-controlled one rather than a worker. See Ziadeh, with a note by Nau, "L'Apocalypse de Samuel, supérieur de Deir-el-Qalamoun," 374–407, especially 386 (Arabic) and 400 (French).

our fruit, the great, holy power in which the living one was clothed when he came forth toward us. Humility: the wall of every virtue and the shield of every good action, about which Paul says, "You have received the shield of faith, with which you will be able to quench every blazing fire of the evil one."* Humility: the saving power, the medicine *Eph 6:16
that heals every wound and supports you in the battle through its wisdom, having overthrown the great walls that the royal tyrant had caused to surround her.* For after the curtain of the tent *2 Cor 10:4-5
was made of gold, linen, and dark blue, it was surrounded with a cord of haircloth to guide it,[20]* *Exod 26

[20] The phrase "cord of haircloth to guide" the curtain (ⲛ̄ⲧⲁⲩⲕⲧⲟ ⲉⲣⲟϥ ⲛ̄ⲟⲩϩⲱⲥ ⲛ̄ϭⲟⲟⲩⲛⲉ ⲉⲧⲣⲉϥⲣ̄ϩⲙ̄ⲙⲉ ⲙ̄ⲙⲟϥ, Lefort, 119, Lantschoot, 277) is interesting because there is no such guiding cord in the Septuagint, which speaks of a curtain to cover the tabernacle (δέῤῥεις τριχίνας in 26:7 and κατακκάλυμμα in 26:14). In *Instruction concerning a Spiteful Monk*, the sentence says, "they covered [the furnishings] with sackcloth" (ⲛ̄ⲧⲁⲩϩⲟⲃⲥⲟⲩ ⲛ̄ ⲟⲩϩⲱⲃⲥ̄ ⲛ̄ϭⲟⲟⲩⲛⲉ, fol. 43a, Veilleux, *Pachomian Koinonia*, 3:35; Budge, *Coptic Apocrypha*, 169; Lefort, *Oeuvres de s. Pachôme*, CSCO 159, p. 19). I was unable to find Exodus 26:7-14 in Sahidic. These verses seem to fall into an unbridged gap in the content of the extant Sahidic fragments of Exodus. See A. Hebbelynck, "Les manuscrits coptes-sahidiques du 'Monastère Blanc': Recherches sur les fragments complémentaires de la collection Borgia," *Le Muséon* 30 (1911): 103–6. But the Bohairic version carries over the word "covering" (ⲉϩⲃⲱⲥ or ⲉϩⲱⲃⲥ in 26:7 and ϩⲱⲃⲥ̄ in 26:14). See Paul de Lagarde, *Der Pentateuch koptisch* (Leipzig: B. G. Teubner, 1867), 190; Melvin K. H. Peters, ed., *Exodus*, vol. 2 of *A Critical Edition of the Coptic (Bohairic) Pentateuch*, Society of Biblical Literature Septuagint and Cognate Studies Series 22, ed. Claude E. Cox (Atlanta: Scholars Press, 1983), 70–71; and London, BL Or. 8787, 111–12, on the right side. Both Lantschoot (290) and Lefort (119) cite Exod 27:9-16 here instead of Exod 26. I cite Exod 26 because the reference

that is, humility, an insignificant thing indeed according to the world, excellent and very precious according to God.[21] So if we acquire this strength in our heart and in our mouth, we will trample on all the power of the enemy and we will quench every fire of evil.* "Upon whom will I look," he# said, "except the gentle and humble person who trembles at my words?"*

*Eph 6:16
#God
*Isa 66:2

So let us not be careless, O brothers, in this time of famine, for boastfulness has multiplied in it. We loved the ease and satisfaction of the flesh, for "the beloved one ate and was satisfied and became fat and kicked."* Let us struggle from now on, O my beloved ones, for our days have become few,* and grief has ceased among people. The time that has passed is sufficient.* A great struggle is set forth for us,* the crown of which does not wither and the scepter of its kingdom does not perish.* You will sit on an eternal throne at the right hand of the glory of God.* If we are victorious, we will receive eternal life, but if we are conquered we will feel regret when we fall into harsh punishments. For, look, he* said, "Today I have placed in front of you life and death, good and evil, so choose life so that you

*Deut 32:15
*Matt 24:22
*1 Pet 4:3
*Heb 12:1
*1 Cor 9:25; 2 Tim 4:8
*fol. 4v (Lantschoot, 278–79; Lefort, 120)
*Moses

seems to be to the curtain of the Tabernacle itself (clasped with gold and covered) rather than to the curtain of the court of the Tabernacle (clasped with bronze and silver), the subject of Exod 27.

[21] Perhaps the *Apa* means to conjure up the image of Pachomian monks in their linen tunics tied with a belt. Elsewhere in the discourse, in sentences left out of *Instruction concerning a Spiteful Monk*, he tells the monks that they are the temple, "the house of God and the resting place of the Holy Spirit." See Lantschoot, "Lettre de saint Athanase," 273; and Lefort, *S. Athanase*, CSCO 150:116.

shall live."* So let us fight against ourselves, O my beloved ones, while repentance is placed before us. For everyone who struggles controls himself in everything.* Paul said, "I fought in the good struggle, I completed the course, I guarded the faith, so now the crown of righteousness is placed before me."*[22] And not for him alone, but for us also, if we endure in grief and humility: grief because of the passions that are at work in the body, and humility because of our neighbor, the image of God.

*Deut 30:19

*1 Cor 9:25

*2 Tim 4:7-8

We promised virginity to God. Let us give it to him sound, not merely a bodily virginity, but a virginity erased of every sin. For virgins in the gospel were rejected because of their laziness, and those who were alert and prepared were received into the bridal chamber.*[23] And may the God of every gift perfect you in every vigilance, so that, having triumphed, you inherit with all the saints, taking pride in yourself confidently in the city of our Lord Jesus Christ, to whom belongs the glory and the power and the honor and the authority and the worship, now and forever, and to the ages of ages. Amen.*

*Matt 25:1-12

*Jude 25

[22] Stephen Davis has studied the use of this biblical passage at the White Monastery in "Completing the Race and Receiving the Crown: 2 Timothy 4:7-8 in Early Christian Monastic Epitaphs at Kellia and Pherme," in *Asceticism and Exegesis in Early Christianity*, ed. H.-U. Weidemann, Novum Testamentum et Orbis Antiquus (Göttingen: Vandenhoeck & Ruprecht, 2013), 354–55.

[23] This is the last common line between this manuscript and *Instruction concerning a Spiteful Monk*.

Appendix A

A Comparison of Three Texts on Wine

The Apocalypse of Samuel of Qalamun[1]	*On Love and Self-Control*[2]	*Instruction concerning a Spiteful Monk*[3]
It is only at the cost of great humiliation that our fathers accomplished their course, suffering hunger and thirst, and abstaining completely from drinking any kind of wine, for the troubles of concupiscence arise in the human members through the excessive use of wine: wine excites concupiscence, rendering it improper, and it is what breaks the flesh of the body. In general, excessive use of wine grieves the	For our fathers all completed their lives in grief and need and great pain and in hunger and thirst, and they became friends with purity. And all the more did they flee from drinking wine, which is full of every sort of harm. All the disturbances and disorders in the members are because of too much wine: the great madness of sin, the excess that makes the fruit fall. Greedy pleasure makes the reasoning foolish	In fact, our fathers passed their lives in hunger, thirst, and great mortification (2 Cor 11:27), by which they acquired purity. Above all, they fled the wine habit, which is full of every evil (Prov 23:31; Sir 19:2; Eph 5:18). Troubles, tumults, and disorders are caused in our members through the abuse of wine (Sir 31:29-30); this is a passion full of sin, it is sterility and the withering of fruit. For sensuality in

The Apocalypse of Samuel of Qalamun	*On Love and Self-Control*	*Instruction concerning a Spiteful Monk*
Holy Spirit,[4] and our fathers knew the numerous sorrows caused by wine from the beginning. Therefore, abstain. But, in small amounts, it could be used with bodily illnesses;[5] for if the great ascetic Timothy[6] was authorized to take a little wine because of his stomach and his numerous weaknesses, what will I do, then, for those who are in the effervescence of youth and who are often subject to great suffering?[7] Truly, my children, it is good to be reserved in everything and there is no greater profit than humiliation;[8] for the one who humbles his soul saves it, and sends it to the harbor of salvation and will	and makes you unashamed and breaks bridle of the tongue [Jas 3:2-5] so that you shall not spare anyone. The enthusiasm for wine is a grief to the Holy Spirit [Eph 4:30].[10] So, let us withdraw from the abundance of wine lest we be dazed with pleasure. "The priest and the prophet were dazed," he [Isaiah] said, because of too much wine [Isa 28:7]. Moses said, "If a person makes a promise to God, that person or priest shall not drink wine all the days of his promise, and he shall not eat anything that comes from the grapevine" [Num 6:2-4], because he knows the lack of restraint in wine; if one	unquenchable thirst stupefies the understanding, makes the conscience overbold, and snaps the rein on the tongue. Total joy is when we do not "grieve the Holy Spirit" (Eph 4:30), or become deranged by sensuality. As it is said, "The priest and the prophet were deranged by wine (Isa 28:7). Wine is licentious, drunkenness is bold; the person who indulges in them will not be exempt from sin" (Prov 20:1). Wine is a good thing if you drink it with moderation (Sir 31:28); "if you set your eyes on cups and goblets you will walk naked as a pestle" (Prov 23:31). Therefore, all who have prepared to become

The Apocalypse of Samuel of Qalamun	*On Love and Self-Control*	*Instruction concerning a Spiteful Monk*
be filled with the good things of the heavenly Jerusalem.[9]	gives himself to it, he will not become wise [Prov 20:1] and he will not preserve his virginity stainless. Wine is good if you drink within measure [Sir 31:27-28], but if you drink more you will be put to shame and you will show contempt for the nobility of your soul. But it is profitable and is a great benefit for everyone who has been prepared to become a disciple of Jesus to withdraw from the excess of wine. So, since our fathers understood the disturbances and deficiencies that are in wine, therefore they withdrew from it, drinking a little within measure. For if this great self-controlled Timothy,[11] whose	disciples of Jesus should abstain from wine and drunkenness. In fact, knowing the great amount of harm caused by wine, our fathers abstained from it. They drank very little of it and only in case of illness.[14] If, indeed, that great worker, Timothy, was given a little of it, it was because his body was full of infirmities (1 Tim 5:23). But what shall I say to the man who is bubbling over with vice and in the prime of youth, weighed down under the impurities of passions?[15] I am afraid to tell him not to drink at all, for fear that some one, mindless of his salvation, might murmur against me. For this language is painful

The Apocalypse of Samuel of Qalamun	*On Love and Self-Control*	*Instruction concerning a Spiteful Monk*
	body had many ailments, was given a little wine [1 Tim 5:23], then what will we say to the one who is strong in the flesh and in the prime of his youth, on whom are many great waves of pollution so that he cannot keep his head up at all [Eph 4:14]?[12] I am afraid to say, "Let him not drink at all," lest the one whose pleasure in wine is great, who hates only the pilot, grumble and slander. For this word is difficult for many. Nevertheless, the caution and the pain itself are good.[13] If one maintains them he will bring his boat safely without disturbance into the harbor of the city of the holy ones.	for many nowadays. Nevertheless, beloved, it is good to be on your guard; and mortification is useful.[16] For the man who mortifies himself will save his ship in the good and holy port of salvation, and will be filled with the good things of heaven (Ps 107:9).[17]

[1] Ziadeh, with a note by Nau, "L'Apocalypse de Samuel, supérieur de Deir-el-Qalamoun," 386 (Arabic) and 400 (French). (My translation is from the French.)

[2] Lantschoot, "Lettre de saint Athanase," 276–77; and Lefort, "Sur la charité et la tempérance," in *S. Athanase*, CSCO 150, Scriptores coptici 19, 118–19. (Lefort provides a French translation in CSCO 151, Scriptores coptici 20, 96–97.)

[3] This is the translation of Veilleux, *Instructions, Letters, and Other Writings of Saint Pachomius and his Disciples*, vol. 3 of *Pachomian Koinonia*, 34–35 (§§45–47). See also Budge, "The Instructions of Apa Pachomius the Archimandrite," in *Coptic Apocrypha in the Dialect of Upper Egypt*, 168–69, with an English translation on 374–75; and Lefort, *Oeuvres de s. Pachôme*, CSCO 159, Scriptores coptici 23, 18–19 (Coptic).

[4] Note that wine is a grief to the Holy Spirit here as in *On Love and Self-Control.*

[5] Note that the *Instruction concerning a Spiteful Monk* likewise concedes that a little wine may be taken by those who are ill.

[6] Note that Timothy is described as an ascetic here as in *On Love and Self-Control*, in contrast to *Instruction concerning a Spiteful Monk*, where he is described as a worker.

[7] In portraying the young, strong wine-enthusiast as one who is impeded by heavy emotions, *The Apocalypse of Samuel* is closer to *Instruction concerning a Spiteful Monk* than to *On Love and Self-Control*, which portrays the young, strong wine-enthusiast as a person drowning because he hates the pilot.

[8] Note the similarity to *Instruction concerning a Spiteful Monk* here and the contrast with *On Love and Self-Control.*

[9] This quotation from Ps 107:9 in the sentence about being filled with "good things" in the heavenly Jerusalem is found also in *Instruction concerning a Spiteful Monk*, but not in *On Love and Self-Control.*

[10] See the similarity with *The Apocalypse of Samuel* on this point.

[11] Note the similarity with *The Apocalypse of Samuel* and the contrast with *Instruction concerning a Spiteful Monk* on this point.

[12] *On Love and Self-Control* here retains its nautical imagery, which is lacking in *The Apocalypse of Samuel* and in *Instruction concerning a Spiteful Monk.*

[13] Note the contrast here with both *The Apocalypse of Samuel* and *Instruction concerning a Spiteful Monk*, which are much closer to each other in this sentence.

[14] Here the *Instruction concerning a Spiteful Monk* is similar to the *Apocalypse of Samuel* in allowing wine to the sick.

[15] Note the similarity here to *The Apocalypse of Samuel* and the contrast with *On Love and Self-Control.*

[16] In the phrase "mortification is useful," the Sahidic word for *useful* is ⲟⲩϩⲏⲩ. Perhaps it stands behind the word *profit* in the phrase "there is no greater profit than humiliation" in *The Apocalypse of Samuel*. There is no equivalent to it in *On Love and Self-Control.*

[17] This quotation is present in *The Apocalypse of Samuel* but absent from *On Love and Self-Control.*

Appendix B

The Contents of the Codex MONB.CP

This appendix contains summaries of the contents of each of the identified texts from the codex MONB.CP. The arrangement of the list is as follows: Texts whose sequence in the codex has been discerned are listed first, in sequential order. Next are listed the texts that have been identified but whose place in the sequence cannot yet be discerned. Information about the catalogue entries and published editions and translations of the texts is provided in the introduction to the translation on pages 113–19.

Sequenced Texts

Gregory of Nyssa, *First Panegyric of Stephen the Protomartyr* (Paris, BnF, copte 131[4], fol. 162) [pages 17–18 of MONB.CP].

In this commentary on Acts 6:8–8:1 Gregory presents Stephen as an athletic champion winning against all odds because he is with Jesus, who overcame death. The beginning is missing. The textual fragment begins with Stephen standing in the midst of his opponents, who personify false wisdom. Gregory says that Stephen brings down this false wisdom with real wisdom, fear with freedom, threats with disregard, bitterness with beneficence, the lie with the truth. Even as his opponents were intent on putting him to death, Stephen saw them as brothers and fathers, saying, "Brothers and fathers, listen." Gregory portrays Stephen as having left his earthly nature even before leaving his body, seeing the heavenly door open and the inner inaccessible places lit up: the divine glory itself and the radiance of the glory, although no one can describe the glory of the Father with words. The glory transformed Stephen, so that even his accusers saw that he had the face of an angel. Stephen tried to give the others a share of what had been shown to him by grace by describing it to them: "I saw the heaven open and the Son of humanity standing at the right hand of God." The text is unfinished.

Severus of Antioch, *Homily 14, on the Virgin Mary* (Paris, BnF copte 131[1], fol. 67; Cairo, IFAO, copte 172+212A; and Cairo, IFAO, copte 174 r°, lines 1–34) [pages 55–59 in MONB.CP].

The sermon was copied in its entirety and remains complete, although scattered. The heading says, "A word of the holy patriarch and archbishop of Antioch, *apa* Severus, that he preached on the ever-virgin Theotokos, Holy Mary, on the day of her holy commemoration. In the peace of God. Amen." The sermon affirms the celebration of all the saints: the prophets, apostles, and martyrs. Each has contributed to the working out of God's plan for human salvation. Mary is held up as an example of all three roles.

As a prophet, Mary fulfills Isaiah 8:3-4, interpreted as a reference to Jesus, who would abolish the tyranny of the devil and the worship of idols, beginning with his calling of the Magi to himself and his entry into Egypt as a child in fulfillment of Hosea 11:1. It should not be astonishing, Severus insists, that a child will do this, because this child is God, the one who makes known the glory of his Father, whose living Word and Image he is. With his Father he created all things, for Son and Father are equal in the glory of divinity and are united inseparably. Together they created humans in their image. Christ is the power of the invisible Father and the Prince of Peace, reconciling heaven and earth by his blood on the cross and sowing the seeds of eternal life in us through the preaching of his coming kingdom, in which Mary rejoices in the words of Luke 1:48-50.

Mary is also an apostle, the head of all the apostles, Severus asserts. He cites Acts 1:14 to demonstrate that Mary was with the disciples when they received the Lord's commission to preach to all in every place and were thus made apostles. Through the preaching of the Word made flesh in her,* Mary is the root and foundation of the gospels.

*John 1:14

Referring to the story of Jesus' birth in Matthew's gospel, Severus says that Mary can also be called a martyr because she bore the initial suspicion of Joseph, she became a refugee in Egypt, she moved back to Nazareth for fear of King Archelaus, and she endured plots against her throughout her life. (Cairo, IFAO, copte 172+212A begins here.) It was as if Mary were saying with Paul, "I die daily."*

*1 Cor 15:31

Since the prophets, apostles, and martyrs themselves all praise Mary, Severus urges his hearers to join them because God the Word took on human flesh from Mary without ceasing to be Immanuel, "God with us," just as Mary gave birth without ceasing to be a virgin. Severus takes aim at the Council of Chalcedon and at Nestorius for dividing into two natures the inexpressible unity of God the Word.

Severus contrasts Mary with Mount Sinai, from which the Law was given. Mary gave birth to the lawgiver, who instead of preaching the Law to one people proclaimed the Gospel to all people and in his coming made earth into heaven. Severus quotes John 1:51: "Amen, amen, I tell you that you will see the heaven open and the angels of God ascending and descending on the Son of Humanity." Severus urges his hearers, therefore, to live in heavenly virtue, practicing virginity or marriage purely and not handing power back to Satan, whose work the Son of God has destroyed,* by defiling the temple of God through fornication or other impurity of body or thought. Severus calls to account in this matter especially all who serve at the altar.

*1 John 3:8

Here Cairo, IFAO, copte 174 r°, lines 1–34, begins with a damaged section in which Severus seems to be putting this speech in the mouth of either Christ or Mary: "I spare you; I spare you. I comfort you. I spare your poor souls." Severus begs his hearers to remember their weakness and powerlessness and the day that God's wrath will pour down, lest they die in their sins. He quotes Proverbs 1:24-27 to warn them that if they ignore God and reject God's words, they will be taken by surprise and panic when their destruction comes suddenly and they are scattered as by a whirlwind. He recommends cleansing through prayer, fasting, charity, and repentance. He takes 1 Thessalonians

4:4 to refer to acquiring self-control in purity and honor.

Severus asserts that those who wear the habit (ⲥⲕⲏⲙⲁ) of Christ are teachers full of God. Those who wear the garment of the angels (ⲑⲉⲃⲥⲱ) are worthy to be in the presence of the angels at the liturgy, the holy offering of "the body and blood of our Lord Jesus Christ." Christ said that where two or three are gathered in his name, he would be in their midst.* Severus wants his hearers to understand that they "gather with our Lord and our God, our Savior Jesus Christ, and the army of angels." He warns them to guard themselves against defilement so that their sins do not condemn them to affliction in hell (ⲁⲙⲉⲛⲧⲉ) and they may hear "that voice" that says, "Let the impious one be taken so that he does not see the glory of God."* Severus hopes that the Virgin Mary will be an ambassador so that his hearers may enjoy eternal goodness in heaven by the grace of Jesus Christ. He closes with a doxology to the Trinity.

*Matt 18:20

*Isa 26:10 in the Septuagint

Constantine of Assiut, *Homily on Isaiah 14:18* (Cairo, IFAO, copte 174 r°, lines 35–174 v° end) [pages 59–60 in MONB.CP].

The heading says, "A word of our holy father, esteemed in every aspect, *apa* Constantine, the bishop of the city of Assiut, that he preached in the presence of fathers of a faithful monastery, very reverent, chosen people and worshipers of God." Constantine begins by introducing the biblical passage of Isaiah 14:18, which follows the Septuagint: "The kings of the nations lie in glory, each in his house." The text that follows is faded, but Constantine seems to be commending the monks for being

filled with all knowledge as they walk faithfully toward their goal, trusting in the God who raises the poor from the ashes and sets them with the
Ps 113:7 "princes of his people." This rising from the ashes occurs when virtuous works are done and the commandments are kept. Since God is generous, God is not hiding anything or begrudging anything, Constantine says. He uses James 1:17 and 2 Peter 1:8 to encourage his hearers to receive the good that has come down from God and to be fruitful in Christ. He quotes "the word of that great voice," Isaiah, to warn them to be like the ox and donkey
Isa 1:2 that know their master.

Since the "head of the apostles, the holy Peter," has reminded them to be prepared at all times to
1 Pet 3:15 give an explanation for the hope that is in them, Constantine is responding to their request for his interpretation of Isaiah 14:18 according to his "poor knowledge." He takes Isaiah 14:18 to mean that people who rule over themselves through virtuous deeds and keeping the commandments will be like the kings of the nations who lie in glory. God has provided support so that sin might not rule over
Rom 6:12 us. When Isaiah says, "The man is in his house," Constantine understands *house* to mean "the Kingdom of heaven," that is, the "heritage that has been prepared for us by the one who promised it from the creation of the world." The page ends here.

End of an unidentified letter (London, BL Or. 3581A(13) r°, lines 1–32 + Cairo, IFAO, copte 301 r°).

The beginning is missing. The writer commends the recipient's community. Because the recipient has given rest to the writer during a time of persecution, the writer seeks a blessing for him from the saints for this partnership, by which the recipient has fulfilled the words of the apostle (Paul). The writer's suffering has been for the sake of the "orthodox faith, the pure confession, and the community, so that there might be no mixture in it." He says of the recipient, too, "You do not fear anyone, nor do you limp in your reasoning, and you pay no heed to their favoritism." In an allusion to 2 Corinthians 5:12, he says that it is not the outward appearance that is trustworthy, but the heart. The "holy Archbishop of Alexandria," too, "in the power of God . . . spoke boldly about the faith that was disputed and provoked." Doing away with the impiety, "he was not ensnared in anything; nor was he afraid." The writer quotes Hebrews 10:39 to say that his group is not destined for destruction but for the salvation of their souls by faith.

He sends greetings to the brothers, indicating that he is in conversation with Antios (?) and Victor about letters to the holy nuns (ⲛϩⲉⲗⲗⲁ ⲉⲧⲟⲩⲁⲁⲃ). Someone named Mena, who is working to support the community of the orthodox church that is under persecution, will speak to the recipient about ⲕⲩⲣⲟⲥ ⲡⲑⲉⲛⲛⲏⲥⲓⲱⲧⲏⲥ (Cyrus from Tinnis). Mena spared no effort to go down to the monastery of Pelusium, which the author reports is now truly writhing.[1] The author also wrote a promised

[1] On Pelusium, see *The Coptic Encyclopedia*, s.v. "Faramā, Al-," by Randall Stewart. The use of the title "archbishop of Alexandria" dates this fragment to no earlier than the fifth century. It seems to stem from a time of imperial effort to impose Chalcedonian adherence on Egypt. By the middle of the sixth century, Pelusium had a Chalcedonian bishop.

letter to Paul, the soldier, who has honored him and whom he honors. But he disapproves of Paul's dining room, since Christ never reclined or stretched out his hand at the table there. The food is spread sparingly, and apparently Paul is full of gloom and needs to be reminded that "God loves a
2 Cor 9:7 cheerful giver." In writing these things, the writer has gracious intentions and aims toward virtue. He warns against the devil and then closes.

Severus of Antioch, *Letter to Probus the General*(London, BL Or. 3581A(13) r°, lines 33–48).

The heading says, "A letter from the holy Patriarch and Archbishop . . . written to Probus the General, in peace." There are fourteen lines of text. Less than half of the text is legible, because the right corner is missing and the left side has been damaged, blotched, and stitched. Walter Ewing Crum gives the first line as, "I know your power (ἐξουσία), and that ye strive after (ἐπιθυμεῖν) good."[2] Severus goes on to write of the generation (or the kindred: ⲧⲥⲩⲛⲅⲉⲛⲓ̈ⲁ) of someone; he seems to quote from John 1:5 about the light illuminating the darkness; he mentions someone's word; he speaks of casting judgment (perhaps a reference to Romans 12:19) and of Christianity. The subject of light illuminating the darkness is also discussed in a Syriac fragment of a letter of Severus of Antioch to Probus the General.[3] It could be that the

[2] Crum, *Catalogue of the Coptic Manuscripts in the British Museum*, #185, p. 74.

[3] Brooks, *A Collection of Letters of Severus of Antioch from Numerous Syriac Manuscripts*, PO 67, tome XIV, fasc. 1, 125–26.

Coptic provides the beginning of the letter, which is lacking in the Syriac.[4]

Liberius of Rome, *On the Fast* (London, BL Or. 3581A(13) v° + Cairo, IFAO, copte 301 v°; and Cairo, IFAO, copte 173).

The heading says, ". . . Liberius the archbishop speaking about the Holy Fast. In peace." Liberius makes ten calls to the fast, each starting with the phrase ⲡⲉⲟⲩⲟⲉⲓϣ ⲡⲉ ⲡⲁⲓ ("This is the time"). It is the time for the forgiveness of sins, the day of salvation.* Liberius quotes Nahum 1:15 to call on his hearers to fulfill their vows. In quotations from Zechariah 14:20 and Psalm 32:9 (31:9 in the Septuagint), he says it is the time to bridle the horse to make it holy to the Lord and to muzzle the ignorant foal, by which he means that his beloved community should enslave their bodies, not their souls.* This will lead to their resurrection and illumination by Christ.* Liberius feels bold to say, "I got up and I am with you."* It is time for the negligent to get up.# So Liberius calls his beloved ones to struggle in the fast of the forty days so that the one lying down rises, the idle one works, the negligent one is eager, the timid one becomes courageous, and the gentle one becomes a fighter against pleasure.

*2 Cor 6:2

*1 Cor 9:27

*Eph 5:14

*Ps 139:18/ Ps 138:18 in the Septuagint

#Prov 6:9

[4] A marginal note in the commentary on 2 Samuel 21:17 (2 Kings 21:17 in the Septuagint) of Theodoret of Cyrus (ca. 393–ca. 460) refers to Severus's letter to Probus in Greek, stressing the idea that there is nothing so important as the life in the darkness. See Robert Devreesse, *Les Anciens Commentateures grecs de l'Octateuch et des Rois (fragments tirés des chaînes)*, Studi e Testi 201 (Vatican: Biblioteca apostolica vaticana, 1959), 199.

Then Liberius turns to Zechariah 8:19, where he takes "the fast is four" to refer to the four gospels, in which Jesus accomplishes a forty-day fast. He takes "the fast is five" to refer to five of the commandments: You shall not commit adultery, kill, steal, lie, or covet. In this way, his hearers will be prepared for every good work, pleasing in God's sight.* Liberius understands "the fast is seven" to refer to keeping the Sabbath holy, and "the fast is ten" to refer to the ten commandments given to Moses. In the fragmentary section at the bottom of London, BL Or. 3581A(13) v°, Liberius seems to be reviewing the story of Exodus 33–34, in which Moses experiences the mystery of God, and the regulations of God's covenant with the people are renewed after their infidelity. Some lines appear to be missing at the bottom of the page.

*2 Tim 2:21; 1 Tim 5:4

At the top of Cairo, IFAO, copte 173 r°, the subject is Jesus, the God who holds the power of the world and pilots (ⲣϩⲉⲙⲙⲉ) all. Even though "God our Savior did not need to fast," he did fast when he was in the body, and pressed out "the poison of the dragon" for us. This demonstrates for Liberius that demons are driven out through prayer and fasting. He gives the example of a man whose restriction of food put pressure on the demon inside him, which came out of him crying, "I burned!" He uses Exodus 32:6 and Matthew 24:6 to warn against satisfying the lust for food and drink. He talks about how a magician gives a woman something to eat to cause her to conceive, but her womb becomes "the grave of her child." It is not the fed one but the one with failing eyes and a hungering soul who gives God glory.*

*Bar 2:18

Then he rehearses the story of the Ninevites and Jonah, "the prophet whose words did not happen." When the people of Nineveh heard Jonah preach that the cry of their evil had come before God and that God would destroy them, they turned God's wrath back in forty days. Ashamed of their food and drink, they fasted and repented with ashes on their heads. Even the animals wore sackcloth until "the whole city was saved." Liberius personifies the fast, which also comes before God and shuts the mouth of the evil crying out. It bows before God with ashes on its head until it wins over the God who had threatened destruction.

Liberius presents the people of Israel in the wilderness for forty years as a contrast to the Ninevites, using Isaiah 58:3-8, in which God rejects the fast that is accompanied by violence and injustice and desires the fast that releases the oppressed. Liberius points to the seizure of Naboth's vineyard,* the burning of Baruch's book,# and the imprisonment of Jeremiah§ as examples of violent fasting. Liberius holds the people of Jerusalem, gathered for the feast of the Passover, responsible for the unjust death of Jesus, "the one who holds the power of the world and pilots it." In a series of paradoxes, Liberius says, "They bound the one who bound the chariot wheels of Pharaoh";* they "brought the one who brought them out of the servitude of Pharaoh into the praetorium of the unlawful king Herod." They crowned with thorns the one who planted the grapevine, and they gave vinegar to the one who makes the plants sprout to make honey. "They crucified the one who drove out before them Sihon and Og, the kings of the

*1 Kgs 21
#Jer 36:4-26
§Jer 26:9; 37:15

*Exod 14:25

Deut 31:4 Amorites," and the one who made Jerusalem the center of the nations was put between two robbers. Liberius chastises the Jews for repaying good with evil, citing Psalm 109:5 / Psalm 108:5 in the Septuagint, and Proverbs 17:13. He ends with a lament for the Jews based on Isaiah's words (10:1 and 3:10 in the Septuagint, "Let us bind the righteous one because he is difficult for us"), since the Jews do not recognize their Messiah, who would bring them out of their sins. Liberius chides the Israelite ancestors because they did not fast during their forty years in the desert. The next page is missing.

Athanasius, *Fragments on the Moral Life* (Manchester, J. Rylands Lib. 25, fols. 2, 5, 6) [last page of MONB.CP].

The beginning is missing. In folio 2, Athanasius is talking about bearing fruit in Christ* by not swearing, which is to use God's name lightly. Christians should provide a better example to leaven the world. Athanasius compares life in the Lord Jesus to the life of the angels because Christians put to death the desires of the flesh.* They eat a few vegetables and drink water instead of eating big meals with meat and wine. They replace long sleep with long prayer.

*John 15:8

*1 Cor 15:31; Gal 5:24; Rom 13:14

Even those who cannot achieve the heights of such a life all at once should make a start, Athanasius says, pointing to Lot, who was rescued by angels from the destruction of Sodom and Gomorrah.* Lot was afraid to go up the mountain as the angels told him to, so he asked for a small city of refuge instead. From there he was able to ascend the mountain later.

*Gen 19:15-30

Athanasius calls people away from the world's indulgence in wine, food, and fornication, so that they are not consumed by these things. Then comes a paragraph quoted by Besa, Shenoute's successor at the White Monastery:

> Let no one see you disgracing yourself and say, "This is the person who is practicing discipline to achieve the gift of heaven; this is the disciple and pupil of the wise teacher; this is the person who has been chosen out of the world* and reckoned with the angels in heaven." You who look to the king of heaven, hoping to stand next to him, let Christ be glorified through you, and let him not be blasphemed on your account. For he speaks in this way: "Whoever glorifies me I will glorify; whoever despises me I will despise."* You despise him when you honour him with your words yet blaspheme him with your deeds.[5]

*John 15:18

*1 Sam 2:30

Athanasius refers to 1 Corinthians 6:15, 1 Corinthians 3:16-17, and 2 Corinthians 6:14 to assert that the body of a Christian is the temple of the Holy Spirit and should be morally clean. Sexual intercourse should be within marriage and for the purpose of procreation. Christ is patient with sinners now, but fear of the day of his wrath should keep a person from sin.* Athanasius prohibits drunkenness, "in which there is intemperance," by

*Jas 2:12; Rom 8:13

[5] Translation by Brakke, "Fragments on the Moral Life," in *Athanasius and Asceticism*, 315–16; see also Lefort, *S. Athanase*, CSCO 150, p. 123, and CSCO 151, pp. 103–4; Kuhn, *Letters and Sermons of Besa*, CSCO 157, p. 82, and CSCO 158, p. 79.

quoting Ephesians 5:18-19, but does not demand total abstinence from wine. God's medicines are found in the fullness of the Spirit, through God's words, songs, and psalms.

Addressing both the baptized and catechumens, Athanasius says that all should prepare themselves for the king's return through repentance, just as John the Baptist taught.* They should flee from sin rather than returning to it* and gain control over their natural impulses so that God's handiwork is not corrupted and they do not forfeit the eternal good things to come for a temporary pleasure: "For while we are in the body, brothers, repentance remains for us," along with prayer that no one continue as a stranger to God or, worse, return to being a stranger to God. At Christ's wedding banquet there will be no more grieving over the lost.* Athanasius recommends the fear of God to combat negligence.*

*Luke 3:7-8
*2 Pet 2:22
*Matt 22:12
*Jer 48:10 / Jer 31:10 in the Septuagint, and Jer 17:5

Christ loved us and ascended a cross to save us from these things, Athanasius preaches. This Savior is also the Creator of all things,* the one to whom the Father said, "Let us make a human being according to our image and likeness."* Jesus took his human flesh from Mary, while remaining the same forever.* "Jesus, the immortal one . . . died in the flesh" like us, but rose and sits at God's right hand. When the risen Jesus appeared to his disciples, he had to reassure them that they were not seeing a Spirit; the body that died is the body that will rise.* Thus Athanasius urges his hearers to put on Christ, as Mary did. This means to remove themselves from "arrogance, quarreling, enmity," and other vices listed in the Pauline letters. He says that monks will be judged even

*John 1:13
*Gen 1:26
*Ps 102:27/ Ps 101:28 in the Septuagint
*Luke 24:39; John 5:29

more strictly for disdaining God's commandments than laypeople. The martyrs are lifted up as the prime example of those who triumphed in Christ.* Athanasius speaks specifically of those martyred in Alexandria. They preferred to fall into human hands rather than into "the hands of the living God."* They trusted that Jesus would return their bodies incorruptible. The sermon closes with this doxology: "Let it be for us all that we attain the forgiveness of our sins through the love for humans of our Lord Jesus Christ. Glory to the Father, with him and the Holy Spirit, the giver of life and of one substance, for ever and ever. Amen."[6]

*Matt 10:28, 32-33

*Heb 10:31

Texts that Have Been Identified but not yet Sequenced

Athanasius (?) (London, BL Or. 8802, fols. 1-4 v°, line 24).

See the translation of *On Love and Self-Control.*

Severus of Antioch, *Letter to Theognostus* (London, BL Or. 8802, fol. 4 v°, line 25–6 r°, line 20).

The heading refers to *On Love and Self-Control* when it says, "*Likewise,* An epistle of the holy patriarch and archbishop of Antioch Apa Severus, which he wrote to a certain Theognostus, with whom he had friendly relations (συνήθεια), when he heard that he had fornicated (πορνεύω) with a

[6] Translation by Brakke, "Fragments on the Moral Life," in *Athanasius and Asceticism,* 319; see also Lefort, *S. Athanase,* CSCO 150, p. 129, and CSCO 151, p. 109.

woman; and he wrote to him to upbraid him with guidance and wisdom (σοφία)."[7]

Severus's letter begins with an acknowledgment of three letters he has received from Theognostus, in which Severus sees Theognostus's God-loving character reflected. So when Severus heard the following sad news of Theognostus, he could not believe it.

An Egyptian visited Severus, and they discussed vice contrasted with virtue in the Christian life, and the future Day of Judgment. Severus quoted Matthew 11:30 and Romans 8:18 to indicate that the virtuous life in this world and the glory of the world to come are open not only to monks but also to those who enter by a different route. God does not want
Ezek 33:11 any to be lost. Severus held up Theognostus as an exemplary layperson and read from his letters.

But Severus's visitor sat silent. When Severus asked him why, he said that virtue is in deeds,
1 Cor 4:20; Matt 7:21 not words. He accused Theognostus of putting on the appearance of respectability with his wife and children while he committed adultery with women who frequented the theaters and with those for hire. When Severus heard this, he wanted to throw his visitor out. He insisted that someone like Theognostus would not do such a thing, since Theognostus understood the Scriptures that prohibit such behavior, like 1 Corinthians 6:15, Matthew 5:28, Ephesians 5:3, 1 Thessalonians 4:3-5, and 1 Corinthians 7:4. How could someone

[7] The translation of the heading is by Layton, in *Catalogue of Coptic Literary Manuscripts in the British Library*, 217 (italics in quotation mine).

who knew the love of the Trinity, the beauty of the divinity, the angels, the patriarchs, the suffering of the only-begotten One, the preaching of the apostles and fathers, and the eternal punishments commit such abomination?

Nevertheless his guest asserted that what he had said about Theognostus was true. Severus suspected him of being jealous of Theognostus, but he is writing to Theognostus to ascertain the facts. He closes by expressing confidence that, if Theognostus is truly guilty, he will confess his sins readily and seek forgiveness, according to Psalm 32:5 (31:5 in the Septuagint) and Jeremiah 8:4.

Severus of Antioch, *Letter to Caesaria* (London, BL Or. 8802, fol. 6 r°, line 21–6 v°).

The heading links this text to the *Letter to Theognostus* with "Likewise, another epistle of the patriarch and archbishop of Antioch Apa Severus, which he wrote also to the patrician lady Caesaria, on how it is good for one to forcibly restrain one's thoughts for the peace of one's neighbor."[8] Severus begins by recounting how a holy ascetic monk interpreted Hebrews 9:22, "Without the shedding of blood there is no forgiveness." The monk said that "the shedding of blood" means killing one's own desire in order to acquire "peace and love toward his neighbor." Those who know this grasp the rudder that turns in the direction of life, and they pilot (ⲣϩⲙⲙⲉ) their boats with compassion.

[8] The heading was translated by Layton, *Catalogue of Coptic Literary Manuscripts in the British Library*, 217.

Severus then enters into a lengthy discussion of 1 Corinthians 5:9-13 to say that friendly, everyday interaction with "the world," even with sinners, is necessary and not forbidden for the Christian community. But the heretic *within* the Christian community should be cast out, according to Titus 3:10-11. Severus explains that he is talking about the "Phantasiasts," by which he means those who hold to "the fantasy that Julian the Wretched [Julian of Halicarnassus] is currently proclaiming," such as the monk Eustathius, who has gained entry to Caesaria's monastery.[9] Severus urges Caesaria to cast Eustathius out because "he wants to beguile those who are standing well into the heresy of the Manichaeans." The letter to Caesaria is incomplete.

[9] This dates the letter to Caesaria to the 520s, the active years of a controversy between Severus of Antioch and Julian of Halicarnassus, both anti-Chalcedonian bishops who took refuge in Egypt from Emperor Justin (518–527). There they disputed about whether Christ's body was incorruptible, with Severus arguing that it was not because that would detract from Christ's real humanity. On the controversy, see Aloys Grillmeier and Theresia Hainthaler, *Christ in Christian Tradition*, vol. 2, part 2, translated by John Cawte and Pauline Allen (Louisville, KY: Westminster John Knox, 1995), 25–26, 79–111; Stephen J. Davis, *The Early Coptic Papacy: The Egyptian Church and Its Leadership in Late Antiquity*, The Popes of Egypt 1 (Cairo: The American University of Cairo Press, 2004), 99–101; and René Draguet, *Julien d'Halicarnasse et sa controverse avec Sévère d'Antioche sur l'incorruptibilité du corps du Christ*, Universitas Catholica Lovaniensis, series 2, vol. 12 (Louvain: P. Smeesters, 1924). Around the year 530 Eustathius wrote a "Letter to Timothy the Scholar on the two natures, against Severus." The letter is in PG 86.1:901–42. See O. Bardenhewer, *Geschichte der altkirchlichen Literatur* (Freiburg in Bresgau and St. Louis, MO: Herder, 1932), 5:16.

Basil of Caesarea, Proemium in regulas fusius tractatas (Preface to the Longer Rules) (Manchester, J. Rylands Lib. 25, fol. 3).

The heading says: "Likewise, the holy Basil, the Bishop of Caesarea of Cappadocia, teaching the beloved brothers, encouraging them to struggle in works of asceticism, which will acquire for us eternal life. In the peace of God." Basil begins by beseeching his community "through the love of our Lord Jesus Christ, who gave himself for our sins" to live in repentance while there is still time, so they are not cast out of the bridal chamber later. He quotes 2 Corinthians 6:2, "Now is the acceptable time; now is the day of salvation." Later, God will appear as Judge. Those on God's right will enter the kingdom of heaven, while those on God's left will "be enveloped in the fire of Gehenna," where there is "weeping and gnashing of teeth."* Basil uses 2 Timothy 2:5 to say that only those who work enjoy the harvest and only those who compete get the prize, and he uses Matthew 24:46 / Luke 12:43 and Genesis 4:7 to urge his hearers to do right. This means keeping *all* of the commandments. Basil refers to the parable of the servant entrusted with one talent who was condemned for not increasing it.* When the Lord commissioned his disciples in Matthew 28:19, he told them to teach all nations to "observe all things whatsoever I command you." Thus Paul, he says, wants to be commended as a minister of God "in all things."* For "what do my other virtues profit me, if, through calling my brother a fool, I am condemned to Gehenna?"* Basil quotes John 8:34 to say that anyone who sins is a servant of sin. Even Peter, who "had done so

*Matt 25:30

*Matt 25:14-30

*2 Cor 6:3-4

*Matt 5:22

many good deeds," received a rebuke when he objected to letting Jesus wash his feet.*

*John 13:8

To those who might quote Joel 2:32, "Whosoever shall call on the name of the Lord shall be saved," Basil replies that it is not enough to call on the Lord's name.* Whatever we do should be done out of belief and a disposition of love.* Then Basil moves to a discussion of three dispositions, the first of which is fear of punishment. Here the manuscript ends.[10]

*Rom 10:4; Matt 7:21
*Matt 6:5; 23:5; 1 Cor 13:3

John Chrysostom, *Homily 31 on the Gospel of Matthew* (Paris, BnF, copte 131[1], fol. 37; and Paris, BnF, copte 131[4], fol. 163).

The heading is only partially extant. It says, "word of . . . John . . . bishop of Constantinople . . . the gospel according to Matthew," after which the scribe seems to be asking God for a holy death. The homily concerns Matthew 9:23-26, in which Jesus raises the daughter of the ruler of a synagogue. Chrysostom puts the girl's story in parallel with Lazarus's.* He notes that Jesus prepares his hearers for resurrection in both cases by saying that the deceased is only sleeping. This is a preview not only of Jesus' own resurrection but also of the resurrection of all his disciples. Second, Jesus did not rebuke the people for laughing when he said the girl was sleeping because, as in the case of Lazarus,* he wanted the greatest possible contrast between their certainty of death and the fact of the risen life to come. (Chrysostom also draws in

*John 11:11
*John 11:34, 39

[10] It is very likely that on another page the text continued to discuss the other two dispositions: desire for reward, and love. Quotations in this summary are from Clarke, *The Ascetic Works of Saint Basil*, 145–51.

Moses here. God made sure that Moses identified his staff as a staff before God turned it into a snake in Exodus 4:2.) Third, Jesus does everything to convince the parents of their daughter's resurrection, from lifting her up to commanding that she be fed, just as Jesus commanded that Lazarus be brought out and unbound, and later ate with him.* But because Jesus was humble, he also commanded that the witnesses of the girl's resurrection say nothing to anyone.

*John 11:44; 12:2

Then Chrysostom turns to the lives of his hearers, especially those who have lost children to death. The child in Matthew's gospel died again, Chrysostom notes, but because of Jesus' resurrection, resurrection is now permanent, and thus Christians have no cause for exorbitant grief at death. Chrysostom accuses his listeners of hiring professional mourners from among pagan women to stir up emotion at funerals; he cites 2 Corinthians 6:13 to make them stop. Even the pagans, who do not know about the resurrection, console the bereaved and urge mourners to bear what cannot be undone, he says. Christians should remind mourners that God will undo death and raise the dead.

In the meantime, the child sleeps.* Only the devil has a reason to mourn. For Christians, death leads to a crown and rest in a fair haven, safe from the troubles of this world.* Chrysostom then describes that future rest, citing Isaiah 35:10 and Matthew 8:11.

*Ps 116:7/ Ps 114:7 in the Septuagint

*Gen 3:16, 19; John 16:33

(Paris, BnF, copte 131[4], fol. 163 begins here.) To the person who retorts that grief is only natural, Chrysostom points again to the pagans, some of whom put crowns on their deceased children and dress them in white to mark them as heirs, even though they do not know anything about the resurrection. He insists that the Christian child who dies was never truly heir of the parents' perishable goods but, even better, was "joint-heir with Christ" of God's eternal things.* If the parents long to see their child again, Chrysostom advises, they should "live the same life with him."[11] In the meantime, they should bear the pain, like the Son of God. Although he prayed that God would let the pain pass,* Jesus went through it all the way to a shameful death. But he was raised in glory, a reason for hope. God is transforming all things. Chrysostom goes on to say that God would not have taken the child if he or she had not been in a state of repentance or righteousness. (Since the last line is close to the end of the sermon, it probably continued onto another page.)

*Rom 8:17

*Matt 26:39

John Chrysostom, *Homilies 4 and 5 on the Epistle to the Hebrews* (Manchester, J. Rylands Lib. 25, fol. 4; and Manchester, J. Rylands Lib. 25, fol. 1).

The heading says, "Likewise, the sixth word of remembrance that the blessed John, the Golden Mouth and Archbishop of Constantinople, preached, interpreting the Letter to the Hebrews, in peace."[12] After introducing the text of Hebrews

[11] The English is from the translation of George Prevost, NPNF 10:209.

[12] Translated by Crum, *Catalogue of the Coptic Manuscripts in the Collection of the John Rylands Library*, #62, pp. 25-26. The content of this sermon, however, does not correspond with

2:14a the text has, "Let all the heretics be ashamed, the ones who divide the Logos from his flesh, and let the Phantasiasts also be ashamed, the ones who say, 'He did not become truly and unalterably human,' ascribing to him a fantasy and a deceit." Chrysostom goes on to say that the purpose of Jesus' taking flesh was to "free those who all their lives were held in slavery by the fear of death."[13] The Coptic text explores what it means to be in slavery to the fear of death in contrast to what it means to be free from this fear on account of Christ. Those who are servants of God and not of the fear of death are ready to die at any time. They are patient in all trouble, difficulty, trial, danger, and persecution. They do not live according to the flesh. They avoid all jealousy, and they are worthy of eternal joy and freedom. Their hope is

---

that of the sermon now known as the sixth, presented in Migne's edition (PG 63:53–58). Instead, as Louis points out in her forthcoming *Catalogue raisonné des manuscrits littéraires coptes conserve à l'IFAO du Caire*, the beginning is similar to the portion of what is now known as Homily 4, dealing with Hebrews 2:14-15 but with additional comments (PG 63:41, lines 20-46). I have been able to spot the continuation of Chrysostom's sermon in what is now known as Homily 5, dealing with Hebrews 3:6 (PG 63:50, line 40–51, line 31). In the English translation of the Greek by Frederic Gardiner in *Saint Chrysostom: Homilies on the Gospel of St. John and the Epistle to the Hebrews*, NPNF 14, ed. Philip Schaff (New York: Charles Scribner's Sons, 1889), the part loosely corresponding to Manchester, J. Rylands Lib. 25, fol. 4, is on pages 385, column 1, lines 6–42, and 391, column 1, line 40–column 2, line 49.

[13] PG 63:41, lines 39–41; NPNF 14:385, end of §6. From here on the Coptic manuscript diverges from the Greek text preserved in Migne, only touching it lightly at points until PG 63:42, line 34.

not in this world but in "the other aeon." The devil has power only over those who fear death and hope only for the good things of this world. "For in hope we were saved. Now hope that is seen is not hope. For who hopes for what is seen? But if we hope for what we do not see, we wait for it with patience."*[14]

*Rom 8:24

The preacher acknowledges that it is hard to see wicked people at ease and in plenty while good people suffer and hunger, but he urges his listeners not to be troubled by this:

> Yea, and in another point of view, it is not possible either that a bad man should be altogether bad, but he may have some good things also; nor again that a good man should be altogether good, but he may also have some sins. When therefore the wicked man prospers, it is for evil on his own head, that having received the reward of those few good things, he may hereafter be utterly punished yonder; for this cause does he receive his recompense in this life.[15]

1 Corinthians 11:30 is cited, along with Hebrews 12:6, to the effect that suffering in this life is meant to spare one eternal suffering in "that place." Then the story of Lazarus and the rich man in Luke 16:25 is cited, where Abraham says to the rich man, "Child, remember that during your lifetime you received your good things and Lazarus in like manner evil things."[16]

[14] Here the Coptic text shifts from Homily 4 to Homily 5.

[15] Translation by Gardiner, NPNF 14:391.

[16] PG 63:51, lines 29–31.

(Manchester, J. Rylands Lib. 25, fol. 1 begins here.) Chrysostom recalls Christ's telling his disciples that they would be afflicted.* Like athletes, they are in the middle of a hard contest and cannot spare a thought for the comforts of life. Even when there is no persecution, we try each other, he says, and experience other afflictions, too, all of which should be borne with joy. "No testing has overtaken you that is not common to everyone."*

*John 16:33; 2 Tim 3:12

*1 Cor 10:13

Nevertheless, Chrysostom reminds his hearers, they pray not to come into temptation and should not seek it by throwing themselves into danger. But if the Gospel calls them to danger, they should endure it courageously. This is to obey Christ, who commanded his disciples both to pray that they "may not come into the time of trial"* and to take up their cross and follow him.* Like soldiers, they should not incite war, but they should be armed and ready to fight the devil and shed their own blood if it is necessary. To prepare for this, Chrysostom tells them to let go of all worldly attachments, quoting Galatians 6:14b: "The world has been crucified to me and I to the world."

*Matt 26:41

*Matt 26:24

On the verso, Chrysostom says that there is presently no persecution, and he prays to God that there will never be. The war he is talking about is the "war of the passions," bitter enemies of humanity. The "passions of the killer" include wrath, jealousy, arrogance, empty glory, and slander in the war that extends evil over humans. He then cites Ephesians 6:12-13a, regarding God's armor against spiritual enemies. Chrysostom points out that the war attacks the eyes, ears, tongues, hands, and feet. He explains why Paul says to wear the

Eph 6:14 belt of truth, "because lust is a mockery and a lie"
(a thought he supports with "the prophet's" words
in Psalm 38:7 / Psalm 37:8 in the Septuagint), and
it is fitting to fight it with temperance. Chrysostom
cautions that we should be strengthened in the
fear of God, lest God pierce us in wrath. God the
Creator can sap sinners of their strength, burning
Job 31:12 them with fire. Thus the helmet of salvation is
Eph 6:17 also necessary, to protect the reasoning faculty in
the head, from which come both good and evil. He quotes Ephesians 6:15-16 to urge the listeners to wear the shoes of the Gospel and carry the shield of faith as they use their hands to pray and work. In this way they will overcome their enemies and acquire eternal life through the grace and love that Jesus Christ has for humans. The sermon closes with a doxology.

John Chrysostom, *Homily 7 on the Epistle to the Hebrews* (Vienna, K 9170; and Cairo, IFAO, copte 171).

The damaged fragment begins with what seems to be a discussion of Hebrews 4:14-15: "Since, then, we have a great high priest who has passed through the heavens, Jesus, the Son of God, let us hold fast to our confession. For we do not have a high priest who is unable to sympathize with our weaknesses, but we have one who in every respect has been tested as we are, yet without sin." On the recto, there is mention of believing in his words (ⲡⲓⲥⲧⲉⲩⲉⲉⲛⲉϥϣⲁϫⲉ) and of resurrection. The sentence "He is God" (ⲛⲧⲟϥⲡⲉⲡⲛⲟⲩⲧⲉ) is discernible, as is mention of sin and of testing (ⲡⲓⲣⲁⲥⲙⲟⲥ). The verso, much more legible, discusses Hebrews 4:16, "Let us therefore approach the throne of grace with boldness, so that we may receive mercy and find grace to help in time of need." The idea that *now* is the time for repentance is stressed. One day "the Son of Humanity is coming, sitting on the throne of his glory," and "he will give to each according to his works."* In the present, the high priest's throne is one of grace, the gift "that we received through baptism. Let it not be lost through our negligence . . . . For this reason the prophet said, 'In a time of favor I have answered you, and on a day of salvation I have helped you.'"* The bridal chamber has not yet been shut.

*Matt 25:31; 16:27

*Isa 49:8

Then the text previews Hebrews 12:1-2 to speak of the Christian life as a race in front of a stadium full of spectators. "Let us run," the preacher urges. (Cairo, IFAO, copte 171 begins here.) The runner, he says, does not pay any attention to the surroundings or to the spectators, "whether they be rich or poor, whether one mock at him, . . . whether one insult" him, whether one cry out to him, "cast stones at him," or take his possessions and scatter them.[17] The runner seeks only the prize.

Chrysostom then applies this message particularly to the elderly who excuse themselves by saying that they are no longer able to fast. Chrysostom concedes that they may not be able to run (that is, to fast) as they could in their youth but that, despite bodily weakness, they can keep their souls vigorous. In fact, old age drives away the passions of youth and sets the soul free from them in expectation of death and Judgment.

[17] English translation by Gardiner, in NPNF 14:401.

Chrysostom finds it shameful when old people act as if they had never grown up. He says that such people have no right to pray, "Do not remember the sins of my youth and my ignorance" (following the text of Psalm 24:7 in the Septuagint), because they have never outgrown them. An old person should exhibit self-respect in order to gain respect from others. For gray hair is a gift from God and not a shame if the gray-haired one behaves in a way befitting the gray hair and not like a child. How could a childish old person teach the young? he asks, and here the page ends.

Severian of Jabalah, *The Washing of the Feet* (Paris, BnF, copte 132^4, fol. 346; and Oxford, Cl. Pr. b. 25, fol. 1–2^r, line 15).

Enzo Lucchesi describes Paris, BnF, copte 132^4, fol. 346 as a tiny fragment torn vertically, with only about a dozen letters visible. From these he has been able to discern a correspondence to §§8–10 and 12–14 of the edition of the Greek text of this homily made by Antoine Wenger.[18] Paragraphs 8–9 say that everything in the world was created for the glory of God and for service to the human "or, rather, the image of God."[19] Just as people greet an

[18] Lucchesi, "Un témoin copte de l'homélie de Sévérien de Gabala sur le lavement des pieds," 306; Wenger, "Une homélie inédite de Sévérien de Gabala sur le lavement des pieds," 226–28 (Greek) and 231–33 (French). Wenger found twenty-five manuscripts of this text (which he lists on page 221), all attributed to John Chrysostom and all very much alike. He chose to edit and translate Paris, BnF, grec. 582 (tenth century) as representative.

[19] Wenger, "Une homélie inédite," 226 (Greek) and 231 (French).

image of the emperor with reverence for what it represents, so the creation respects the heavenly image in humans.

Paragraph 10 stresses God's care for all that God has made by quoting the Wisdom of Solomon 11:23a, 24: "But you are merciful to all, for you can do all things, . . . for you love all things that exist, and detest none of the things that you have made, for you would not have made anything if you had hated it."

In §§12–14, Severian says that, even though all visible things witness to the generosity of God, there is no stronger witness than God's coming among us as a human, and not only a human, but a slave. He refers to the fact that he is preaching on the Thursday of Holy Week, on which day Jesus' washing of his disciples' feet is recalled. Severian is awed by this mystery: "Even though he was in the form of God, he did not regard equality with God as something to be exploited, but emptied himself, taking the form of a slave."*

*Phil 2:6-7a

The text moves here to Oxford, Cl. Pr. b. 25, fol. 1–2ʳ, line 15, which is in very good condition. It begins with a parallel to §16 of Wenger's edition and follows the text closely to the end at §23.[20] Severian marvels that disciples like Peter, Matthew, and Philip, men of the earth, sat boldly with Jesus while the army of angels, like Michael and Gabriel, assisted Jesus in fear. But even more marvelous is the fact that Jesus, "the one wrapped in light as with a garment,"* "got up from supper and took

*Ps 104:2/ Ps 103:2 in the Septuagint

[20] Wenger, "Une homélie inédite," 228–29 (Greek), 233–34 (French).

off his outer robe."* Jesus, "the one who wrapped the heavens in clouds,"* "wrapped a towel around himself";# the one who made the nature of the waters flow in pools and rivers "poured water into a basin";* "the one to whom 'every knee shall bend, in heaven and on earth and under the earth'"* bent his knee before his disciples. The Lord of all washed the feet of his disciples, not thereby disgracing the worthiness of his divinity but revealing his love for humanity.

*John 13:4
*Ps 147:8/ Ps 146:8 in the Septuagint
#John 13:4
*John 13:5
*Phil 2:10

Although all the disciples recognized these truths about Jesus, most of them allowed Jesus to wash their feet because they did not want to reject his authority. But Peter objected, saying, "Lord, you are not washing my feet; you will never wash my feet."* Severian remarks that, although Peter meant well, he did not understand God's "economy." Identifying his hearers with Peter, Severian says, "You object as a human, and you change your mind as a lover of God."

*John 13:8

When the Savior saw the fight Peter was putting up, he countered it with an objection that outweighed Peter's: "Amen, amen, I tell you, unless I wash you, you have no share in me."* Peter regretted what he had done in haste and hastily repented, saying, "Lord, not my feet only but also my hands and my head.* Wash me entirely so that I may say with the psalmist David, 'Wash me, and I shall be whiter than snow.'"* Jesus replied, "One who has bathed does not need to wash except for the feet, but is entirely clean."*

*John 13:8
*John 13:9
*Ps 51:7/ Ps 50:9 in the Septuagint
*John 13:10

Severian raises the question of why Jesus washes specifically the feet of the disciples. He answers that it was not only to cleanse them but also to empower their heels to run into the world: "How beautiful are the feet of those who bring the good news of peace and proclaim what is good."* *Isa 52:7 Severian finds yet another mystery in the washing of the feet. In Genesis 3:15 God said to the serpent, "He will strike your head and you will strike his heel." God cursed humanity "so that the physician might put his hands on that place and the poison of the snake might not have power from that time on, and so that you might understand that when he cleansed the feet" he gave power over demons. Severian says that before, the heel was vulnerable to the serpent, but now, by the hand of God, it tramples on the deceiver. The one who gave power to the feet says, "See, I have given you authority to tread on snakes and scorpions."* *Luke 10:19 The closing doxology affirms that the Word of truth has washed the thoughts of the listeners and calls on them to live in purity to the glory of the Holy Trinity.

Severus of Antioch, *Homily 28, on Thomas* (Oxford, Cl. Pr. b. 25, fol. 2^r, line 16–2^v; and Strasbourg, BNU, Kopt. 100 [b]).

The heading says, "A word of the holy patriarch and archbishop of Antioch, *apa* Severus, that he preached on blessed Thomas the apostle on the New Sunday, after the resurrection of our Lord."[21]

[21] The scribe is incorrect about this. Severus originally preached this sermon in Seleucia in 513 not eight days after Easter but on the day that the Syrian church commemorated Thomas the apostle, July 3. See Maurice Brière, Introduction to Brière and Graffin, *Les Homiliae cathedrales de Sévère d'Antioche,* PO 138, tome 29, fasc. 1, 53. From this mistake of the scribe's,

Severus begins with the story of a victorious general reliving in his mind former conquests. Severus is thinking of Acts 13:4, where Barnabus and Saul go to Seleucia on their way to Cyprus. From there they ran like "spiritual horses" to the whole world, preaching the Gospel. It was as the prophet Habakkuk said: "You trampled the sea
Hab 3:15 with your horses, churning the mighty waters."
The apostles churned the waters by destroying the love of pleasure and possessions and turning it into self-control (ⲧⲉⲕⲣⲁⲧⲁ) and good sense. So the harbor of Seleucia is blessed; it is the place where the apostles knelt and prayed in their own language. They set sail from Seleucia, Severus says, but their blessing remains: "For the gifts of God
Rom 11:29 are irrevocable."

Severus speaks of the promise of the "God-loving emperor"[22] to maintain and redevelop the city of Seleucia. He notes that Seleucia carries on commerce with the great city of Antioch and its surroundings: "But since the time that the harbor received and sent the apostles. . . ." The sentence is unfinished.

The sermon continues in Strasbourg, BNU, Kopt. 100 [b], but the manuscript is a severely damaged fragment.[23] On the *recto* Severus recalls

---

however, we can discern the liturgical context in which his own community may have used this sermon.

[22] This would be Anastasius I (491–518).

[23] Lucchesi has pointed out that what is legible in Strasbourg, BNU, kopt. 100 [b] corresponds to lines 5–9 on page 579 and lines 10–17 on page 581 of the French translation of the Syriac by Brière and Graffin, *Les Homiliae cathedrales de Sévère d'Antioche*, PO 170, tome 36, fasc. 4.

the story of how the people of Israel thirsted in the desert and demanded water. Moses struck a rock at God's command so that water flowed out. But because Moses hesitated, God was angry and swore that Moses would not lead the people into the land God had given them.*

*Exod 17:1-2; Num 20:7-12

When the Coptic is next available, on the *verso*, it is emphasizing the true humanity of Jesus, the one who came to help the descendants of Abraham,* who was of the root of Jesse and David and of the race of the holy Virgin according to the flesh. Thomas's touching him proves that he was not a phantom.

*Heb 2:16

Select Bibliography

Manuscripts

Cairo, IFAO, copte 171, 172+212A, 173, 174, and 301
London, BL Or. 3581A(13)
London, BL Or. 8802
Manchester, J. Rylands Lib. 25, fols. 1–6
Oxford, Cl. Pr. b.25, fols. 1–2
Paris, BnF, copte 131[1], fols. 37 and 67
Paris, BnF, copte 131[4], fols. 162–163
Paris, BnF, copte 132[4], fol. 346
Strasbourg, BNU, Kopt. 100 [b]
Vienna, K 9170

Primary Sources

Amélineau, Émile. "Fragments de la version thébaine de l'Écriture (Ancien Testament)." *Recueil de travaux relatifs à la philologie et à l'archéologie égyptiennes et assyriennes* 9 (1887): 101–30.

———. *Monuments pour servir à l'histoire de l'Égypte chrétienne aux IVe, V^e^, VIe, et VIIe siecles*. Mémoires publiés par les membres de la mission archéologique française au Caire (Tome 4, fasc. 2). Paris: Ernest Leroux, 1888–1895.

———. *Oeuvres de Schenoudi: Texte copte et traduction française.* 2 vols. Paris: Ernest Leroux, 1907–1914.

———. *Vie de Abraham.* In *Monuments pour servir.* 742–53.

———. *Vie de Schnoudi.* In *Monuments pour servir.* 289–478.

Athanasius Werke. Edited by Hans-Georg Opitz, et al. 2 vols. Berlin: Walter de Gruyter, 1935–2006.

Atiya, Aziz Suryal, Yassa 'Abd al-Masih, and O. H. E. Khs-Burmester, eds. *History of the Patriarchs of the Egyptian Church, Known as the History of the Holy Church, by Sawīrus ibn al-Muḳafa', Bishop of al-Ašmūnīn*. Vol. II. Textes et documents. Cairo: La Société d'archéologie copte, 1943–1959.

Basset, René. *Le Synaxaire arabe jacobite (rédaction copte) II: Les Mois de Hatour et de Kihak*. Patrologia orientalis 13 (Tome III, fasc. 3). Paris: Firmin-Didot, 1909.

———. *Le Synaxaire arabe jacobite (rédaction copte) III: Les Mois de Toubeh et d'Amchir*. Patrologia orientalis 56 (Tome XI, fasc. 5). Paris: Firmin-Didot, 1915.

Boon, Amand. *Pachomiana latina: Règle et épitres de s. Pachome, Épitre de s. Theodore et "Liber" de s. Orsiesius, Texte latin de s. Jérôme*. Bibliothèque de la Revue d'histoire ecclésiastique 7. Louvain: Bureaux de la Revue, 1932.

Brière, Maurice, and René Graffin, with C. Lash and J. M. Sauget. *Les Homiliae cathedrales de Sévère d'Antioche, Traduction syriaque de Jaques d'Édesse*. Patrologia orientalis 170 (Tome XXXVI, fasc. 4). Turnhout: Brepols, 1974.

Brooks, E. W. *A Collection of Letters of Severus of Antioch from Numerous Syriac Manuscripts*. Patrologia orientalis 58 (Tome XII, fasc. 2) and 67 (Tome XIV, fasc. 1). Paris: Firmin-Didot, 1919–1920.

Budge, E. A. Wallis. *Coptic Apocrypha in the Dialect of Upper Egypt*. Oxford: Oxford University Press, 1913.

———. *Coptic Martyrdoms, &c., in the Dialect of Upper Egypt*. Vol. 4 of *Coptic Texts*. London: British Museum, 1914.

Camplani, Alberto. *Atanasio di Alessandria: Lettere festali, Anonimo: Indice delle Lettere festali*. Letture cristiane del primo millennio 34. Milan: Paoline, 2003.

Clarke, W. K. L. *The Ascetic Works of Saint Basil*. Translations of Christian Literature, Series 1, Greek Texts. London: Society for Promoting Christian Knowledge, 1925.

Crum, Walter Ewing. "Inscriptions from Shenoute's Monastery." *The Journal of Theological Studies* 5 (1904): 552–69.

Depuydt, Leo. *Catalogue of Coptic Manuscripts in the Pierpont Morgan Library*. Vol. 1. Corpus of Illuminated Manuscripts 4, Oriental Series 1. Louvain: Peeters, 1993.

Evetts, Basil. *History of the Patriarchs of the Coptic Church of Alexandria II: Peter I to Benjamin I (661)*. Patrologia orientalis 4 (Tome I, fasc. 4). Edited by René Graffin and François Nau. Paris: Firmin-Didot, 1907.

Forget, Iacobus. *Synaxarium alexandrinum*. Corpus scriptorum christianorum orientalium 49 and 78; Scriptores arabici 5 and 12. Louvain: L. Durbecq, 1953–1954 (= Corpus scriptorum christianorum orientalium, Scriptores arabici, series 3, vol. 18).

Gardiner, Frederic, trans. *Saint Chrysostom: Homilies on the Gospel of St. John and the Epistle to the Hebrews*. A Select Library of Nicene and Post-Nicene Fathers of the Church, edited by Philip Schaff, vol. 14. New York: Charles Scribner's Sons, 1889.

Halkin, Francis. *Sancti Pachomii vitae graecae*. Subsidia hagiographica 19. Brussels: Société des Bollandistes, 1932.

Horner, George. *The Coptic Version of the New Testament in the Southern Dialect*. Vols. 2 and 7. Oxford: Clarendon Press, 1911, 1924.

Kraemer, Joel L., trans. *The History of Al-Tabari*. Bibliotheca persica, Series in Near Eastern Studies, vol. 34. Albany: SUNY Press, 1989.

Kuhn, K. H, ed. *Letters and Sermons of Besa*. Corpus scriptorum christianorum orientalium 157–58, Scriptores coptici 21–22. Louvain: L. Durbecq, 1956.

Lagarde, Paul de. *Der Pentateuch koptisch*. Leipzig: B. G. Teubner, 1867.

Lanne, Emmanuel. *Le grand euchologe du Monastère Blanc*. Patrologia orientalis 135 (Tome XXVIII, fasc. 2). Paris: Firmin-Didot, 1958.

Lantschoot, Arnold van. *Les Colophons coptes des manuscrits sahidiques*. Vol. 1 of *Recueil des colophons des manuscrits chrétiens d'Égypte*. Louvain: J.-B. Istas, 1929.

———. "Les Textes palimpsestes de B.M., Or. 8802." *Le Muséon* 41 (1928): 225–47.

———. "Lettre de saint Athanase au sujet de l'amour et de la tempérance." *Le Muséon* 40 (1927): 265–92.

———. "Une Lettre de Sévère d'Antioche à Théognoste." *Le Muséon* 59 (1946): 470–77.

Lefort, Louis-Théophile. "Homélie inédite du Pape Libère sur le jeûne." *Le Muséon,* n.s., 12 (1911): 1–22.

———. *Les Vies coptes de saint Pachôme et de ses premiers successeurs.* Bibliothèque du Muséon 16. 1943; reprint, Louvain: Université de Louvain, Institut orientaliste, 1966.

———. *Oeuvres de s. Pachôme et de ses disciples.* Corpus scriptorum christianorum orientalium 159–60, Scriptores coptici 23–24. Louvain: L. Durbecq, 1956.

———. *S. Athanase: Lettres festales et pastorales en copte.* Corpus scriptorum christianorum orientalium 150–51, Scriptores coptici 19–20. Louvain: L. Durbecq, 1955.

———. *S. Pachomii vita bohairice scripta.* Corpus scriptorum christianorum orientalium 89, Scriptores coptici 7. Louvain: L. Durbecq, 1952–1953.

———. *S. Pachomii vitae sahidice scriptae.* Corpus scriptorum christianorum orientalium 99–100, Scriptores coptici 9–10. Louvain: L. Durbecq, 1952.

Lendle, Otto. *Gregorius Nyssenus, Encomium in sanctam Stephanum protomartyrem.* Leiden: Brill, 1968.

Maiberger Paul. *"Das Buch der kostbaren Perle" von Severus ibn al-Muqaffa': Einleitung und arabischer Text (Kapitel 1–5).* Akademie der Wissenschaften und der Literatur, Veröffentlichungen der orientalischen Kommission 28. Wiesbaden: Franz Steiner, 1972.

Maspero, Gaston. *Fragments de la version thébaine de l'Ancien Testament.* Mémoires Publiés par les members de la mission archéologique française au Caire 6, fasc. 2. Paris: Ernest Leroux, 1892.

Migne, J.-P., ed. *S.P.N. Athanasii, archiepiscopi Alexandrini, Opera omnia.* PG 25–26. Paris, 1857–1866.

———. *S.P.N. Basilii, Caesareae Cappadociae archiepiscopi, Opera omnia.* PG 31. Paris, 1857.

———. *S.P.N. Gregorii, episcopi Nysseni, Opera omnia*. PG 46. Paris, 1863.

———. *S.P.N. Joannis Chrysostomi, archiepiscopi Constantinopolitani, Opera omnia*. PG 57 and 63. Paris, 1860–1862.

Morison, E. F. *St. Basil and His Rule: A Study in Early Monasticism*. S. Deiniol's Series III. London: Oxford University Press, 1912.

Peters, Melvin K. H., ed. *Exodus*. Vol. 2 of *A Critical Edition of the Coptic (Bohairic) Pentateuch*. Society of Biblical Literature Septuagint and Cognate Studies Series 22, edited by Claude E. Cox. Atlanta: Scholars Press, 1983.

Pleyte, Willem, and Pieter Adrian Aart Boeser. *Manuscrits coptes du Musée d'antiquités des Pays-Bas à Leide publiés d'apres les ordres du gouvernement*. Leiden: Brill, 1897.

Porcher, Émile. "Sévère d'Antioche dans la literature copte." *Revue de l'Orient chrétien* 12 (1907): 119–24.

———. "Un Discours sur la sainte Vierge par Sévère d'Antioche." *Revue de l'Orient chrétien* 10, no. 20 (1915): 416–23.

Prevost, George, trans. *Saint Chrysostom: Homilies on the Gospel of Saint Matthew*. A Select Library of Nicene and Post-Nicene Fathers of the Church, edited by Philip Schaff, vol. 10. New York: The Christian Literature Company, 1888.

Quecke, Hans. *Die Briefe Pachoms: Griechischer Text der Handschrift W. 145 der Chester Beatty Library*. Textus Patristici et Liturgici 11. Regensburg: Friedrich Pustet, 1975.

Rahlfs, Alfred, ed. *Septuaginta*. Stuttgart: Deutsche Bibelgesellschaft, 1979.

Robertson, Archibald. *Select Writings and Letters of Athanasius, Bishop of Alexandria*. A Select Library of Nicene and Post-Nicene Fathers of the Church, edited by Philip Schaff and Henry Wace, reprinted edition, 2nd series, vol. 4. Grand Rapids, MI: Wm. B. Eerdmans, 1987.

Veilleux, Armand. *Pachomian Koinonia: The Lives, Rules, and Other Writings of Saint Pachomius and his Disciples*. 3 vols. Cistercian Studies Series 45–47. Kalamazoo, MI: Cistercian Publications, 1980–1982.

Wenger, Antoine. "Une homélie inédite de Sévérien de Gabala sur le lavement des pieds." *Revue des études byzantines* 25 (1967): 219–34.

Youssef, Youhanna Nessim. "The Coptic Marian Homilies of Severus of Antioch." *Bulletin de la Société d'archéologie copte* 43 (2004): 127–40.

———. "A Coptic Version of the Homily 28 of Severus of Antioch." *Bulletin de la Société d'archéologie copte* 43 (2009): 121–26.

Ziadeh, J., with a note by F. Nau. "L'Apocalypse de Samuel, supérieur de Deir-el-Qalamoun." *Revue de l'Orient chrétien* 20 (1915–1917): 374–407.

Secondary Sources

Amélineau, Émile. "Catalogue des manuscrits coptes de la Bibliothèque nationale" (unpublished).

———. *La Géographie de l'Égypte à l'époque copte.* Paris: Imprimerie Nationale, 1893.

Atiya, Aziz Suryal, editor-in-chief. *The Coptic Encyclopedia.* 8 vols. New York: Macmillan, 1991.

Bacht, Heinrich. *Das Vermächtnis des Ursprungs.* Studien zum frühen Mönchtum 1. Würzburg: Echter, 1972.

———. "Studien zum 'Liber Orsiesii.'" *Historisches Jahrbuch* 77 (1958): 98–124.

Badger, Carlton Mills, Jr. "The New Man Created in God: Christology, Congregation and Asceticism in Athanasius of Alexandria." PhD diss., Duke University, 1990.

Bernard, Régis. *L'Image de Dieu d'aprés saint Athanase.* Théologie 25. Paris: Aubier, Éditions Montaigne, 1952.

Boud'hors, Anne. *Catalogue des fragments coptes de la Bibliothèque nationale et universitaire de Strasbourg, I. Fragments bibliques.* Corpus scriptorum christianorum orientalium 571, Subsidia 99. Louvain: Peeters, 1998.

Boud'hors, Anne, James Clackson, Catherine Louis, and Petra Sijpesteijn, eds. *Monastic Estates in Late Antiquity and Early Islamic Egypt: Ostraca, Papyri, and Essays in Memory of Sarah*

Clackson (P. Clackson). American Studies in Papyrology 46, edited by Ann Ellis Hanson. Cincinnati, OH: The American Society of Papyrologists, 2009.

Brakke, David. *Athanasius and Asceticism*. Baltimore and London: Johns Hopkins University Press, 1995.

———. "The Authenticity of the Ascetic Athanasiana." *Orientalia*, n.s., 63, no. 2 (1994): 17–56.

Brakmann, Heinzgerd. "Fragmenta graeco-copto-thebaicq: Zu Jutta Henners Veröffentlichung alter und neuer Dokumente südägyptischer Liturgie." *Oriens christianus* 88 (2004): 117–72.

Büchler, Bernward. *Die Armut der Armen: Über den ursprünglichen Sinn der Mönchischen Armut*. München: Kösel, 1980.

Chitty, Derwas J. "A Note on the Chronology of the Pachomian Foundations." In *Papers Presented to the Second International Conference on Patristic Studies held at Christ Church, Oxford, 1955*. Part 2, edited by Kurt Aland and F. L. Cross, 379–85. Studia patristica 2. Texte und Untersuchungen zur Geschichte der altchristlichen Literatur 64. Berlin: Akademie-Verlag, 1957.

Choat, Malcolm. "Athanasius, Pachomius, and the 'Letter on Charity and Temperance.'" In *Egyptian Culture and Society: Studies in Honor of Naguib Kanawati*. Vol. 1, edited by Alexandra Woods, Ann McFarlane, and Susanne Binder, 97–103. Supplément aux Annales du service des antiquités de l'Egypte, cahier no. 38. Cairo: Conseil suprême des antiquités de l'Egypte, 2010.

Coquin, René-Georges. "Le Fonds copte de l'Institut français d'archéologie orientale du Caire." In *Écritures et traditions dans la littérature copte: Journée d'études coptes, Strasbourg 28 mai 1982*, 9–18. Cahiers de la Bibliothèque copte 1. Louvain: Peeters, 1983.

———. "Saint Constantin, évêque d'Asyut," *Studia orientalia christiana collectanea* 16 (1981): 151–70.

Crum, Walter Ewing. *Catalogue of the Coptic Manuscripts in the British Museum*. London: The British Museum, 1905.

———. *Catalogue of the Coptic Manuscripts in the Collection of the John Rylands Library, Manchester*. Manchester: The University Press; London: Bernard Quaritch, and Sherratt and Hughes, 1909.

Dechow, Jon. *Dogma and Mysticism in Early Christianity: Epiphanius of Cyprus and the Legacy of Origen*. Patristic Monograph Series 13. Macon, GA: Mercer University Press, 1988.

Devos, Paul, and Enzo Lucchesi. "Un corpus basilien en copte." *Analecta Bollandiana* 99 (1981): 75–94.

Elm, Susanna. *"Virgins of God": The Making of Asceticism in Late Antiquity*. Oxford Classical Monographs. Oxford: Clarendon, 1994.

Emmel, Stephen. "Robert Curzon's Acquisition of White Monastery Manuscripts." In *Actes du IV*[e] *Congrès copte, Louvain-la-Neuve, 5–10 septembre 1988*, edited by Marguerite Rassart and Julien Ries. Vol. 2. Publications de l'Institut orientaliste de Louvain 41. Louvain-la-Neuve: Université catholique de Louvain, Institut orientaliste, 1992.

———. *Shenoute's Literary Corpus*. 2 vols. Corpus scriptorum christianorum orientalium 599–600. Subsidia 111–12. Louvain: Peeters, 2004.

Evetts, Basil T. A., and Alfred J. Butler. *The Churches and Monasteries of Egypt and Some Neighboring Countries, Attributed to Abû Sâlih, the Armenian*. Oxford: Clarendon, 1895; reprint, London: Butler & Tanner, 1969.

Gabra, Gawdat, and Hany Takla. *Akhmim and Sohag*. Vol. 1 of *Christianity and Monasticism in Upper Egypt*. Cairo: The American University in Cairo Press, 2008.

Garitte, Gérard. "Constantin, évêque d'Assiout." In *Coptic Studies in Honor of Walter Ewing Crum*. Bulletin of the Byzantine Institute 2. Boston: The Byzantine Institute, 1950. 287–304.

Geerard, Maurice. "#2187: Homilia adversus Arium, de s. genetrice dei Maria." In *Clavis patrum graecorum*, vol. 2: *Ab Athanasio ad Chrysostomum*. Turnhout: Brepols, 1974.

Goehring, James E. *Ascetics, Society, and the Desert: Studies in Early Egyptian Monasticism*. Studies in Antiquity & Christianity. Harrisburg, PA: Trinity, 1999.

———. "Remembering Abraham of Farshut: History, Hagiography, and the Fate of the Pachomian Tradition." 2005 NAPS

Presidential Address. *The Journal of Early Christian Studies* 14, no. 1 (2006): 1–26.

———. "The Ship of the Pachomian Federation: Metaphor and Meaning in a Late Account of Pachomian Monasticism." In *Christianity in Egypt: Literary Production and Intellectual Trends: Studies in Honor of Tito Orlandi*, edited by Paola Buzi and Alberto Camplani. Studia ephemeridis augustinianum 125. Rome: Institutum patristicum augustinianum, 2011. 289–303.

Goehring, James E., and Janet Timbie, eds. *The World of Early Egyptian Christianity: Language, Literature, and Social Context, Essays in Honor of David W. Johnson*. CUA Studies in Early Christianity. Washington, DC: The Catholic University of America Press, 2007.

Hamman, A.-G. *L'Homme, Image de Dieu*. Relais-études 2. Paris: Desclée, 1987.

Harmless, William. *Desert Christians: An Introduction to the Literature of Early Monasticism*. New York: Oxford University Press, 2004.

Hasan, Sana S. *Christians versus Muslims in Modern Egypt: The Century-Long Struggle for Coptic Equality*. Oxford and New York: Oxford University Press, 2003.

Hyvernat, Henri. "Catalogue of the Clarendon Press Sahidic Fragments Deposed in the Bodleian Library." Unpublished manuscript, Oxford, 1886–1887.

Iskander, John. "Islamization in Medieval Egypt: The Copto-Arabic 'Apocalypse of Samuel' as a Source for the Social and Religious History of Medieval Copts." *Medieval Encounters* 4, no. 3 (1998): 219–27.

Joest, Christoph. "Die Pachom-Briefe 1 und 2: Auflösung der Geheimbuchstaben und Entdeckungen zu den Briefüberschriften." *Journal of Coptic Studies* 4 (2002): 25–98.

———. "Die sog. 'Règlements' als Werk des Pachomianers Horsiese († nach 386)." *Vigiliae christianae* 63 (2009): 480–92.

———. "Horsiese als Redaktor von Pachoms Katechese 1 'An einen gröllenden Mönch': Eine stilkritische Untersuchung." *Journal of Coptic Studies* 9 (2007): 61–94.

———. "Pachoms Katechese 'an einen gröllenden Mönch.'" *Le Muséon* 120 (2007): 91–129.

Kelly, Stephen, and John J. Johnson. *Imagining the Book*. Medieval Texts and Cultures of Northern Europe. Turnhout, Belgium: Brepols, 2005.

Kennedy, Hugh. "Egypt as a Province in the Islamic Caliphate, 641–868." In *Islamic Egypt, 640–1517*, edited by Carl F. Petry. Vol. 1 of *The Cambridge History of Egypt*, edited by M. W. Daly. Cambridge: Cambridge University Press, 1998. 62–85.

Lane-Poole, Stanley. *A History of Egypt in the Middle Ages*. 2nd rev. ed. London: Methuen, 1914; reprint, Karachi, Pakistan: S. M. Mir, 1977.

Layton, Bentley. *Catalogue of Coptic Literary Manuscripts in the British Library Acquired since the Year 1906*. London: The British Library, 1987.

———. "Some Observations on Shenoute's Sources: Who Are Our Fathers?" *Journal of Coptic Studies* 11 (2009): 45–59.

Lefort, Louis-Théophile. "S. Athanase écrivain copte." *Le Muséon* 46 (1933): 1–33.

Lent, Jos van. "The Apocalypse of Samuel of Qalamun Reconsidered." Paper presented at the Tenth International Congress of Coptic Studies, Rome, September 17–22, 2012.

———. "Les Apocalypses coptes de l'époque arabe: Quelques réflexions." In *Études coptes V: Sixième journée d'études, Limoges 18–20 juin 1993 et septième journée d'études, Neuchâtel 18–20 mai 1995*, edited by M. Rassart-Debergh. Cahiers de la Bibliothèque copte 10. Paris and Louvain: Peeters, 1998. 181–95.

Louis, Catherine. *Catalogue raisonné des manuscrits littéraires coptes conservés à l'IFAO du Caire*. L'Institut français d'archéologie orientale, forthcoming.

Lucchesi, Enzo. "Deux commentaires coptes sur l'évangile de Matthieu." *Le Muséon* 123, nos. 1–2 (2010): 19–37.

———. "L'Homélie XIV de Sévère d'Antioche: Un second témoin copte." *Aegyptus* 86 (2006): 199–205.

———. "Un corpus basilien en copte." *Analecta Bollandiana* 99 (1981): 75–94.

———. "Un fragment sahidique du premier panégyrique d'Étienne le protomartyr par Grégoire de Nysse." *Analecta Bollandiana* 124 (2006): 11–13.

———. "Un témoin copte de l'homélie de Sévérien de Gabala sur le lavement des pieds." *Analecta Bollandiana* 127 (2009): 299–308.

Lucchesi, Enzo, with an Introduction by Paul Devos. *Répertoire des manuscrits coptes (sahidiques), publiés de la Bibliothèque nationale de Paris*. Cahiers d'orientalisme 1. Geneva: Patrick Cramer, 1981.

Lundhaug, Hugo, and Lance Jenott. *The Monastic Origins of the Nag Hammadi Codices*. Studien und Texte zu Antike und Christentum 97. Tübingen: Mohr Siebeck, 2015.

MacCoull, Leslie S. B. *Coptic Perspectives on Late Antiquity*. Variorum Collected Studies. Aldershot, Hampshire, UK, and Brookfield, VT: Variorum, 1993.

Martin, Annick. *Athanase d'Alexandrie et l'église d'Égypte au IVe siècle (328–373)*. Palais Farnèse: École française de Rome, 1996.

Maspero, Gaston. *Fragments de manuscrits coptes-thébains provenant de la bibliothèque du deir Amba-Schenoudah*. Mémoires publiés par les members de la mission archéologique française au Caire (tome 6, fasc. 1). Paris: Ernest Leroux, 1892.

McNary-Zak, Bernadette. *Letters and Asceticism in Fourth-Century Egypt*. Lanham, MD: University Press of America, 2000.

———. "Pachomian Remission." *Coptic Church Review* 23, no. 4 (2002): 107–10.

Meinardus, Otto F. A. *Two Thousand Years of Coptic Christianity*. Cairo and New York: The American University in Cairo Press, 1999.

Mikhail, Maged S. A. "Egypt from Late Antiquity to Early Islam: Copts, Melkites, and Muslims Shaping a New Society." PhD dissertation, The University of California, Los Angeles, 2004.

Orlandi, Tito. "Coptic Literature." In *The Roots of Egyptian Christianity*, edited by Birger A. Pearson and James E. Goehring.

Studies in Antiquity & Christianity. Philadelphia: Fortress, 1986. 51–81.

———. *Elementi di lingua e letteratura copta*. Milan: La Goliardica, 1970.

———. "Gregorio di Nissa nella letteratura copta." *Vetera christianorum* 18 (1981): 333–39.

———. "The Library of the Monastery of Saint Shenoute at Atripe." In *Perspectives on Panopolis: An Egyptian Town from Alexander the Great to the Arab Conquest, Acts from an International Symposium Held in Leiden on 16, 17 and 18 December 1998*, edited by A. Egberts, B. P. Muhs, and J. van der Vliet. Papyrologica Lugduno-Batava 31. Leiden: Brill, 2002. 211–32.

———. *Corpus dei manoscritti copti letterari*. http://rmcisadu.let.uniroma1.it/~cmcl (accessed Jan. 2, 2012).

Papaconstantinou, Arietta. "'They Shall Speak the Arabic Language and Take Pride in It': Reconsidering the Fate of Coptic after the Arab Conquest." *Le Muséon* 120, nos. 3–4 (2007): 273–99.

Porcher, Émile, with an Introduction by Henri Hyvernat. "Analyse des manuscrits coptes 131^{1-8} de la Bibliothèque nationale, avec indication des textes bibliques." *Revue d'égyptologie* 1 (1933): 105–60, 231–78.

Quecke, Hans. *Untersuchungen zum koptischen Stundengebet*. Publications de l'Institut orientaliste de Louvain 3. Louvain: Institut orientaliste, Université catholique de Louvain, 1970.

Roldanus, J. *Le Christ et l'homme dans la théologie d'Athanase d'Alexandrie*. Studies in the History of Christian Thought 4. Leiden: E. J. Brill, 1968.

Rousseau, Philip. *Pachomius: The Making of a Community in Fourth-Century Egypt*. The Transformation of the Classical Heritage 6. Edited by Peter Brown. Berkeley: University of California Press, 1985.

Rubenson, Samuel. *The Letters of St. Antony: Monasticism and the Making of a Saint*. Studies in Antiquity and Christianity. Minneapolis: Fortress, 1995.

———. "Translating the Tradition: Some Remarks on the Arabization of the Patristic Heritage in Egypt." *Medieval Encounters* 2, no. 1 (1996): 4–14.

Samir, K. "Témoins arabes de la catéchèse de Pachôme 'A propos d'un moine rancunier' (CPG 2354.1)." *Orientalia christiana periodica* 42 (1976): 494–508.

Schneider, Carolyn. "The Image of God in *On Love and Self-control* and *Instruction concerning a Spiteful Monk*." In Coptic Society, Literature and Religion from Late Antiquity to Modern Times: Proceedings of the Tenth International Congress of Coptic Studies, Rome, September 17–22, 2012, and Plenary Reports of the Ninth International Congress of Coptic Studies, Cairo, September 15–19, 2008. Vol. 2. Edited by Paula Buzi, Alberto Camplani, and Federico Contardi. Orientalia Lovanievia Analecta 247. Leuven: Peeters, 2016. 929–36.

Schroeder, Caroline T. "'A Suitable Abode for Christ': The Church Building as Symbol of Ascetic Renunciation in Early Monasticism." *Church History: Studies in Christianity & Culture* 73, no. 3 (2004): 472–521.

Suciu, Alin. "The Homilies on the Epistle to the Hebrews by John Chrysostom: A Complement to the Coptic Version" (July 12, 2011). Accessed July 6, 2013. http://alinsuciu.com/2011/07/12/the-homilies-on-the-epistle-to-the-hebrews-by-john-chrysostom-a-complement-to-the-coptic-version.

Suermann, Harald. "Koptische arabische apokalypsen." In *Studies on the Christian Arabic Heritage in Honor of Father Prof. Dr. Samir Khalil Samir S. I. at the Occasion of His Sixty-Fifth Birthday*, edited by Rifaat Ebied and Herman Teule. Eastern Christian Studies 5. Louvain: Peeters, 2004. 25–44.

Swanson, Mark. *The Coptic Papacy in Islamic Egypt, 641–1517*. The Popes of Egypt 2. Cairo: The American University in Cairo Press, 2010.

Thomas, David, Barbara Roggema, and Alex Mallett, eds. *Christian-Muslim Relations: A Bibliographic History*. Vols. 1–2. History of Christian-Muslim Relations 11 and 14. Leiden and Boston: Brill, 2009–2010.

Timbie, Janet. "A Liturgical Procession in the Desert of Apa Shenoute." In *Pilgrimage and Holy Space in Late Antique Egypt*, ed. David Frankfurter. Religions in the Graeco-Roman World 134. Leiden, Boston, and Cologne: Brill, 1998. 415–41.

Timm, Stefan. *Das christlich-koptische Ägypten in arabischer Zeit*. Part 2, Beihefte zum Tübinger Atlas des vorderen Orients, Series B (Geisteswissenschaften), no. 41/2. Wiesbaden: Dr. Ludwig Reichert, 1984.

Werthmuller, Kurt J. *Coptic Identity and Ayyubid Politics in Egypt, 1218–1250.* Cairo and New York: The American University in Cairo Press, 2010.

Wipszycka, Ewa. "Les Terres de la congrégation pachômienne dans une liste de payments pour les apora." In *Le Monde grec: Hommages á Claire Préoux*, edited by Jean Bingen, Guy Cambrier, and Georges Nachtergael. Brussels: Éditions de l'Université de Bruxelles, 1975. 625–36.

———. "Moines et communautés monastiques en Égypte (IVe–VIIIe siècles)." *The Journal of Juristic Papyrology*, Supplement XI. Warsaw: Warsaw University, Faculty of Law and Administration, Chair of Roman and Antique Law, Institute of Archaeology, Department of Papyrology, and the Raphael Taubenschlag Foundation, 2009.

Zanetti, Ugo. "Bohairic Liturgical Manuscripts." *Orientalia christiana periodica* 61, no. 1 (1995): 65–94.

General Index

Scripture Index